Globalisation, Diaspora and Belonging

GLOBALISATION, DIASPORA AND BELONGING

Exploring Transnationalism and Gujarati Identity

Edited by

Sharmina Mawani

Anjoom A. Mukadam

RAWAT PUBLICATIONS

Jaipur • New Delhi • Bangalore • Hyderabad • Guwahati • Kolkata

ISBN 978-81-316-0632-2

Published by
Prem Rawat for **Rawat Publications**
Satyam Apts, Sector 3, Jawahar Nagar, Jaipur 302 004 (India)
Phone: 0141 265 1748 / 7006 Fax: 0141 265 1748
E-mail: info@rawatbooks.com
Website: www.rawatbooks.com

New Delhi Office
4858/24, Ansari Road, Daryaganj, New Delhi 110 002
Phone: 011 2326 3290

Also at *Bangalore, Hyderabad, Guwahati* and *Kolkata*

Typeset by Rawat Computers, Jaipur
Printed at Chaman Enterprises, New Delhi

Everything exists in relation to other things,
in a state of interdependence.
There is nothing that exists in and of itself.
It is therefore impossible to conceive of one's own
personal interests independently of those of others.

—***Dalai Lama***

Contents

Foreword – Farouk Topan ix

Contributors xiii

Introduction – Circles of Belonging:
Reflections on Gujarati Identities 1
Sharmina Mawani and Anjoom A. Mukadam

Part I : Globalisation and Migration

1 Gujarat and the Dialectics of Globalisation 21
Sylvie Guichard

2 Gendering the Gujarati Diaspora: Oral Narratives and Identity 42
Sandhya Rao Mehta

3 Being Ismaili in the Democratic Republic of the Congo: Identity Maintenance among Gujarati Ismailis in Kinshasa 58
Sahir Dewji

4 Buying and Selling an Illusion: Multinational Corporations and Young Gujaratis in Mumbai 78
Sharmina Mawani

Part II
Language and Culture

5 The Administrator and the Poet: Language and Globalisation in Nineteenth Century Gujarat 103
Arvind Bhatt

6 Indobrits: Cultural Hybridity as a Constantly Negotiated Lived Reality 118
Anjoom A. Mukadam

7 Identity and Belonging: The Case of the Gujarati Diaspora Community in the United Kingdom, Singapore and South Africa 145
Sheena Shah

Part III
Inclusion/Exclusion

8 Contesting 'Purity' and Zones of Inclusion and Exclusion among the Gujaratis in Contemporary Zanzibar 169
Akbar Keshodkar

9 'Wherever there is one Gujarati, there is Gujarat': The Integration of Hindus in the United Kingdom 190
John Mattausch

10 A Religious Education Curriculum: Addressing the Challenges Faced by Canadian Adolescents of Gujarati Ancestry 210
Shezeleen Kanji

11 Space, Representation and Belonging: A Swaminarayan Temple in Sydney, Australia 236
Laura Beth Bugg

12 From Ahmedabad to Karnavati: Cultural Roots and Socio-Spatial Aspects of Intolerance 255
Tommaso Bobbio

Index 277

Foreword

Farouk Topan

This volume is a welcome addition to the two books edited previously by Sharmina Mawani and Anjoom A. Mukadam, namely, *Gujaratis in the West: Evolving Identities in Contemporary Society* (2007) and *Gujarati Communities across the Globe: Memory, Identity and Continuity* (2012). There are three key features pertaining to Gujarati identity that emerge from the discussions in this collection and I mention them here as they provide a valuable backdrop to the papers in this volume.

First, there is the link between identity and culture, a bond which played a crucial role in the evolving identities of the Gujaratis as individuals initially migrated from Gujarat, or India generally – the 'cultural' centre – to places which had their own indigenous cultures. East Africa is a notable example of such a contact zone as it features quite considerably in the discussions, though I think a similar process would also have taken place in other Gujarati settlement areas around the Indian Ocean. In interacting with indigenous cultures, peoples and their languages, Gujarati settlers adopted other perspectives into their worldview and allowed some of their own to gradually fade away. What was retained and what was eventually discarded depended upon the religious and secular outlook of each particular community. As Gujarati settlers were diverse in both, there was no uniformity in the type and manner of cultural appropriation and adaptation that occurred, especially in the second and succeeding generations. Ways of greeting, for instance, became less formal, though not any less respectful; prohibitions and protocol surrounding food preparation and consumption were modified to take account of local conditions.

The second feature has proved to be long lasting and more enduring in its impact. The colonial presence in East Africa (from the 1890s to the 1960s) gave rise to a process of Westernisation through which members of different East African communities, particularly the urban middle- and upper-classes, adopted various aspects of Western lifestyle, values and aspirations. Prominent among these was Western education, whose key prerequisite was the learning and mastery of English. As decades went by, the importance of English increased. Gujarati parents, no less than other parents in similar positions, embraced English as a tool of personal and communal progress. Schools, which had previously used Gujarati as a medium of instruction, switched to English in the late 1950s. Gujarati remained for a time as a core subject in schools but by the early 1960s it had been removed from the curriculum entirely in some schools. This meant that succeeding generations of Gujarati children spoke Gujarati at home but were unable to read or write it – a reverse of the Swahili situation where later generations of Arab settlers on the East African coast stopped speaking Arabic but have retained the ability to read it because of Quran classes. Embedded in Western education, English became a useful bridge to the West from the mid-1960s onwards when the Gujaratis, along with other South Asians, migrated from East Africa, and more particularly, when they were expelled from Uganda in 1972. The aftermath of that experience in the West, and its effect on identity, forms the third feature.

A generation of Gujaratis has emerged by now who have known no other home than the one in the West, having been either born or raised and educated there from a young age. Their identity and sense of belonging has been shaped by factors different from their fathers and grandfathers in India, or in East Africa. It is interesting that quite a few of the scholars studying the various Gujarati communities around the world are in this category. One already discerns in their works an endeavour to rethink and reposition themselves as individuals in a Western context, whose 'zone of belonging' is the West: even the term 'diaspora' is being politely distanced. Such a confluence of generational insights and perceptions from diverse vantage points has generated an exciting atmosphere both for explaining and defining self-identities, and for creating a fresher framework of scholarship for Gujarat studies. This volume contributes substantially to that discourse.

In putting together this book, the editors have made it possible for readers to gain a better understanding of the challenges and successes of the Gujaratis. The authors of the individual chapters also need to be commended for sharing their insights, research and perspectives and offering us a glimpse into the everyday lives of this community. It is my hope that this volume will stimulate further research on the Gujaratis.

Farouk Topan

Aga Khan University-Institute for the
Study of Muslim Civilisations, London, UK

School of Oriental and African Studies, University of London, UK

Contributors

Arvind Bhatt has worked in the field of bilingualism, focusing on community languages and complementary schools, for over 25 years. He has taught English, mathematics and Gujarati in mainstream schools. For a number of years he led and trained a team of minority language teachers in Leicester. Arvind has been involved in major research projects with the Universities of Leicester, Lancaster and East London where he was a Research Fellow. He has argued the case for minority languages locally and nationally and was the lead author of the curriculum guide for Gujarati as a modern language. Arvind has contributed research papers for several books and journals and is now engaged in research on the emergence of modern Gujarati in the mid-nineteenth century.

Tommaso Bobbio obtained his PhD at Royal Holloway, University of London, and is now a post-doctoral fellow in the Department of Culture, Politics and Society, University of Torino. He has conducted extensive research on the city of Ahmedabad, from the late-nineteenth century to contemporary times, focusing on issues relating to the production of inequality and socio-spatial marginalisation, collective violence and citizenship. His first monograph, *Urbanisation, Citizenship and Social Change in India,* will be published by Routledge in 2014.

Laura Beth Bugg is a lecturer in the Department of Sociology and Social Policy at The University of Sydney. Her research interests include the intersection of religion, place and welfare governance. She is particularly interested in the experiences of new immigrant groups in the establishment of places of worship and religious schools, and the ways in which contestations around minority places of worship and schools are mediated and controlled by local governance processes. Recent research projects have examined forms of social organisation and belonging in transnational migrant religious communities in Australia, and comparative research on faith-based asylum-seeker welfare organisations in Australia and the UK that examines the way in which faith-based organisations address the religious experience and cultural specificity of asylum seekers in programme delivery.

Sahir Dewji graduated from Harvard University with a Master's in the History and Culture of the Islamic World, specialising in the study of Indo-Muslim culture. He is currently pursuing a PhD at Wilfrid Laurier University in Religion and Culture. His research focuses on cosmopolitan ethics and contemporary Islam in Canada. Previously, Sahir graduated from the Institute of Ismaili Studies' Graduate Programme in Islamic Studies and Humanities and obtained a Bachelor of Science from the University of Waterloo in 2007. His intellectual interests lie in the study of Ismaili thought and history, as well as Muslim identity and expressions in the North American context. He also devotes his time to other areas of interest, including the study of religions, philosophy, Islamic intellectual and political traditions as well as music.

Sylvie Guichard is a lecturer at the Department of Legal History, University of Geneva, Switzerland. She studied political science in Geneva, Berlin and London and holds a doctorate in political science from Sciences Po., Paris and the University of Geneva. Recently, she was a fellow at the Center for the Study of Law and Governance, Jawaharlal Nehru University, New Delhi, India. Her teaching focuses on religion and politics and religious fundamentalism. Her doctoral research on the Indian history textbook controversy looked at the links between nation-building, history, school education and textbooks. She has published a book (*The Construction of History and Nationalism in India*, Routledge, 2010/paperback edition 2012) and several articles on the subject. Currently, she is working on the political role of the Indian Supreme Court, and is also a close follower of politics in Gujarat.

Shezeleen Kanji obtained a Master of Arts in Education (Muslim Societies and Civilisations) and a Master of Teaching from the Institute of Education, University of London. She is currently employed as a Secondary Religious Education Teacher with the Ismaili Tariqah and Religious Education Board for Canada teaching students from grades seven to twelve in Edmonton, Alberta. Her areas of interest include studying the ways in which students choose to identify or not identify with aspects of their ancestral culture and the role of faith and culture in providing adolescents a sense of belonging.

Akbar Keshodkar is Assistant Professor of Anthropology in the Department of Humanities and Social Sciences at Zayed University, Dubai, United Arab Emirates. He acquired his doctorate degree from the Institute of Social and Cultural Anthropology at Oxford University. His research interests include examining the impact of historical and contemporary transnational networks on the movements of identities in Muslim communities in the western Indian Ocean region and the experience of the South Asian diaspora in Zanzibar and other parts of East Africa. His most recent monograph, published in October 2013 by Lexington Books, is titled, *Tourism and Social Change in Post Socialist Zanzibar: Struggles for Identity, Movement and Civilization.*

John Mattausch is a lecturer in the Department of Politics and International Relations, Royal Holloway College, University of London. For the past twenty years he has been researching diverse topics concerning the joint social history of Britons and Gujaratis from 1608 to the present day. His publications and academic interests are listed at: http://pure.rhul.ac.uk/

portal/en/persons/john-mattausch%28bf129ac3-a08e-46e2-8fbc-de8aa16a93e2%29.html

Sharmina Mawani obtained her doctorate from the Department for the Study of Religions at the School of Oriental and African Studies (SOAS), University of London. Her thesis investigated the centrality of the *ginans* (devotional songs) in the formation of the ethno-religious identities of the Nizari Ismaili Muslims of Gujarati ancestry in Toronto and Mumbai. Sharmina is particularly interested in the manner in which traditional religious practices are evolving in contemporary Western society. At present, she is a lecturer at the Institute of Ismaili Studies, London and also holds the post of Vice-President of the Gujarat Studies Association, which she co-founded in 2005. Sharmina has co-edited two volumes on the Gujarati community, *Gujaratis in the West: Evolving Identities in Contemporary Society* and *Gujarati Communities Across the Globe: Memory, Identity and Continuity*. Another volume, entitled *Gujarati Realities: Perspectives of Female Researchers*, will be published by Logos Verlag Berlin in 2014.

Sandhya Rao Mehta has a PhD in the literature of the Indian diaspora. She is an Assistant Professor in the Department of English at Sultan Qaboos University, Oman. Her current research interests include a study of the Indian diaspora in Oman, particularly from the point of view of its women. She has published widely in the areas of emerging literatures as well as worked on the changing role of the English language among various communities. She has recently co-edited a critical anthology entitled *Language Studies: Stretching the Boundaries* published by Cambridge Scholars Publishing.

Anjoom Mukadam is a lecturer in the Department of Graduate Studies at the Institute of Ismaili Studies in London. She received her PhD and Master's degrees in Sociolinguistics from the University of Reading and Bachelor's degree and PGCE in Secondary Education from King's College, University of London. Anjoom brings an interdisciplinary perspective to her research and teaching. Her main research interests are in the arena of ethno-linguistic and religious identities with a particular focus on Muslim youth in the

West, including issues related to migration and 'diaspora', hybridity, adolescent identity formation, discrimination, 'race' and ethnicity, heritage language education, popular culture, multiculturalism and multilingualism. Anjoom has presented various aspects of her research at numerous international conferences. Her publications include a co-edited volume entitled *Gujaratis in the West: Evolving Identities in Contemporary Society* and several book chapters and journal articles. Her most recent publication is a co-edited volume entitled *Gujarati Communities Across the Globe: Memory, Identity and Continuity*.

Sheena Shah obtained her doctorate in Linguistics from Georgetown University, USA. Her thesis examined the factors affecting proficiency among Gujarati heritage learners in the UK, Singapore and South Africa, focusing in particular on whether there is a relationship between heritage language ability and ethnic and cultural identity. She is currently a post-doctoral fellow at the University of Cape Town, South Africa. Her research interests include endangered, minority and heritage languages, language maintenance and shift, language policy, language and education, and language and identity.

Circles of Belonging

Reflections on Gujarati Identities

Sharmina Mawani and Anjoom A. Mukadam

In recent times, academic discourse on belonging, especially as it relates to those from minority ethnic communities, has often been placed within the framework of contemporary tragic events, such as the terrorist attacks of 11 September 2001 (9/11) in New York and 7 July 2005 (7/7) in London. However, discussions on belonging are not a product of the modern world, but were present in the work of early sociologists, as is evident in Émile Durkheim's *The Division of Labor in Society*. Durkheim (1893) stressed the importance of 'collective consciousness' as the main source of a society's identity. It is through the sharing of common values, beliefs and morals that the individual is provided with a sense of connection to others, as well as a feeling of acceptance. The notion of belonging is complex in nature and is applicable to individuals and groups, ranging from the small, for example, membership to a family, to the very large, such as membership in a global religious group. The need to belong is a necessary factor for most individuals in society, and a variety of groups – be they political, social or cultural – meet that very basic human need. It is through the processes associated with achieving a sense of belonging that individuals shape their identities. Identities are always constructed in a specific context and in relation to other individuals and groups, but they are not formed passively. Rather, identities and the process of belonging is something 'that people accept, resist, choose, specify, invent, redefine, reject, actively defend, and so forth' (Cornell and Hartmann 1998: 77).

While shared values of a group can bring together like-minded individuals, this same process can also exclude certain individuals, thereby creating an 'us' and 'them' positioning, resulting in 'othering'. Although 'othering' is a crucial feature of belonging, as it is only by identifying who we are not, that we can comprehend who we are, at its extreme, 'othering' may lead to xenophobia. However, it often also results in the suppression of individualism in favour of the collective to the extent that members of the group may see themselves as one and will defend any threats to the group's cohesiveness. For many, such as the Gujaratis, the collective with which they identify is the ethnic group to which they belong; as it is their ethnicity that highlights that they are different from others, who are often the majority. While this difference can be seen to be a disadvantage, many Gujaratis, especially those in the diaspora and post-diaspora, have gone through the 'process of selecting items, however few, from the cultural past – pieces of ethnic folk art, folk dances, music, a partial use of language, knowledge of some aspects of the group's history – which become symbols of ethnic identity' (Isajiw 1977: 36). A sense of belonging is created through shared meanings and alliances, which allows individuals to feel like they belong to a real, virtual or imagined group. It is through participation in the practices of a specific group that an individual is able to establish and maintain social, political and economic relationships.

The creation of a sense of belonging is a multifaceted dynamic process that does not require an individual to select one solitary group to which they may belong. An individual may belong to multiple groups simultaneously – be they regional or national, religious or ethnic, sporting clubs or political parties. Nevertheless, it is rare to find an individual who belongs to groups with opposing views, as emphasis on 'what one is' and 'what one is not' results in the production of boundaries, which are constructed and maintained, not by a natural process, but by humans. And it is members of the group who decide the permeability, flexibility and fluidity of the group's boundaries. It is often wrongly assumed that the need to belong is unique to new immigrants. The process of belonging is a shared one between new immigrants, the majority population, as well as earlier settlers, thus resulting in transformations in identities, cultural practices, etc., among all three groups. There is no question that new immigrants may feel a sense of displacement as they try to adjust to their new environment. All three groups may identify the path of assimilating, that is, immigrants discarding all aspects of their own culture, as the fastest and most effective way to belong to the local community. But this is in contrast to belonging, which is created by forming links and associations by the newcomer with their neighbours through shared experiences, beliefs, preferences, etc. What is often neglected is the recognition that in a neighbourhood or city with a long-established population, the influx of new immigrants may result in feelings of displacement among the long-time inhabitants, and they may perceive their neighbourhood or city as unfamiliar.

Individuals are constantly engaged in affirming their sense of belonging through interactions with others. Yet, this process has become part of everyday life and, therefore, more often than not, goes unnoticed. One becomes conscious of this sense of belonging only when there is a disruption to familiar patterns, such as when a newcomer joins a group with long-standing members, adjusting to life in a new apartment, neighbourhood or city. It is only at that time, as an individual tries to adapt to his/her new situation, that their consciousness of belonging is heightened. Belonging to one group or another is not a simple matter of membership, but involves social practices in which all members are expected to participate. These social practices can range from formalised rites of passage to more informal behaviour, such as attending office parties and maintaining regular contact with friends and neighbours. Thus, these social 'obligations' are imperative in creating and maintaining a sense of belonging to one's group or neighbourhood. As these social practices become part of an individual's everyday life, they are able to attach spaces with meaning, thereby determining the circles to which they belong. Belonging is essential to human survival, as it is a sense of belonging that provides confirmation of support systems necessary for everyday life, such as adequate shelter, employment and security. Scholars studying migration tend to discuss belonging from one of three perspectives: (i) as an element of legal rights, for example citizenship (Karst

1989; Castles and Davidson 2000); (ii) as a feature of individual or group identity (Lovell 1998; Savage, Bagnall and Longhurst 2005); or (iii) as an aspect in creating a sense of place (Leach 2002; Massey 2005).

While all these studies focus on varying aspects, it can be said that there is a high level of interconnection between all three elements of belonging. This interconnection is perhaps best illustrated by looking more closely at the notion of citizenship. The idea of citizenship implies rights, privileges, as well as responsibilities. The citizen 'belongs' to the state and has the right to influence the development of the nation through various means of participation. The identity of the citizen is created based on their comprehension of the nation and their place within that nation. A sense of belonging and the importance it carries for the individual in everyday living goes beyond discussions of globalisation and migration. It is often the conversations and encounters that occur at a local level between new immigrants and long-term residents that determines the ease and speed of both parties developing and maintaining a sense of belonging.

Such debates are a necessary part of attempting to comprehend one's sense of self. Therefore, it is not surprising that they have been at the forefront of studies on human societies and how individuals perceive themselves in relation to others, locally, nationally and globally. The collection of essays in this volume focuses upon the experiences of belonging of the Gujaratis, highlighting the unique ways that globalisation, migration, language, culture and 'othering' shape perceptions of belonging. The contributors in this volume seek to shed light on the myriad strategies employed by various Gujarati communities in their attempts to belong and find acceptance.

GLOBALISATION AND MIGRATION

In popular discourse, the term 'globalisation' is sometimes misused as a synonym for terms such as Westernisation and the Internet revolution; it is also overused, making it a prevalent feature in everyday life, thereby rendering the term meaningless. It may be fashionable to use the term, but there is also a more serious side to the processes of globalisation, on which there is a growing amount of scholarly literature. One of the more widely cited definitions of globalisation is that by Giddens (1990: 64), who defines it as 'the intensification of worldwide social relations which link distant localities in such a way that local happenings are shaped by the events occurring many miles away and vice versa'. Scholarship on globalisation is vast, and while it is not the intention of this 'Introduction' to provide a comprehensive discussion on the subject, it is imperative to outline essential factors of this phenomenon that are relevant to the chapters in this volume. Steger (2009) has identified four core qualities of globalisation, which may provide some clarity to the complex notion of globalisation. The first is the expansion of existing social networks, alongside the creation of new ones, which transcend geographical, cultural and political boundaries. The second quality is the widening of social associations and global connections. This includes global financial markets, chain stores which offer consumers the same products on numerous continents, as well as non-governmental organisations. The third is the formation of a 'network society', which witnesses the escalation of social exchanges; examples include Internet and satellite communication, which results in local events developing out of distant occurrences. This phenomenon has also been referred to as globality, which 'means that *we have been living for a long time in a world society,* in the sense that the notion of closed spaces has become illusory. No country or group can shut itself off from others' (Beck 2000: 10, original emphasis). The fourth quality highlights the notion that processes of globalisation are both objective and subjective, thereby, they also affect the way humans think about the world, as well as their actions in this global arena.

Globalisation is not a phenomenon that has already occurred; it is, in actuality, still incomplete and therefore, still unfolding, still in process. And, globalisation brings with it its own characteristics, organisations and challenges, in which new forms of social organisation and traditional methods interweave, creating a new structure for social life around the globe.

One of the primary visible effects of globalisation is an increase in migration. Statistics relate that just over 3 per cent of the world's population lives outside their country of origin. While this is an indication that the majority do not undertake migration, more importantly, it signals a rise in migration from 150 million in 2000 to 214 million in 2012 (International Organization for Migration 2012). The reasons why individuals and families migrate are numerous, and will be discussed with reference to specific Gujarati communities in the individual chapters in the first section of this book. The migration of peoples is a phenomenon that has been present throughout history and has continuously affected notions of belonging. Population movements across the globe have created numerous challenges in the processes of migrant integration and acceptance. Making the decision to migrate is a difficult one, and, although advancement in global communication and travel increases the range of possible destinations, complex processes to procure visas and work permits further complicate this decision. These processes often lead migrants to cities where social networks, familial, ethnic, or otherwise, contribute to shared perceptions of belonging, influencing identity construction and the recreation of images of 'home'.

As people migrate and populate neighbourhoods, this process induces changes in the identities of the migrants, as well as in those already settled in specific regions. New migrants often create their homes in enclaves where others from their ethnic community already reside – where stores, restaurants and places of worship have been established by earlier migrants, and often public establishments, such as hospitals and schools have made provisions to accommodate the needs of the changing demography – thereby making the transition from the 'old' to the 'new' less difficult. The appearance of migrants, especially those from minority ethnic communities, is sometimes viewed as being problematic, as they challenge the established norms of a neighbourhood, town or city, thereby upsetting the identities of the long-established residents. Nevertheless, it would be erroneous to assume that globalisation and migration foster a sense a loss, rather, these processes cultivate transformations.

Part I of the book begins with a consideration of globalisation and migration and their impact on specific Gujarati communities. The opening chapter by Sylvie Guichard highlights how, in the post-liberalisation period and in a globalised world, Gujarat interacts with the federal state and with the rest of the world and analyses the ways in which these three levels influence each other and work together. She uses the term 'deterritorialisation' to describe the different processes related to globalisation, often to imply a form of uprooting of economic, social and political interactions. However, according to Guichard, this is only one side of the story of globalisation, as uprooting is accompanied by some sort of re-rooting. This chapter illustrates that this dialectical movement does not stop with one de- and re-territorialisation but triggers a series of changes that have to be understood as mutually reinforcing, each pulling the other along.

The book continues with a discussion by Sandhya Rao Mehta about the role of Gujarati women in Oman. Focussing on the period before the 1970s, when the Gulf nations began to be established, Mehta highlights that while the Gujarati diaspora has been explored from numerous points of view, including the sociological, economic and cultural, one of the least represented areas remains the women of this diaspora. Her contribution adds to the dearth of literature on the Indian community in the Arabian Gulf, where research into the diaspora remains largely limited to its economic effects on the host nation and the exploration of workers' rights. Based on personal interviews and oral narratives, Mehta attempts to trace the origin of the Indian diaspora in Oman, particularly as told by its women, in order to reveal a perspective that has remained relatively unexplored.

In Chapter 3, Sahir Dewji examines the role of religion and ethnicity in the identity formation of Ismaili Muslims of Gujarati descent who have spent a formative portion of their lives in the Democratic Republic of the Congo (DRC). Dewji explores the reasons why these individuals migrated to the DRC and, through the use of personal narratives conveys their experiences in their new home. Through an analysis of in-depth interviews Dewji uncovers that for these individuals religion is the most crucial part of their identity and that the *jamatkhana* (place of worship) serves as a pillar of strength in both spiritual and worldly matters. This chapter also reveals that members of this community have chosen to settle in the DRC in the hopes of a better economic future despite the political instability.

The final chapter in this section by Sharmina Mawani discusses the effects of globalisation and the emergence of multinational corporations in Mumbai on the identities of young adult Ismaili Muslims. Mawani examines how these young adults feel that by consuming global goods, they are identifying with others in the West who are also purchasing these brands. Following a closer analysis of the respondents' preferences and language skills, Mawani concludes that the multinationals are selling an illusory identity, and at the same time, the participants have a false self-perception of a Western identity. What they are being sold is not in fact 'Western', but a glocalised version which appeals to their sense of being Western but which is, in fact, very Indian in nature.

LANGUAGE AND CULTURE

Many individuals, especially the second and subsequent generations, will find something familiar in the chapters in the second section where the focus is not on grammar or syntax, rather in the significance humans attach to language and its impact on belonging and issues of identity. The German philosopher Ernst Cassirer (1945: 30) identifies language, alongside myth, art and religion, as being parts of a symbolic universe, 'the varied threads which weave the symbolic net, the tangled web of human experience'. The questions of why people speak particular languages in specific contexts with certain individuals and how these come to signify aspects of belonging are intriguing. With these ideas come the notions of the role of language in the formation of one's identity; the impact that shifting from one language to another has on the concept of the self and community; the importance of language for the maintenance of traditions; and the effects of language loss on ancestral traditions and one's place within a community. Underlying all of these notions is vital to our understanding of how language is used to create a sense of belonging.

Ethnic groups often lay claim to a particular language, which facilitates and reinforces a sense of belonging. New migrants may cling more tightly to their heritage language as, in many cases, it may be their only means of communication. For some, limited, or no, skills in the dominant language of their newly adopted home may mean that they have restricted, or no, access to healthcare, education and employment and this may also act as a barrier when attempting to communicate with their neighbours. The issues surrounding language do not disappear with the second and subsequent generations, especially in relation to the Gujarati community. For the younger generation the fear is that with the increasing use of the English language in all spheres of life, including the home, at community events and places of worship, this younger generation is likely to lose their heritage language and with it a part of their culture. For some this may also result in a kind of alienation from the Gujarati community, as their ability to communicate with the older generation decreases over time. But the picture is not totally bleak, as there are many who are able to speak and understand English, as well as their heritage language (in varying degrees of proficiency), thereby providing them with a hybrid linguistic identity and at the same time, keeping open the doors to the cultures of both the majority and their own Gujarati community.

There is a strong connection between language and culture as it is through language that culture is expressed. Indeed many will attest to the fact that certain notions expressed easily in one language cannot be translated into another language without losing some of the intended meaning, which are often culturally bound. Thus, the language that is used, the way it is used and with whom it is used, creates speech communities that consist of individuals who use the same linguistic code, again, providing one with a sense of belonging to a particular group. The way language is used reflects the group's cultural values, that is, their views on the appropriate ways of thinking and behaving, views which are shared by all individuals who speak the same language. Therefore, it is the languages that we speak that shape the way we view the world.

Alongside language, many often cite the culture of a group as another major component that affects one's sense of belonging. Judd (2002: 10) defines culture 'as the system of shared objects, activities and beliefs of a given group of people'. Pennycook (1995: 47) takes this definition one step further and states that culture is 'the process by which people make sense of their lives, a process always involved in struggles over meaning and representation'. These definitions can be applied to the chapters discussed in the second part of this book, as they highlight the reality that the

Gujaratis negotiate and belong to multiple cultures and sub-cultures. The culture of a specific community is not one that has come into being in recent times. On the contrary, it draws on a shared history, as well as shared practices and traditions. It is these aspects of shared historical memory that bind a community together, for they shape the group's present and future. This is not to say that culture is static. The culture of a particular community is in a constant mode of evolution, adopting, adapting and discarding aspects, as circumstances require.

> Cultural identity ... is a matter of 'becoming' as well as of 'being'. It is not something which already exists, transcending place, time, history and culture. Cultural identities come from somewhere, have histories. But like everything that is historical they undergo constant transformation. Far from being eternally fixed in some essentialist past, they are subject to the continuous 'play' of history, culture and power. (Hall 1990: 225)

What one must bear in mind, however, is that this is a gradual process, in which cultural artefacts are carefully weighed, measured and considered, before they are adopted, adapted or discarded.

The chapters in Part II explore socio-cultural and socio-linguistic aspects, in varying contexts. Chapter 5 by Arvind Bhatt is an exploration of the reforms and changes instituted by the British after they established their rule in Gujarat following the defeat of the Mughals and the Maratthas in 1818. Bhatt particularly focuses on the literacies introduced by the new administration and on the consequent changes in the Gujarati language and its literature. The chapter takes account of the relationships between the rulers and the ruled, and concentrates on the crucial friendship between the Scottish administrator, Alexander Kinloch Forbes, and the Brahmin poet, Dalpatram. Issues and debates during and following this process of 'modernisation' of language and literature are analysed in the context of social, technological, industrial, political and religious changes.

In Chapter 6, Anjoom Mukadam looks at the manner in which young second-generation Indians of Gujarati ancestry in Britain, whom she terms 'Indobrits', are using hybridity as a constantly negotiated lived reality to overcome imposed boundaries and social inequities. The term 'hybridity' is complex and encompasses a range of possibilities. In order to lead to a more nuanced understanding of how the second generation have utilised hybridity in their everyday lives, Mukadam introduces three types of hybridity.

Chapter 7 by Sheena Shah focuses on three research sites – the UK, Singapore and South Africa – and discusses how the Gujarati School plays a crucial role in passing on various aspects of Indian identity, including ethnic culture, religion and heritage language. Through their personal narratives, we hear how these Gujarati young adults struggle with some of the demands and expectations associated with belonging to the Gujarati community. At times, they feel that these are contrary to the local mainstream mindset to which they are exposed, especially in relation to the search for a life partner and gender role differences in marriage, education and career choices.

INCLUSION/EXCLUSION

A fascinating aspect of group identities is the way in which they perform two functions simultaneously. On the one hand, they provide an individual with a sense of belonging to a group, which instils one with a feeling of security and stability. On the other hand, identifying oneself with a specific group, also requires one to identify who one is not, a process which involves highlighting difference from 'others'. As Neumann and Welsh (1991: 331) have indicated, 'the basic value of the notion of the Other is to remind us that this is not only a positive, but also a negative process'. In the extreme sense, this could result in preference for segregation and discrimination. Nevertheless, one cannot define oneself without the 'other'. For, what an individual perceives as intrinsic in the 'other' and which is identified as being contrary to one's own traits, leads one to see the 'other' as everything that one is not. Having said that, it is imperative to understand that this difference is not an inherent quality but only becomes 'otherness' if it is attributed with meaning and is identified as a significant component in the identity of the 'other'. Another point about the 'other' is that there is never one singular 'other'; rather, there are 'others', in relation to whom individuals define their own identities. As one's identity is in a constant state of flux, who is categorised as the 'other' is also not static, but shifts continuously: 'each age and society recreates its Others' (Said 1979: 322). And this creation and recreation is far from being a natural process, it is one which is socially constructed, 'the Other is never simply given, never just found or encountered, but made' (Hallam and Street 2000: 1). Often, if an individual or group is perceived as the 'other' for a long period of time, even after this 'otherness' no longer holds any significant meaning, the perception of the 'other' still remains, as it has been embedded in historical memory.

The process of excluding the 'other' can be both explicit and implicit. Overt forms of exclusion include racism and stereotypes, while more tacit forms, which are often firmly fixed in the behaviours and attitudes of the members, are less easily recognised. The process of exclusion results in disadvantaging certain members and can lead to the severing of ties between individuals and families, communities and even society at large. Individuals who face exclusion are unable to participate in the main areas significant to living in a society, including the economic, social and cultural spheres. Levitas (2005) has highlighted three approaches to exclusion. The first is the redistributive discourse (RED), in which the focus is on the ways in which poverty is the main component of exclusion, which restricts participation. In this sense, then, exclusion is 'the dynamic process of being shut out, fully or partially, from any of the social, economic, political and cultural systems which determine the social integration of a person in society' (Walker and Walker 1997: 8). The second approach is the moral underclass discourse (MUD), where particular attention is given to moral misconduct and lawlessness, either by an individual, entire neighbourhoods or communities, as being the primary cause of exclusion. This approach argues that individuals exclude themselves by participating in delinquent behaviour, thereby separating themselves from mainstream society and becoming part of the 'underclass'. The third approach is the social integrationist discourse (SID), which concentrates on paid employment as the key factor of integration. Here, exclusion is equated with exclusion from the labour market. Conscious of oversimplifying this complex notion, Levitas (2005: 27) summarises these three approaches by outlining what is absent in individuals who are excluded: 'in RED they have no money, in SID they have no work, in MUD they have no morals.'

There are three components that frequently emerge in definitions of exclusion: relativity, agency and dynamics (Atkinson 1998). Relativity refers to inclusion or exclusion as being context-specific and varying in degrees. Therefore, it is not static and cannot apply to all times and in all places. The notion of agency indicates that an individual, group, society or institution is, knowingly or unknowingly, responsible for the exclusion. While voluntary or self-exclusion is also plausible, it is difficult to identify when exclusion is really voluntary. Dynamics refers to the perception that exclusion is a dynamic process, existing over time and, is perhaps, even passed down from one generation to the next. This results in exclusion being influenced by aspects from the past and the present (ibid.).

> Exclusion consists of dynamic, multi-dimensional processes driven by unequal power relationships interacting across four main dimensions – economic, political, social and cultural – and at different levels including individual, household, group, community, country and global levels. It results in a continuum of inclusion/exclusion characterised by unequal access to resources, capabilities and rights. (Popay et al. 2008: 2)

The idea of exclusion, then, focuses on one primary theme – the lack of participation in society.

The opposite of exclusion is the notion of inclusion, whose primary aim is to prevent exclusion, which is 'crucially about changing the processes that produce and reproduce exclusionary outcomes' (Marquez et al. 2007: 14). Inclusion may be defined as 'the attempt to re-integrate or increase the participation of marginalised groups within mainstream goals' (Barry 1998: 1). While inclusion is often seen to be of a positive nature, scholars (Rodgers 1995; Goodin 1996; Kronauer 1998) have pointed out that implicit in the notion of inclusion is the idea of the normative. The aspects that an individual or group includes as part of the normative framework are not static, but differ over time and with changing contexts, for example, the workplace, place of the worship, etc. This means that inclusion is fluid, diverse and dependent on changing conditions. Inclusion will often be experienced in varying degrees in different domains, and this too will change with time. Furthermore, the consequences of inclusion are not the same in homogeneous and heterogeneous societies. In a heterogeneous society, if an individual is excluded from one sub-group, he/she can be included in another. In a homogeneous society, this is more difficult, and, sometimes, impossible. Nevertheless, the inclusion of an individual in one sphere does not guarantee inclusion in all spheres. One of the key factors of inclusion is participation, as this satisfies the need to 'fit in', thereby creating fulfilling social lives: 'The opportunities you have for full social engagement and participation are crucial for health, well-being and longevity' (Marmot 2004: 2). Thus, an individual's experience of inclusion is connected with a sense of belonging.

Part III of the volume focuses on issues related to inclusion and exclusion. A discussion by Akbar Keshodkar on notions of 'purity' among Gujaratis in Zanzibar, Tanzania opens this part of the book. Based on several years of ethnographic research in Zanzibar, this chapter examines how the Gujarati descendants of inter-ethnic marriages cope with their stigmatisation in the community and the strategies they employ to transform their position vis-á-vis other Gujaratis in contemporary Zanzibar. Keshodkar examines how membership in a *jat* (caste) historically shaped the politics of belonging among the Gujarati community in the multi-ethnic landscape of Zanzibar. Being a minority on the island, notions of *jat* offered different Gujarati communities, both Hindu and Muslim, in Zanzibar a means to construct zones of inclusion and exclusion between themselves as well as from other Zanzibaris. Their ability to maintain these zones of inclusion and exclusion were compromised in the aftermath of the 1964 Revolution, as a consequence of which, the majority of Gujaratis fled Zanzibar. Those remaining behind aimed to reformulate these social boundaries in the following decades, but in the process of doing so, now exclude those Gujaratis who are descendants of marriages with non-South Asian Zanzibaris. Keshokadar explains how the derogatory label *chotardas* (half-caste), used by numerous Gujaratis in Zanzibar, serves as a powerful reminder to descendants of mixed marriages of their place in the community.

John Mattausch, in Chapter 9, examines the position of British Gujaratis, the great majority of whom are Hindus, and who have shown themselves to be remarkably successful in many fields of endeavour, in a very short period of time. He points out how, after the debacle over East African Asians quietened down, neither they nor their religion have been characterised by the media nor by politicians as a problem – in sharp contrast to British South Asian Muslims. There have been no accusations made that they are excluded, or have excluded themselves, from British society. However, Mattausch argues that this immunity from accusations of exclusion is not because British Gujarati Hindus are 'integrated', rather it is because their fortuitous placement in the British public/private polity permits their religious culture to be sustained, untroubling to the wider British community. This chapter demonstrates how British Gujarati Hindus contentedly 'belong' in Britain, as well as throughout the diaspora, and, according to Mattausch, this, paradoxically, has been effected by their ascribed religion and good fortune.

The discussion by Shezeleen Kanji in the next chapter concentrates on the discrimination faced by Ismaili Muslim adolescents in Toronto, Canada. Drawing on her own experiences as a professional religious education teacher, she explores how a religious education curriculum, which focuses on ethical development, can assist these adolescents in learning to appreciate and embrace their Gujarati culture. Kanji examines how through an understanding and acceptance of ethical values these adolescents can then use these tools to combat the discrimination they face, thus becoming active agents of change in multicultural Canada.

In Chapter 11, Laura Beth Bugg examines the submission of a development application for a Swaminarayan Hindu temple on the semi-rural fringe of Sydney, Australia in 2009. The application encountered significant opposition from local residents and was denied planning approval by local government planners for reasons of incompatibility with the rural area. Using the Hindu temple as a case study and Soja's (1996) spatial trialectic as a theoretical lens, Bugg considers the way in which a minority place of worship serves as a contested site of belonging for transnational Gujarati migrants. While local residents ensure the stability of their position as White Anglo-Australian elites through discursive strategies that celebrate Anglo-Australian values, heritage and elite lifestyle pursuits, these strategies are challenged by the Swaminarayans. In the process of contesting a hegemonic representation of rural space, the Hindu community negotiates strategic alliances that resist cultural expectations through boundary crossing moves, while at the same time creating new cultural practices that reinforce group solidarity and create new ways of belonging, both as Swaminarayans and Australians.

The final chapter of the book by Tommaso Bobbio focuses on the state of Gujarat as a case study, and investigates the rise of subnational cultures in India in the last two decades of the twentieth century. Given the success of politics stressing local specificities in recent times, Bobbio aims to analyse the phenomenon in relation to both changes in the political economy, after the 1991 neo-liberal reforms, and the rise of Hindu nationalism as a dominant political force, both at the national and regional levels. This chapter shows how the success of a subnational propaganda favoured the consolidation of an idea of 'Gujaratiness' as the key element of a new form of middle-class culture in the state. Moreover, the emergence of such a public culture is strictly related to the political fortune of its main promoter, Narendra Modi, who is projected to become a key actor on the national political stage.

The contributors in this volume discuss the various circles to which Gujarati communities belong, or desire to belong, and the challenges they face when trying to create a sense of belonging in varied sites around the globe. The aim of this volume is to inform, as well as stimulate thought, reflection and discussion on Gujarati identities. It offers various lenses by which these circles of belonging can be viewed.

REFERENCES

Atkinson, Anthony Barnes. 'Social Exclusion, Poverty and Unemployment', in *Exclusion, Employment and Opportunity*, edited by Anthony Barnes Atkinson and John Hills, London: Centre for Analysis of Social Exclusion, London School of Economics, 1998, pp. 1–20.

Barry, Monica. 'Social Exclusion and Social Work: An Introduction', in *Social Exclusion and Social Work: Issues of Theory, Policy and Practice*, edited by Monica Barry and Christine Hallett, Dorset: Russell House, 1998, pp. 1–12.

Beck, Ulrich. *What is Globalization?*, Cambridge: Polity Press, 2000.

Cassirer, Ernst. *Essay on Man: An Introduction to a Philosophy of Human Culture*, New Haven, CT: Yale University Press, 1945.

Castles, Stephen and Alistair Davidson. *Citizenship and Migration: Globalization and the Politics of Belonging*, New York: Routledge, 2000.

Cornell, Stephen and Douglas Hartmann. *Ethnicity and Race: Making Identities in a Changing World*, Thousand Oaks, CA: Pine Forge Press, 1998.

Durkheim, Émile. *The Division of Labor in Society* (1893), New York: The Free Press, 1984.

Giddens, Anthony. *The Consequences of Modernity*, Cambridge: Polity Press, 1990.

Goodin, Robert. 'Inclusion and Exclusion', *European Journal of Sociology*, Vol. 37, No. 2 (1996): 343–71.

Hall, Stuart. 'Cultural Identity and Diaspora', in *Identity, Community, Culture, Difference*, edited by Jonathan Rutherford, London: Lawrence & Wishart, 1990, pp. 222–37.

Hallam, Elizabeth and Brian V. Street. 'Introduction', in *Cultural Encounters: Representing Otherness*, edited by Elizabeth Hallam and Brian V. Street, London: Routledge, 2000, pp. 1–10.

International Organization for Migration. 'Facts and Figures', <http://www.iom.int/jahia/Jahia/about-migration/facts-and-figures/lang/en> (24 April 2012).

Isajiw, Wsevolod W. 'Olga in Wonderland: Ethnicity in a Technological Society', *Canadian Ethnic Studies*, Vol. 9, No. 1 (1977): 77–85.

Judd, Elliot L. *Cross-Cultural Communication*, Chicago: Office of Language and Cultural Education, 2002.

Karst, Kenneth L. *Belonging to America: Equal Citizenship and the Constitution*, New Haven: Yale University Press, 1989.

Kronauer, Martin. '"Social Exclusion" and "Underclass": New Concepts for the Analysis of Poverty', in *Empirical Poverty Research in a Comparative Perspective*, edited by Hans-Jürgen Andreß, Aldershot: Ashgate, 1998, pp. 51–75.

Leach, Neil. 'Belonging: Towards a Theory of Identification with Place', *Prospecta*, Vol. 33 (2002): 126–33.

Levitas, Ruth. *The Inclusive Society? Social Inclusion and New Labour*, Basingstoke: Macmillan, 2005.

Lovell, Nadia (ed.). *Locality and Belonging*, London: Routledge, 1998.

Marmot, Michael. *Status Syndrome: How Your Social Standing Directly Affects Your Health*, London: Bloomsbury, 2004.

Marquez, Gustavo et al. (eds). *Outsiders: The Changing Patterns of Exclusion in Latin America and the Caribbean*, Washington, DC: Inter-American Development Bank, 2007, <http://idbdocs.iadb.org/wsdocs/getdocument.aspx?docnum=1154386> (9 June 2013).

Massey, Doreen B. *For Space*, London: Sage Publications, 2005.

Neumann, Iver B. and Jennifer M. Welsh. 'The Other in European Self-Definition: An Addendum to the Literature on International Society', *Review of International Studies*, Vol. 17, No. 4 (1991): 327–48.

Pennycook, Alastair. 'English in the World/the World in English', in *Power and Inequality in Language Education*, edited by James W. Tollefson, Cambridge: Cambridge University Press, 1995, pp. 34–58.

Popay, Jennie et al. *Understanding and Tackling Social Exclusion: Final Report of the Social Exclusion Knowledge Network of the Commission on Social Determinants of Health*, 2008, <http://www.who.int/social_determi-ants/knowledge_networks/final_reports/sekn_fina l%20 report_042008.pdf> (19 June 2013).

Rodgers, Gerry. 'What is Special about a Social Inclusion Approach?', in *Social Exclusion: Rhetoric, Reality, Responses*, edited by Gerry Rodgers, Charles Gore and Jose B. Figueiredo, Geneva: International Institute for Labour Studies, 1995, pp. 43–55.

Said, Edward. *Orientalism*, New York: Vintage, 1979.

Savage, Mike, Gaynor Bagnall and Brian J. Longhurst. *Globalization and Belonging*, London: Sage Publications, 2005.

Soja, Edward. *Thirdspace: Journeys to Los Angeles and Other Real-and-Imagined Places*, Malden, MA: Blackwell, 1996.

Steger, Manfred B. *Globalization: A Brief Insight*, New York: Sterling, 2009.

Walker, Alan and Carol Walker (eds). *Britain Divided: The Growth of Social Exclusion in the 1980s and 1990s*, London: Child Poverty Action Groups, 1997.

Part I

GLOBALISATION AND MIGRATION

CHAPTER 1

Gujarat and the Dialectics of Globalisation

Sylvie Guichard

One specificity of the modern world is that the earth has been mapped, recovered by several levels of administrative units (Anderson 1991). This is 'a product of historically determinate strategies of parcelization, centralization, enclosure and encaging' (Brenner 1999a: 49). The higher unit in this system is the state that is supposed to control or at least to have sovereignty over the territory within its boundaries.[1] Yet the current round of globalisation has had an impact on this hierarchy of boundaries. The world is still represented by several layers of grids, the different levels remain, but the hierarchy has been put into question, disorganised. As a consequence, Amin (1997: 129) notes, we should '[replace] a territorial idea of the local, national and the global as separate spheres of social organisation and action, by a relational understanding of each as a nexus of multiple and asymmetric interdependencies involving local and wider fields of influence'. Following this idea of 'relational understanding', the aim of this chapter is to analyse in the post-liberalisation period and in a globalised world how Gujarat interacts with the federal state and with the rest of the world and how the three levels influence each other or work together. How is Gujarat 'Indian' and, at the same time, global?

Writing about Gujarat and globalisation brings us to this hybrid space that has been called 'glocal'. The idea of glocalisation[2] surfaced as a reaction to studies on globalisation that overemphasised the global reach of certain phenomena (see Mawani's chapter in this volume). As a counterweight, other studies considered it necessary to underline that these phenomena had local consequences and local expressions. The 'glocal' is thus the result of a double movement of deterritorialisation and reterritorialisation. However, this dialectical movement does not stop with one de- and reterritorialisation. On the contrary, it triggers a cascading of de- and reterritorialisation.

In this chapter, I will look at a series of these movements with a focus on the regional state of Gujarat (see Figure 1.1). Following the first section of the chapter that aims to clarify the terms and processes of de- and reterritorialisation, the second section attempts to map the movements of de- and reterritorialisation, beginning at the central state level and its consequences at the regional state level. The third section turns to the sub-regional level and shows how de- and reterritorialisation operate between economic development and land liberalisation. The final section is dedicated to the emotional power of the territory and to reterritorialisation through subnationalism.

In order to take both sides of the story into account as well as their consequences, I will look to the work of scholars (notably Brenner 1999a, 1999b; Ó Tuathail 1998; 1999) who have shown that deterritorialisation has to be understood and analysed as only one moment, only one part of the processes of de- and reterritorialisation.[3] Ó Tuathail (1998: 82) put forth that '[t]he problematic of deterritorialization is also the problematic of reterritorialization; it is not the presence or absence of state territoriality but its changing status, power and meaning in relationship to postmodern technological constellations, speed machines and global webs of capitalism'. According to this view, globalisation does not cause a loss of importance of territoriality but brings about modifications in its status, power and meaning. In the same vein, I propose to conceptualise the dialectical movements of de- and reterritorialisation as a spiral of changes in the conception of territory and territoriality, as a series of rescalings of the territorial organisation and of the control over the territory. Thus, deterritorialisation has to be understood *in conjunction with a movement of reterritorialisation*, as describing a process of change of scale of reference or change in the scale of control over the territory.[4]

Figure 1.1 *Gujarat and the Movements of De- and Reterritorialisation*

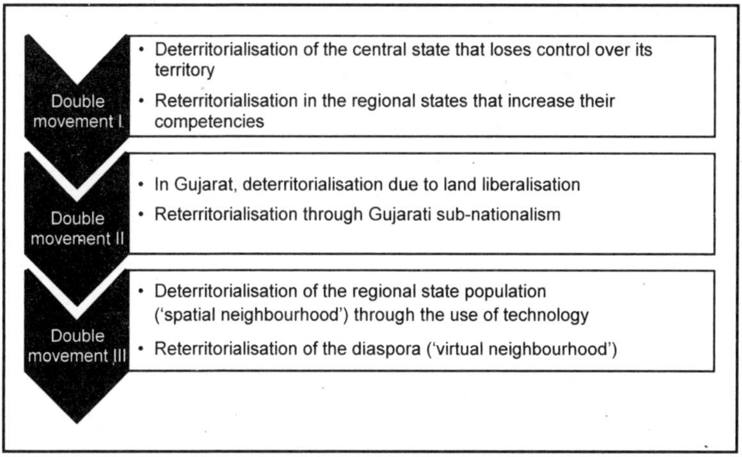

The processes of de- and reterritorialisation concern material as well as cultural and emotional factors. Writing about territoriality, Penrose (2002: 280) distinguishes the material side and the emotional side of territoriality. He emphasises that '[w]hen people create territories, they create boundaries that both unite and divide space along with everything that it contains. By combining some people and certain resources and separating them from other people and other resources, the creation of territories gives physical substances and symbolic meaning to notions of "us" and "them" and "ours" and "theirs"'. The material side of territoriality refers to resources present on a certain territory that become then 'our' or 'their' resources. Thus, the material power of the territory goes with an emotional appropriation of this materiality. People feel attached to a certain territory, whether or not they live there, but they consider it to be their homeland (Connor 2001), or the place where they have their roots (Malkki 1992) (see Dewji's chapter in this volume). Studies on nations and nationalism have shown the strength that attachment to a territory can have as people's identity is linked with a place, with its landscapes and the meaning it has for those who identify with it (Paasi 1995; Smith 1996, 1999; Storey 2012). The emotional power of territoriality can be linked with the processes of de- and reterritorialisation as changes in territoriality induce emotional responses.

DE- AND RETERRITORIALISATION

Softening of the Hierarchy of Boundaries

Globalisation designates an 'increasing interlinking of political, economic, institutional, social, cultural, technical, and ecological issues at the global level' (Backhaus 2003: 6). This increased interlinking results in states losing some of their power over their territory. In a more interlinked world, states have less control on what happens in their territory and on what is entering or leaving it – be it information, goods, people or money. Yet, studies have noted that globalisation does not only mean less power to the central states, but that it also causes a redistribution of power (Brenner 1999a; Randeria 2002; Rodriguez-Pose and Gill 2003). Somewhat paradoxically, globalisation has resulted in decentralisation: by diminishing the power of the states (their possibility to control what is happening in their territory) and has led to an increased power of the regions (Rodriguez-Pose and Gill 2003). There are several reasons for that: one is devolution, the fact that the central state has ceded a number of what were its competencies to the regions; another is that regional states often re-regulated domains that had been deregulated by the central state.

In this new configuration of power, the regions, with increased competencies and a weakening control of the central state, gained direct access to the world. This put into question the hierarchy of boundaries according to which the federal state managed most of what was linked with the international level (be it contacts with other countries, with international organisations, or foreign enterprises). Traditionally, municipalities had to refer to the region and the regions had to go through the union when faced with questions with international implications. Yet, with decentralisation, the regional states and municipal authorities have gained more control on their territory. Now, regions have become direct interlocutors with foreign governments and international organisations (Sinha 2004). The hierarchy of boundaries has been *flattened*. This flattening or horizontalisation of the boundaries results in the central state symbolically losing its territory, as its boundaries no longer represent the limit between the country and the rest of the world. This makes the centre just another interlocutor and one that has neither its own territory nor its own people. It becomes a deterritorialised unit. The level of the central state remains, but it is weakened given that many of its competencies have been reterritorialised at the regional level.[5]

We can observe how this movement developed in India. With the liberalisation of its economy in the 1990s, India joined the processes of globalisation more directly. Until then, the country was far from insulated from the global trends and issues but its investment, trade and banking policies restricted the penetration of foreign money and goods into its territory. This controlled economy prevented or protected India from being fully globalised. But the fiscal deficit of 1990–91 forced the government to introduce important changes. Through economic reforms and deregulation, the central government lost control over many areas that were previously tightly regulated. The reforms included, among other measures, 'the abolition of industrial licensing and other types of control over private investment' (Ahluwalia 2002: 101). Since July 1991, investors have been free to choose in which regional state they want to invest. Before that, they had to petition the government for their investment proposal and the final decision on the location of the investment was reserved to the central government. This allowed for an equitable regional distribution of industries (Chakravarti 2009).

In 1990–91, the fiscal deficit required the government of the Union to increase revenues and to cut spending (Corbridge and Harriss 2004). In the process of diminishing its budget, it transferred many competencies to the states but without transferring the corresponding resources (Rodriguez-Pose and Gill 2003). However, much of what was done and decided at the central state level until the 1990s became the prerogative of the regional states. The regions have become central in economic as well as in political terms.[6] India thus moved from a central dirigisme to what Rudolph and Rudolph (2002: 58) called 'a federal market economy'. According to these authors, '[t]he decline of central public investment and the growth of private investment have given the federal states a greatly expanded role in economic liberalisation and in promoting investment and economic growth' (ibid.: 59). This has also resulted in growing competition between the states of the

Indian Union to attract domestic and foreign investments. As Sinha (2004: 49) points out, '[d]irect attraction of foreign investment by states has contributed to de facto authority to approve foreign investment projects, establish tax rates for foreign investment firms, and establish rules of the game. Thus, state-level actors are shaping foreign economic relations'. Here, we see how liberalisation of the Indian economy accelerated decentralisation and devolution of power to the regional states.

In the summer of 2012, Narendra Modi, the Chief Minister of Gujarat, visited Japan to promote Japanese investment in Gujarat. The Indian press noted that it was the first time that a Chief Minister was invited for an official visit by the Japanese government, as the honour is normally reserved for presidents or prime ministers. In 2012, Modi was also visited by an American envoy who praised the economic development of the state and at the same time mentioned that Modi was a very controversial Chief Minister (I will come back to Modi's double image later) (see Bobbio's chapter in this volume). And, in October 2012, the British High Commissioner visited Gujarat after ten years of a no-contact policy.[7]

We could think that these examples are only an expression of the political climate in which representatives of foreign governments enter into contact with a Chief Minister – and potential candidate for Prime Minister – of a state welcoming foreign investments. These examples are, however, also an expression of the horizontalisation of boundaries; an expression of a situation in which the representative of a regional state can deal directly with officials of another country; an expression of a more interconnected world in which regional states have direct access to the rest of the world, unmediated or much less mediated by their central government than previously.

The hierarchy of boundaries has been flattened or softened but not erased. Gujarat's access to the rest of the world no longer depends on the central government. Gujarat now has the autonomy to be an international player. Yet, Gujarat's contact with the world is still, in certain areas, mediated by its inclusion in the Indian Union. Gujarat's position in India still has a large influence because a number of competencies remain on the 'Union List' in the

Constitution. Moreover, in a feedback loop, Gujarat's contacts with the world and its visibility on the world map influence the place of Gujarat within India.

So far, we have noted, first, that globalisation transforms the relations that the regional states can have with the rest of the world and, second, that their position in the world has an impact on their position within India. The more 'direct access' the regional states developed, the more their dependence on the federal state diminished. But this has had a further consequence on the relations between the states. Before liberalisation, states were already competing with each other for central resources but this competition increased in the post-reform era in which states competed to attract national and international funds (Sinha 2004). Moreover, now, regional states not only compete against each other for resources but they also compete with the central state for resources and for control over their territory. The regional states, with their increased powers, are less willing to let go of their resources to the centre. This can be exemplified with the issue of tax transfer.

On several occasions, Modi accused the centre of stealing Gujarat's money. In November 2007, he even proposed that the centre stop collecting taxes from the state for a year and that, in return, Gujarat would forgo central aid for that period.[8] Modi reiterated his point on several occasions. During his *Sadbhavna* fast, while he was in Jetpur in the Rajkot district, he declared that the people of Gujarat 'would not tolerate Delhi repeat[ing] its loot[ing] of the nation in Gujarat'. And that he will not 'allow anybody else [to] put ... [a] hand on the treasury of Gujarat' (*Deshgujarat* 2012). With these polemical statements, Modi presents himself as the champion of Gujarat against the Delhi Sultanate stealing Gujarat's money and not offering anything in exchange. In a message posted on his blog on 25 January 2012 for Republic Day and entitled *Co-operative, not coercive federalism for strong republic*, Modi wrote:

> There is even larger destruction of the federal structure in fiscal areas. In the name of 'public good' or 'people's rights', more and more funds are making their way to New Delhi. The Finance Commission allocated substantially lesser resources to the states keeping a lion's share of funds with the Centre.

> The Centre has become adept at passing populist schemes but there is no financial support given to the states for their execution. Adequate central funds are not an obligation from New Delhi but the right of every state to pursue development (Modi's Blog 2012).

The position of Narendra Modi on the transfer of taxes to the centre rests on a claimed sense of territoriality, mixing the material and emotional power of the territory. It operates a strong reterritorialisation at the state level of the power and meaning of territoriality. This reterritorialisation might have been particularly strong in Gujarat as the state government under the chief ministership of Modi has fought hard for the rescaling and reterritorialisation of competencies at the regional state level. It has fought to attract and retain the material and emotional power of the regional state territory.

DETERRITORIALISATION, LAND LIBERALISATION AND ECONOMIC DEVELOPMENT

The reterritorialisation at state level was accompanied by a simultaneous movement of deterritorialisation. In effect, reterritorialisation occurred in Gujarat due to its (controversial) economic success. This resulted in land liberalisation and can be considered to be a form of deterritorialisation. Sud (2010) shows how the government of Gujarat passed gradually from developmentalism with its policy of 'land to the tillers' (a policy of land redistribution that took place before the 1970s) to land liberalisation and expropriation of agricultural land for setting up industries and Special Economic Zones (SEZs). Sud (ibid.) argues that the economic development of Gujarat rests for the most part on the deregulation of land propriety. This deregulation began in 1988, when the Chief Minister Amarsinh Chaudhary revoked, only for drought stricken areas, the rule that in order to buy agricultural land one had to reside within an eight-kilometre radius and be an agriculturist. Moreover, the (then Bharatiya Janata Party (BJP)) government decided to simplify the process through which up to 10 hectares of agricultural land could be converted to non-agricultural land for industrial purposes. By 1995, the eight-kilometre restriction had been withdrawn for the entire state and the land market was open to entrepreneurs. Yet, as demonstrated by Sud (ibid.: 127), the state did not simply 'withdraw from making decisions about who would buy land and where' as 'the state started to facilitate the land needs of entrepreneurs who expressed interests in investing in the economy'. In order to do that, in several cases the state intervened invoking the outdated Land Acquisition Act of 1894 that allows it to acquire private land for public purposes and then transferred the ownership of the land to private developers.[9] 'After all, in the reasoning of the state, liberalization induced industrialization is a public purpose which will generate employment and prosperity' (ibid.: 129).[10]

Thus, the reterritorialisation we observed in the previous part of this chapter went hand in hand with a movement of deterritorialisation notably by making public land available for industry and even by deterritorialising in the first sense of putting some parts of the land of Gujarat outside the territory with the creation of SEZs. A SEZ is a 'specifically delineated duty free enclave and shall be deemed to be foreign territory for the purpose of trade and operations and duty and tariffs' (Government of Gujarat 2012). SEZs are seen as instruments of development to attract foreign investors and to allow Indian investors to be more competitive to export. They are not new, the first SEZ was opened in 1965 in Gujarat, but their number has grown at a quicker pace since the 1990s.[11] SEZs are indeed 'zones of exception' due to tax exemption but also because, in these zones, many labour and environment laws do not apply (Büschi 2012). These exceptions, as was the case for liberalisation in general, have been justified as promoting growth and generating employment in the state.[12] Yet, this deterritorialisation has also created worries, disapproval and opposition. In an interview in 2007, Gopal Krishna Pillai, the then chairman of the Board of Approval for SEZs and Commerce Secretary, listed what he saw as unjustified fears towards the foreign territory status of SEZs:

> The SEZs are deemed to be 'foreign territory' only for the purpose of the Customs Act. It means, there you get duty-free items. But otherwise every single law of the land will be applicable to SEZs. Some NGOs have come and told me that if a

> murder is committed in an SEZ, you will have to file a complaint with the Interpol! You have seen the articles stating that Jamaat-e-Islami thinks that 'SEZs are against Muslims'. In Gujarat, people are saying that SEZs will increase the flow of liquor. Someone else said that you are bringing back the East India Company. All these allegations are not true.
>
> Every single law of India will apply there (in SEZs) .... A gate pass is required only in the processing area, the rest of the area will be open for the public. (Rediff.com 2007)

But one issue related to the creation of SEZs has been particularly contentious: land acquisition or expropriation. There have been several cases in India when the land acquired for new SEZs was agricultural land which meant that people lost their livelihoods and were not given compensation or alternative employment opportunities that were promised when these SEZs were agreed upon. In 2007 two cities in West Bengal where the government planned to acquire prime agricultural land for setting up a chemical hub (in Nandigram) and a motor car plant by Tata Motors (in Singur) faced similar issues. In the latter case, the strong mobilisation of people that either did not want to sell their land or refused the inadequate compensation led Ratan Tata to finally renounce the opening of the plant in Singur and to accept Modi's offer to set up in Sanand, Gujarat. There, Tata could install his factory on land that was already the property of the government. Thus, the state of Gujarat did not build its reputation solely on SEZs, but also on a general climate favourable to investment, and a crucial factor for this was the availability of land.

RETERRITORIALISATION AND SUBNATIONALISM

Deterritorialisation, through land liberalisation and the controversial economic success of Gujarat that accompanied it, led to a form of reterritorialisation through subnationalism. The dialectic developed as follows: a first movement of deterritorialisation through liberalisation was followed by a second movement of reterritorialisation through heightened subnationalism. The economic success of Gujarat aroused a renewed pride for their region, especially among the Gujarati middle class (Nandy 2008; Majumdar 2012), and in some parts of the diaspora (Parmar 2012).

In the last twenty years, subnationalism in Gujarat has taken the form of a Gujarati-type of Hindu nationalism. Since 1995, the state has been governed mainly by the Hindu nationalist Bharatiya Janata Party (BJP). Hindu nationalism is based on a unifying and homogenising discourse that overlooks regional differences, as it aims to construct a Hindu nation gathering people together from different castes and different regions. In this respect, it is a type of deterritorialised discourse. Yet, in Gujarat, as well as in other states, this general discourse has been re-rooted into particular forms of subnationalism.[13] In Gujarat, this began towards the end of the 1980s when the BJP in the state 'took the basic elements of neoliberal economic propaganda – liberalization, privatization of services and infrastructure management, deregulation of the labour market, globalization of investment – and enclosed them in an ethno-nationalist frame' (Bobbio 2012: 663). This Gujarati version of Hindu nationalism was strengthened when Narendra Modi became Chief Minister in 2001. He developed a discourse linking Hindu nationalism, liberalisation and *asmita* (Gujarati pride or identity). A central part of *asmita*, in the way Modi has constructed it, is based on the successful economic development of Gujarat that happened, in Modi's view, due to the policies he put in place. Modi uses *asmita* as a shield against criticisms, turning reproaches made to him in particular as condemnations against Gujarat and Gujaratis in general. Thus, in September 2011, after observers noted the irony of Modi undertaking a fast for communal peace and harmony, he replied that '[f]or 10 years, we did not hit back, but collected all the stones and brickbats thrown at us and used them as the stepping stone to take Gujarat to the new heights of development' (Modi quoted in Dasgupta 2011).

Modi nurtured this Gujarati brand of Hindu nationalism focusing his political discourse on development and nurturing his image of *vikas purush* (man of development). This image is strongly linked with the Vibrant Gujarat Summits that have been organised every two years since 2003. The first summit took place less than a year after the anti-Muslim post-Godhra violence. It marked the beginning of the rhetoric of economic development that Modi has been using since then trying to rise above the dark stains that marked his arrival in power. The polarisation that followed the

2002 violence has played in his favour for his first electoral victory but an unstable situation in the state would certainly have had a negative effect on his chances at winning a second time. Modi projected himself as being the 'developer of Gujarat' and this has allowed him to survive and strive politically.[14]

Modi has been particularly successful in advertising his achievements even if the success story he put forth leaves many sceptics. Some question the role played by the Chief Minister in this success, as Gujarat was already an industrially developed state well before Modi arrived on the scene. Others question the success in itself, noting that the economic growth of the last ten years did not create employment and did not translate into improvements of most aspects of human development in the state (Hirway and Shah 2011; Chandhoke 2012; Sood 2012). This is another case of the unequal development brought about by glocalisation that Bauman described in 1998. According to him, glocalisation brings 'concentration of capital, finance and all other resources of choice and effective action – but also and in the first place ... concentration of freedom to act' (Bauman 1998: 43). This concentration in the hands of a few at the cost of all others is particularly strong in Gujarat as it has been reinforced by the actions of the state through the 'high state-big-business alliance' (Sud 2010: 134). Modi's model of development is certainly popular among industrialists who benefit from it and among the middle class who hope to benefit from it, but it excludes a large part of the population. In 2008, for a growing portion of the people of Gujarat less food was available than in 1980, placing Gujarat thirteenth in the 'Indian State Hunger Index'; behind states like Uttar Pradesh, Rajasthan and Assam (Goswami 2009). In April 2011, when Anna Hazare (the social activist who, in the same year, initiated the movement demanding a strong anti-corruption bill) praised Modi for his efforts at rural development, farmers protested once again in Gujarat (Yadav 2011). Before the 2012 assembly elections, many observers also pointed to the unequal growth of Gujarat that resulted in the state going down in the Human Development Index from fifth in 1996 to ninth in 2006 (Chandhoke 2012), despite its much advertised economic growth.

However, in the context of the 'federal state economy', Modi has successfully promoted the image of Gujarat as a business destination for Indian and foreign investments. Thus, after attracting national and international media attention because of the 2002 anti-Muslim violence, the state garnered recognition due to the success of its economic development. The report of the (United States) Congressional Research Service (CRS) on India that came out in September 2011 made special mention of Modi and Gujarat. Modi was presented as a potential BJP prime ministerial candidate for the 2014 general elections and as someone 'who has overseen impressive development successes in his state, but who is also dogged by controversy over his alleged complicity in lethal anti-Muslim rioting there in 2002' (CRS 2011: 41). A few months later, Modi was on the cover of *Time* magazine (the 26 March 2012 issue) with the headline *Modi means business but can he lead India*. In the same month, the Brookings Institution published a long interview with the Chief Minister (Antholis 2012) that critics considered to be far too positive (Dharker et al. 2012). In the three cases, it was economic success that was the centre of attention, even if a mention of the post-Godhra violence was always made. This gives Narendra Modi a Dr Jekyll and Mr Hyde personality where one facet is linked with violent Hindu nationalism and the other with economic development. Modi remains marred by the 'original sin' that allowed him to come to power, but it is undoubtedly his Dr Jekyll side that is currently under the spotlight.

Modi has, thus, successfully constructed his image of being a Gujarati leader playing in a globalised world for the good of Gujarat. When he was reproached for being 'only' a regional leader, he replied that he was proud of being unlike Rahul Gandhi who is, according to Modi, not a regional nor a national leader, but an international one, as he could campaign in India as well as in Italy (Dasgupta 2012). However, the balance between subnationalism and liberalisation is difficult to keep and inevitably brings contradictions. For example, Modi, who is known for trying hard to attract foreign investments in Gujarat, recently said that he was opposed to the Congress' initiative to open the Indian market to foreign direct investment (FDI) in the retail sector. Besides, attracting FDI was also the aim of his 2012 visit to Japan during which he publicised the compliments that Japanese functionaries made to him for his 'visionary leadership'. Khare (2012) points out the incoherence of Modi's pride after the Chief Minister had said in 2004 that '[a]fter years of suppression, we have got into the habit of taking certificates from foreigners. Should we be taking certificate from this lady in Japan who came here only for a few days?' (Modi quoted in Khare 2012). This reply that Khare (2012) recalls as 'vintage Modi, massaging Gujarati subnationalism' was triggered by a comment from Verghese Kurien, the director of Amul, who said that the 2002 communal violence had marred the reputation of the state as shown by the negative comment of a visiting Japanese dignitary.

As we have seen, Modi is aware of the power of image; he is aware of the image he projects (his image as a political leader as well as the image of his achievements in Gujarat) and he is in control of it. He uses all types of media and technology to target different sectors of the public, especially the young and urban middle class. He has a blog and is active on Twitter. To increase his presence during the 2012 assembly elections campaign, he set up a cable TV channel called *Namo Gujarat*. Moreover, his presence was multiplied with the help of 3D technology and holographic projection, which assisted him in addressing public meetings in different places simultaneously. This way he did not need to criss-cross the territory of the state to cover it with his image. The day before the end of the election campaign, he addressed people through holographic projections in 53 different places (*Indian Express* 2012). On Modi's website (2012), it was reported that '[t]he Chief Minister affirmed that this is for the first time that people are connecting like this using technology and added that technology is only the medium – the bond he shares with the people is that of the heart'. Yet connecting technology has been in use for a long time to keep the 'bond of the heart,' but mainly between the diaspora and its homeland (Anderson 1994). Thus, in terms of territory and 'its changing status, power and meaning' (Ó Tuathail 1998: 82), the reterritorialisation through subnationalism has been accompanied by yet another form of deterritorialisation, resting on a broad and generalised use of media and technology to communicate within, what Appadurai (1996: 194) called the 'spatial neighbourhood' (in opposition with the 'virtual neighbourhoods' of the diaspora). This further blurs the distinction and makes the links between spatial and virtual neighbourhoods (or the diaspora) more complex.

CONCLUSION

In this chapter, I followed a series of de- and reterritorialisations at play when looking at globalisation and its influence on the way Gujarat is in India and in the world. This demonstrates that globalisation is not only synonymous with deterritorialisation, that it does not mean only an uprooting of people and economic and financial processes, but that it means a change of scale, and is thus accompanied by a movement of reterritorialisation. I have also argued, looking at the state of Gujarat and at the interactions between the subregional, regional, national and international levels, that one should not stop with the observation of one double movement of de- and reterritorialisation, as one movement is followed by subsequent movements that should be examined together to get a better grasp of the phenomenon. It is a process, a series of movements that have to be understood as mutually reinforcing, each pulling the other along. Moreover, this process of change of scale of reference or change in the scale of control over the territory concerns the territory as a material place, but it also concerns the emotional component that is involved and plays a role in the process of de- and reterritorialisation.

NOTES

1. I do not imply that the state had complete control over its territory but only that the organisation was clearly pyramidal.
2. The concept of glocalisation indicates 'the combined process of globalization and local-territorial reconfiguration' (Swyngedouw 1992: 61 quoted in Brenner 1999b: 436).
3. The concept of deterritorialisation was first used by Deleuze and Guattari (1972, 1980, 1991), who emphasised that deterritorialisation goes hand-in-hand with reterritorialisation. In their work, the concept of deterritorialisation refers, however, to a very wide range of phenomena mostly not linked with the territory of the state.

4. My definition differs slightly but is inspired by Brenner (1999b: 432) who considers reterritorialisation to be 'the reconfiguration and rescaling of forms of territorial organisation such as cities and states'.
5. There is also a movement of reterritorialisation 'upwards' in supranational entities such as international organisations (Brenner 1999a; Randeria 2002) as well as in the supranational regions (Ching 2001).
6. On the growing importance and autonomy of politics at the state level, see Yadav and Palshikar (2008).
7. Several observers considered that the visit of the British High Commissioner just two months before the Gujarat assembly elections looked like an endorsement of Modi. The High Commissioner, however, replied that contact was made with the state and not with one person in particular (*Firstpost* 2012).
8. It is true that the state of Gujarat pays much more than it receives through various transfers from the centre. In 2008 Gujarat gave INR 40,000 crores in taxes to the centre and got only 2.5 per cent in return (PT 2008).
9. An agreement has been arrived at on the bill to reform the outdated Land Acquisition Act. The bill has now to be approved by the Parliament (see *The Times of India* 2013).
10. Studies on Gujarat demonstrated that despite the growth of the GDP few jobs were created and the indicators for the human development index in the state did not improve (see, among many other studies, Hirway and Shah 2011).
11. This demand for the creation of new SEZs has, however, stopped with the Parliament voting a new fiscal law in 2009 (that has not yet come into force) that withdraws the fiscal advantages accorded to SEZs in the Special Economic Zone Act 2005 (Büschi 2012).
12. For a more general view on the debate on SEZs, see Aggarwal (2006).
13. On the adaptation of the BJP discourse in Kerala, see Chiriyankandath (1996); in Bengal, see Gillan (2003); and in Maharashtra, see Hansen (1996).
14. Several authors (Jaffrelot 2007; Spodek 2010) argue that the BJP and Modi were aware of the limits of using violence for electoral gains, as violence can polarise the population and bring electoral results in the short term, but, if it lasts too long, it will be seen as the failure of the state to bring back peace and order.

REFERENCES

Aggarwal, Aradhna. 'Special Economic Zones: Revisiting the Policy Debate', *Economic and Political Weekly*, Vol. 41, No. 43/44 (Nov. 2006): 4533–36.

Ahluwalia, Montek S. 'State-Level Performance under Economic Reforms in India', in *Economic Policy Reforms and the Indian Economy*, edited by Anne O. Krueger, Chicago: The University of Chicago Press, 2002, pp. 91–128.

Amin, Ash. 'Placing Globalization', *Theory, Culture and Society*, Vol. 14 (1997): 123–37.

Anderson, Benedict. *Imagined Communities*, London and New York: Verso, 1991.

——. 'Exodus', *Critical Inquiry*, Vol. 20 (1994): 314–27.

Antholis, Wiliam J. 'India's Most Admired and Most Feared Politician: Narendra Modi', *Brookings*, 16 March 2012, <http://www.brookings.edu/blogs/up-front/posts/2012/03/16-modi-antholis> (2 April 2012).

Appadurai, Arjun. *Modernity at Large: Cultural Dimensions of Globalization*, Minneapolis and London: The University of Minnesota Press, 1996.

Backhaus, Norman. 'The Globalisation Discourse', Swiss National Centre of Competence in Research North South, Working Paper No. 2, 2003, <http://www.dsgz.geo.uzh.ch/pdfs/Backhaus_GlobalisationDiscourse.pdf> (12 November 2012).

Bauman, Zygmunt. 'On Glocalization: Or Globalization for Some, Localization for Some Others', *Thesis Eleven*, Vol. 54 (1998): 37–49.

Bobbio, Tommaso. 'Making Gujarat Vibrant: *Hindutva*, Development and the Rise of Subnationalism in India', *Third World Quarterly*, Vol. 33, No. 4 (2012): 657–72.

Brenner, Neil. 'Beyond State-Centrism? Space, Territoriality, and Geographical Scale in Globalization Studies', *Theory and Society*, Vol. 28, No. 1 (1999a): 39–78.

——. 'Globalisation as Reterritorialisation: The Re-scaling of Urban Governance in the European Union', *Urban Studies*, Vol. 36, No. 3 (1999b): 431–51.

Büschi, Michaela. 'Urbanization, Law and SEZ (Special Economic Zones) in India', Unpublished PhD Thesis, Graduate Institute of International and Development Studies, Geneva, 2012.

Chakravarti, Ritadhi. 'An Empirical Analysis of Investment Determinants in Indian States: 1998–2006', *The Michigan Journal of Business*, Vol. 2, No. 2 (2009): 9–53.

Chandhoke, Neera. 'Modi's Gujarat and its Little Illusions', *Economic and Political Weekly*, Vol. 47, No. 49 (Dec. 2012): 10–11.

Ching, Leo. 'Globalizing the Regional, Regionalizing the Global: Mass Culture and Asianism in the Age of Late Capital', in *Globalization*, edited by Arjun Appadurai, Durham and London: Duke University Press, 2001, pp. 279–306.

Chiriyankandath, James. 'Hindu Nationalism and Regional Political Culture in India: A Study of Kerala', *Nationalism and Ethnic Politics*, Vol. 2, No. 1 (1996): 44–66.

Congressional Research Service (CRS). 'India: Domestic Issues, Strategic Dynamics, and US Relations', 1 September 2011, < http://www.fas.org/sgp/crs/row/RL33529.pdf> (2 May 2012).

Connor, Walker. 'Homelands in a World of States', in *Understanding Nationalism*, edited by Montserrat Guibernau and John Hutchinson, Oxford: Polity Press/Blackwell, 2001, pp. 53–73.

Corbridge, Stuart and John Harriss. *Reinventing India: Liberalization, Hindu Nationalism and Popular Democracy*, New Delhi: Oxford University Press, 2004.

Dasgupta, Manas. 'Modi Holds Fast with Eye on National Political Stage', *The Hindu*, 17 September 2011.

——. 'Modi Rakes up Rahul's Roots', *The Hindu*, 17 September 2012.

Deleuze, Gilles and Félix Guattari. *Qu'est-ce que la philosophie?*, Paris: Editions de Minuit, 1991.

——. *Mille Plateaux*, Paris: Editions de Minuit, 1980.

——. *L'Anti-Œdipe*, Paris: Editions de Minuit, 1972.

Deshgujarat. 'People Won't Allow Centre Repeat Nation's Loot in Gujarat: Modi', 30 January 2012, <http://deshgujarat.com/2012/01/30/people-wont-allow-centre-repeat-nations-loot-in-gujaratmodi/> (21 June 2012).

Dharker, Anil, Cyrus Guzder, Nandan Maluste and Teesta Setalvad. 'An Aarti from Time: A Brookings Chalisa', *Outlook*, 2 April 2012.

Elden, Stuart. 'Missing the Point: Globalisation, Deterritorialisation and the Space of the World', *Transactions of the Institute of British Geographers*, Vol. 30, No. 1 (2005): 8–19.

Firstpost. 'Engaging with Gujarat, Not Endorsing Modi: UK High Commissioner', 22 October 2012, <http://www.firstpost.com/

world/engaging-with-gujarat-not-endorsing-modi-uk-high-commissioner-499073.html> (12 December 2012).

Gillan, Michael. 'Bengal's Past and Present: Hindu Nationalist Contestations of History and Regional Identity', *Contemporary South Asia*, Vol. 12, No. 3 (2003): 381–98.

Goswami, Rahul. 'The Hunger Index', January 2009, <http://infochangeindia.org/agriculture/analysis/the-hunger-index.html> (8 January 2012).

Government of Gujarat, Industries Commissionerate. 'Special Economic Zone (SEZ)', <http://ic.gujarat.gov.in/?page_id=430> (23 November 2012).

Hansen, Thomas Blom. 'The Vernacularisation of Hindutva: The BJP and Shiv Sena in Rural Maharashtra', *Contributions to Indian Sociology*, Vol. 30, No. 2 (1996): 177–214.

Hirway, Indira and Neha Shah. 'Labour and Employment in Gujarat', *Economic and Political Weekly*, Vol. 46, No. 44/45 (Nov. 2011): 62–64.

Indian Express. 'Modi: PM Sowing Communal Seeds, People Won't Forgive', 11 December 2012.

Jaffrelot, Christophe. 'The 2002 Pogrom in Gujarat: The Post 9/11 Face of Hindu Nationalist Anti-Muslim Violence', in *Religion and Violence in South Asia, Theory and Practice*, edited by John R. Hinnells and Richard King, London and New York: Routledge, 2007, pp. 173–92.

Khare, Harish. 'What's in a NaMo? A Troubling Cult', *The Hindu*, 27 October 2012.

Majumdar, Dipesh. 'Middle Class Makes Narendra Modi Urban Legend', *DNA*, 10 December 2012.

Malkki, Liisa. 'National Geographic: The Rooting of People and the Territorialization of National Identity among Scholars and Refugees', *Cultural Anthropology*, Vol. 7, No. 1 (1992): 24–44.

Modi's Blog. 'Co-operative, Not Coercive Federalism for Strong Republic', 25 January 2012, <http://blogs.timesofindia.indiatimes.com/narendra-modis-blog/entry/co-operative-not-coercive-federalism-for-strong-republic> (22 December 2012).

Modi's Website. 'Connecting with People Innovatively', 19 November 2102,<http://www.narendramodi.in/connecting-with-people- innovatively-shri-narendra-modi-addressed-public-meetings-at-4-places-at-a-time-using-3-d-technology/> (21 November 2012).

Nandy, Ashis. 'Blame the Middle Class', *The Times of India*, 8 January 2008.

Ó Tuathail, Gearóid. 'Borderless Worlds? Problematising Discourses of Deterritorialisation', *Geopolitics*, Vol. 4, No. 2 (1999): 139–54.

——. 'Political Geography III: Dealing with Deterritorialization', *Progress in Human Geography*, Vol. 22, No. 1 (1998): 81–93.

Paasi, Anssi. 'Constructing Territories, Boundaries and Regional Identities', in *Contested Territory: Border Disputes at the Edge of the Former Soviet Empire*, edited by Tuomas Forsberg, Aldershot: Edward Elgar, 1995, pp. 42–61.

Parmar, Vijaysing. 'Foreign Hand Being Lent to Narendra Modi', *The Times of India*, 20 November 2012.

Penrose, Jan. 'Nations, States and Homelands: Territory and Territoriality in Nationalist Thought', *Nations and Nationalism*, Vol. 8, No. 3 (2002): 277–97.

PT, Sebastian. 'Thanks, but No Thanks', *Outlook Business*, 12 July 2008, <http://business.outlookindia.com/article.aspx?101310> (3 December 2012).

Randeria, Shalini. 'Globalising Gujarat: Environmental Action in the Legal Arena', in *Development and Deprivation in Gujarat: In Honour of Jan Breman*, edited by Ghanshyam Shah, Mario Rutten and Hein Streefkerk, New Delhi: Sage Publications, 2002, pp. 249–69.

Rediff.com. 'Rivalry between Business Houses has Blown up the SEZ Issue', 21 February 2007, <http://www.rediff.com/money/2007/feb/21sez.htm> (3 December 2012).

Rodriguez-Pose, Andrés and Nicholas Gill. 'The Global Trend Towards Devolution and its Implications', *Environment and Planning C: Government and Policy*, Vol. 21 (2003): 333–51.

Rudolph, Susanne H. and Lloyd I. Rudolph. 'New Dimensions of Indian Democracy', *Journal of Democracy*, Vol. 13, No. 1 (2002): 52–66.

Sinha, Aseema. 'The Changing Political Economy of Federalism in India: A Historical Institutionalist Approach', *India Review*, Vol. 3, No. 1 (2004): 25–63.

Smith, Anthony D. 'Culture, Community and Territory: The Politics of Ethnicity and Nationalism', *International Affairs*, Vol. 72, No. 3 (1996): 445–58.

Smith, Anthony D. *Myths and Memories of the Nation*, Oxford: Oxford University Press, 1999.

Sood, Atul. 'Poverty Amid Prosperity', *The Hindu*, 30 November 2012.

Spodek, Howard. 'From Gandhi to Modi: Ahmedabad, 1915–2007', in *The Idea of Gujarat: History, Ethnography and Text*, edited by Edward

Simpson and Aparna Kapadia, New Delhi: Orient Blackswan, 2010, pp. 136–52.

Storey, David. *Territories: The Claiming of Space*, London: Routledge, 2012.

Sud, Nikita. 'The Politics of Land in Post-Colonial Gujarat', in *The Idea of Gujarat: History, Ethnography and Text*, edited by Edward Simpson and Aparna Kapadia, New Delhi: Orient Blackswan, 2010, pp. 120–35.

Swyngedouw, Erik. 'The Mammon Quest: 'Glocalisation', Interspacial Competition and the Monetary Order: The Construction of New Scales', in *Cities and Regions in the New Europe*, edited by Mick Dunford and Grigoris Kafkalas, New York: Belhaven Press, 1992, pp. 39–67.

The Times of India. 'Finally a Consensus on Land Acquisition Bill After Six Years', 19 April 2013.

Yadav, Anumeha. 'Rural Modiland is No Model, Anna', *Tehelka*, 30 April 2011.

Yadav, Yogendra and Suhas Palshikar. 'Ten Theses on State Politics in India', *Seminar*, Vol. 591 (November 2008): 14–22.

CHAPTER 2

Gendering the Gujarati Diaspora

Oral Narratives and Identity

Sandhya Rao Mehta

Around the year 1650 a Portuguese commander is said to have asked for the hand of the daughter of a Baniya trader in the erstwhile kingdom of Muscat. This trader, offended and angered at the presumptuousness of the Portuguese, went to the ruling family, the Ya'ribahs, and eventually helped to expel the Portuguese from the kingdom of Muscat, much to the relief of the rulers who were themselves looking for ways to ward off this external threat (Allen 1978). This tiny slice of history, narrated in Allen's (ibid.) exploration of the history of the Indian trading community in Oman, is based on historical narratives pointing to the way in which the Gujarati Banyan traders were then able to use their clout with the ruling family to exempt themselves from paying the *jiziyah* (poll tax). More importantly, however, this anecdote points to a very little known fact about Indian presence in the coastal city of Muscat in which traders appear to have lived along with their families, often for long periods of time. Current anecdotal evidence also points to the fact that some of these families, most of whom were Gujaratis, continued to live in various towns of Oman even during and after the First World War when Indian presence otherwise dwindled in these parts. By the beginning of the Second World War, large groups of Indian merchants from the Kutch area of Gujarat are said to have resettled here, often with women following their trader-husbands upon marriage.

In this way, women came to be an integral part of the Indian diaspora in some parts of the Arabian Gulf, particularly in Oman.

And yet, theirs is a tale which has waited to be told, for, while the Indian diaspora in the Middle East is itself an area little explored by academics, whatever research does exist privileges a tale which is essentially a meta-narrative of commerce and economy. While limited research on the Indian trading community in Oman appears occasionally, it is the women of this narrative who are entirely absent and, therefore, silent. As the economy develops and the community asserts itself more vocally, it is the women who remain behind the shadows of statistics and economic data, often hiding tales of displacement, loss and re-creation of homes with a paucity of resources and emotional support. The way in which these women experience the process of migration and create, unknown to themselves, an identity which negotiates the two homes, the one left behind and the one to be created in the new land, establishes a way in which diasporas could be explored in new patterns, giving voice to the women whose unrecorded and unrecognised roles could assume centre stage. This process of gendering the diaspora could thus create ways in which a hitherto silent group of women could assume agency and, thus, create identities.

FEMINISING DIASPORA: AN OVERVIEW

One of the most striking features indicative of the metanarratives of diaspora, which most often include the expulsion of the Jews from the Middle East, the trans-Atlantic slave trade that centred much of seventeenth century American history, and the lesser known exile of the Mesenians under Spartan rule, is the predominantly masculine nature of this experience. Discourses on diaspora most famously include, among many others, those of Safran (1991), Tölölyan (2007) and Cohen (1997). Most studies of the diaspora revolve around defining varying versions by framing it historically, examining a host of diasporic features including issues of identity and the self, and choices made between marginal and multicultural constructions. In the literary field, these studies have manifested themselves in the iconic works of Salman Rushdie, whose celebration of not belonging lent diaspora a new form of vocabulary with which to explore its predilections. Parallel studies in these postcolonial areas of migration also soon led to the exploration of the nature of travel as seen by women. In this context, 'diaspora' is itself seen as a masculine concept, both etymologically and symbolically, with the notion of 'dispersal' giving procreative powers to male narratives (Parker 2009). Emerging voices in the diaspora, and the extent to which they were capable of expressing themselves, was most famously suggested by Spivak (1988: 28), who said, '[i]f, in the context of colonial production, the subaltern has no history and cannot speak, the subaltern as female is even more deeply in shadow'. The resulting emphasis on women in the diaspora led to an increased focus on marginal women's literary writings, represented through the works of Buchi Emecheta in the United Kingdom, Maxine Kingston in the United States and Hiromo Goto in Canada. This 'feminisation' of the diaspora largely takes credence from the reality that migration as a feminine act has been hitherto unexplored and that lending a voice to these voiceless narratives becomes a social, cultural and literary imperative. As Jain (2006: np) points out:

> In diasporic settings, such issues as to who is a citizen, who can enter the family networks after obtaining which kind of visa are also located in family domains. Women in diasporas collaborate, acquiesce, co-opt and at time subvert the communicative channels in family networks in order to negotiate economic hardships and gender based oppression. In the process they tend to either become victims or emerge as stronger, more empowered and innovative beings.

Much of diaspora studies on women point to the notion that this is an area which has yet to be fully explored. Hua (2010), for example, looks at the idea of diasporic Asian feminism for the way in which it explores memory, home and identity. She speaks of the twin desires of the diaspora to 'resist assimilation to the host country and ... avoid the social amnesia of their collective histories' (ibid.: np). Hua goes on to focus on the idea of memory and highlights the selective nature of public memory, very often choosing to remember only that which suits the dominant group: 'In particular, the ruling class frequently dominate and manipulate collective memory for their own gains and interests' (ibid.). This is significant, not only in terms of the native/European divide that she uses, but also for the privileging of masculine narratives in the tales of diaspora. Identities thus could be transformative, because diaspora assumes not only a shift in identities but a presumption of 'multiplicity and difference of identities' (ibid.). Such centering of women's narratives are facilitated by the exploration of the ways in which home and self are constructed by women in ways which help them to create specific identities. Thus, Hussein (2005: 1) optimistically states, 'South Asian women have redefined the very idea of South Asianness and South Asian womanhood within both the minority and majority cultures as they give voice to their resistance to oppression'. Brah (1996: 84), too, notes in *Cartographies of Diaspora: Contesting Identities* that power remains an important aspect of diasporic experience, determining the way in which specific fates are sealed: 'All our fates are linked within this system, but our precise position depends on a multiplicity of factors such as gender, class, colour, ethnicity, caste, whether we practice a dominant or subordinate sexuality, and whether we live in a rich, industrially advanced society or a poor country of the third world'.

DIASPORA IN THE ARABIAN GULF

It is this context in which the binaries of home and the not-home, of belonging and not belonging and the various attempts at creating identities within the framework of diaspora that the experience of women in the 'marriage diaspora' need to be considered. The struggles of these women at creating identities in a foreign land very often leads to possibilities which are empowering and creative, albeit often unconsciously. In the context of the Middle East, almost no research exists focusing on the narratives of women. The few personal stories which have been explored include those of Vohra (2009, 2011) whose work on the Indian middle class and the Indian business class in the United Arab Emirates focuses on individual tales, the latter of which she sees as helping to maintain the social status quo of an already unequal society. Gardner (2008), in his study of the Indian business class in Bahrain, also dwells on individual stories of second- and third-generation Indians and their shifting lives, often being in connivance with the local authorities in order to maintain their own privileged position vis-à-vis the floating, labour population. Research on Indians in the Persian Gulf, most of whom were originally from the Kutch region of Gujarat, has primarily focused on economic data of annual remittances as well as trading possibilities (Karayil 2007; Rahman 2009; Pradhan 2010). The few studies on cultural contacts have been linguistic (Ahmed 2011) and historical (Hussein 2011). The occasional success story of the expatriate businessman is also recognised by the Indian government's *Pravasi Bharati* scheme in which a few members of the Indian expatriate community are annually felicitated by the Ministry of Overseas Affairs. Even Deffner and Pfaffenbach's (2011: np) study of the Indian diaspora in Muscat focuses on the way in which the community has created an isolated existence for itself, separated geographically and linguistically from its host nation: 'The close knit circle of friends is distinctly limited to the national community. An individuals's network in the Indian community is shaped by his or her social position and not by regional, or religious affiliation'. Although a well-researched account of the Indian expatriate community, the paper leaves a lacuna in so far as it fails to identify the problems specifically encountered by the women in this diaspora, most of whom arrived following their marriage and had to cope with the novelty of their circumstances as well as the new land in which they found themselves.

An attempt to examine the history of the Bhattia traders more closely automatically leads to Allen's (1978) study entitled *Sayyids, Shets and Sultan: Politics and Trade in Masqat Under the Al Bu-Said, 1785–1914*. In a section discussing the role of Indian merchants in the continuing of trade after the Al Bu'saidi dynasty moved to Zanzibar, Allen (ibid.: 110) traces the history of the Bhattia merchants in the following passage:

> Two examples will serve to demonstrate the early development of the Kutchi Bhattias of Masqat. Virji Purushottam Toprani today owns a small shop in Mattrah, but his family has had contacts with Masqat for seven generations. The family originated in the vicinity of the Rann of Kutch and moved to Mandvi ... . Once settled in Mandvi, the family turned to commerce and late in the eighteenth century, one Aranji sailed to Masqat to conduct his business. He was followed in later years by his son and then grandson, Umarsi, who established a business house in Masqat.

Allen (ibid.) then goes on to describe three other families who he said were considered to be 'the four pillars' of the Indian community at that time: the Bhimanis, Ratansi Purushottam and Virji Ratansi. This exhaustively researched account of the early Gujarati settlers in the coast of Oman is unique in the way in which it sheds light on one of the least explored areas, not only of Omani history, but also of the Indian diaspora anywhere in the Gulf.

Further exploration of these accounts of the trading classes in Oman and the way they settled and subsequently influenced local Omani politics and the economy brings into focus a major gap in this research. In the course of further investigation into these families to understand their narratives more fully, the material evidence which was produced was interesting and revealing. Mr Arvind Toprani's father, Virji Toprani, currently 83 years old, conversed about the way in which trade used to be carried out at the time of the Second World War, as the ships in the Bay of Sidab were bombed by the Japanese navy. Evidence was offered of the early life of the India traders, most of which was in the form of photographs, trading records, passports and customs stamps. All these accounts, interesting as they were, belonged firmly to the public domain. Almost all of these narratives excluded the voice of the women who never seemed to be part of the social fabric of the community at that time. Yet, on deeper probing, it seemed as if they were, for these successful merchants often married women who were related to each other back in Gujarat (in Kutch or Surat) and were brought to Muscat following the men's first or second trip to Gujarat. An integral part of the community, therefore, their presence in the master-narrative of the Gujarati diaspora remained more in the background, as if their presence was always assumed and never particularly recognised. Further conversations with the Kutchi families, particularly of the older women of the community who had travelled to Oman following their marriage in the 1940s, revealed a fascinating narrative of travel, memories and home, of attempts at creating homes away from home coupled with a sense of acquiescence, as if the domestic roles they performed were of little, or even no, consequence and that their untiring attempts at creating a home in the arid new land did not warrant recognition or acknowledgment. When approached for their stories, most of these women were hesitant and rarely knew where to begin. Almost all the conversations occurred in the form of interviews, most often with a few women in the temple or in their homes, over afternoon tea. The interviews were primarily conducted in Hindi as it was the language common to the interviewer and the participants. The oral narrative was, therefore, the primary mode of communication with some women of the community.

CREATING IDENTITY THROUGH ORAL NARRATIVES

These conversations with the Gujarati women echo the notion that that oral narratives help in the creation of identity, in this case, diasporic female identity. In general, oral narratives have been coded for their differences in approach by Eastern and Western societies. Thus, Resenhoeft (2011) discusses the way in which Easterners tend to downplay themselves more often than not and stress shared community values. The Westerner's approach, on the other hand, appears more individualistic, more personal and situates itself on specific tales of achievement as well as problems. Oral narratives are primarily 'forms of communication (which) may draw upon the fundamental human capacity to transfer experience from one person to another through oral narratives of personal experience' (Labov 2001: 5). They can be viewed linguistically as well because '(s)elf concepts and knowledge about the self (including memoirs of personal experiences, or autobiographical memories) are closely ... associated cognitive constructs' (Resenhoeft 2011: 3). Oral narratives have been viewed from a socio-linguistic angle by Labov (2001) and Norrick (2000) who focused on specific markers such as 'I'll' or 'nay' in oral narratives. Nelson (1990) suggests that narratives could be personal with a focus on the role of the 'I' or more community based memories. These narratives are further problematised when placed in the context of gendered narratives as the tone, note as well as content of the text itself differs widely. Niles (1999) examines the way in which the teller of an oral tale could be examined more specifically for physical expression, voice intonation, rhyme and rhythm, for dress, dance and rituals used. He suggests that from a tale, one can obtain a sense of shared common values, an analysis of ritual and alternate tales. Gender plays an equally important role in the analysis of oral narratives. Resenhoeft (2011: 6), in her study on this area, concludes that 'women's and men's memory narratives tend to cluster around gender stereotypical topics and thereby confirm the cultural expectations for gender role conformity'. Alemu's (2007: 53) study of oral narratives in Africa point to a similar sense in which gender defines the nature of the tale being told and the way in which it is being told as well:

> The stories people tell about their lives and those of others are of considerable importance, for there is an intimate connection between the ways in which people construe themselves and others, and the ways in which they are likely to behave, i.e., how we view and think of ourselves strongly influences our behaviour. This makes studying and challenging the stories that people tell about themselves a worthwhile undertaking.

As previously noted, Hua (2010: 3) also makes the point that diasporic women's practices of remembering and documenting these memories enable marginalised women to not only challenge the established tropes of victimisation but 'act as a catalyst for self-recovery and community building'. Oral narratives as rendered by women themselves, have often been seen to be mechanisms of empowerment, a process through which women make possible a subversion of existing assumptions of gender roles and expectations through symbolic, closed door tales, relying heavily on a mutually understood code of reference from where, very often, alternate identities emerge. Oral narratives can thus be seen to be agents of empowerment and a way in which women, at time knowingly and at times not, gain a perspective from which to access the realities of their lives in ways which prioritise their stories, their opinions, and their assumptions over the master male narrative.

GUJARATI WOMEN IN OMAN

In an attempt to frame the rhetoric of oral narratives in a specific diasporic context, a series of interviews were held with women in the Gujarati community of the Muscat region of Oman in the winter of 2011. These women were primarily from historically established families whose narratives had been earlier studied by

Jr. Allen (1978). Women were met in their homes as well as in the Shiv temple where the weekly Monday morning gatherings form an important social ritual. These women, of whom seven stayed on for a detailed discussion, ranged from 30 to 85 years and belonged to Kutchi families in Gujarat. Some of the issues which were framed as significant points of discussion included: (1) their primary reaction to their marriage and arrival in Oman; (2) their view of Oman in their early years and how these perceptions may have changed; (3) what their lives were like in the early years of their diasporic life in Oman; (4) which memories about their early years they treasured; (5) the ways in which their community and the wider society viewed them and their contribution to the familial set up; (6) the role of daily rituals in the creation of 'homes'; and (7) what they felt had been the major setbacks and victories as they take stock of their lives in Oman. The attempt in these conversations was always to look out for details which remained unsaid, assumptions about the women themselves which could be questioned in an attempt to view the situation in a new light and to look out for moments and gestures which would indicate autonomy, agency and self-reflection.

In response to Allen's (1978) geneology of the male line in the Toprani household, a family tree was drawn up with the help of Neeru Toprani, the wife of Arvind Toprani and her mother-in-law, Shanti Behn. Shanti Behn narrated the story of her five sisters, all of whom were married into prominent families in Muscat except for one of them who went to Zanzibar. Thus, Shanti Behn's family tree looked somewhat like the following:

Goki Behn	m	Gokaldas Khimji
Kamla Behn	m	Dharamsinh Khimji
Shanti Behn	m	Virji Toprani
Jassu Behn	m	Rattansinh Sutaria (in Zanzibar)
Ratan Behn	m	Vijay Sinh Toprani

The conversations for the purpose of this study revolved primarily around Shanti Behn, the 85 years old matriarch of the Toprani household, her niece, 67 years old Bhanu Behn and

Shanti's daughter-in-law, Neeru Toprani. All of them narrated the way in which Oman was at once a distant place in their imagination before their marriage but, at the same time, a place which they had vaguely heard about as they had cousins and other family relatives who were already living there. Thus, being married off to go and live in Oman was not a very scary prospect for these women as the family network had already ensured that they would not be in a totally new place. Shanti Behn, in fact, said that when she came to Oman in 1948, she knew her cousin who had been married the previous year and had come to live in the Muttrah area of Muscat which is where all these women lived in the initial years. Bhanu Behn too said that the presence of her aunt Shanti was consolation enough and that she had received a lot of emotional support in the initial years as someone who was educated (she had finished a degree in commerce before she married) but found herself in a very traditional community with few options to further herself. Neeru, on the other hand, knew Oman because her family had been living in Sur, a smaller town about 200 km from Muscat and she had left it as a child to continue her schooling in India. Her return to Muscat, therefore, although new and scary, was cushioned by her earlier memories of the place and the expectations she already had of the city.

All these women offered fascinating vignettes of their early life in the walled city of Muttrah where the Gujarati, indeed the entire Indian community, lived at that time. Muttrah continues to be an important part of the old town, bustling with traditional souks and markets selling frankincense and other Omani goods such as *abayas* (long robes) and *kummas* (handmade caps) for women and men to wear. Until 1970, this area was the centre of the kingdom of Muscat, walled away from the wild desert but also facing the Arabian Sea. Shanti Behn gave a detailed account of the way in which their houses were all adjoining each other with a common terrace where the women would often go to dry clothes as well as make pickles and *papads* (traditional Gujarati savouries). The housing complex shared a common well and washing zone and it is here that Shanti Behn remembers spending long morning hours washing clothes and indulging in community gossip, often about events back home and impending marriages and other functions.

The washing of the clothes and the making of the *papads* and pickles were often accompanied by much singing and chanting, often songs in praise of Laddu Gopal (Lord Krishna as a child), who is the presiding deity of this community. There was always a conscious attempt at creating the kind of homes in which they had been born, decorating their interiors with traditional Gujarati mirror work cushion covers, having a separate temple area for the family deity and singling out a place in the kitchen for rolling out chapattis. The common terraces provided a much needed succor from the heat inside the house and the women were even able to sleep on the terrace, enjoying the sea breeze in the evenings, accompanied as they were by their children who would be playing around them.

Life was tough in those early years for the women of the Kutchi diaspora who were used to a life of plenty in their homes. As all of these women came from prosperous families, they found that having to cook with a limited variety of vegetables and spices severely restricted their cooking repertoire. In fact, as Neeru explained, 'We wanted to cook good things for our husband and children when they came back from school. If the ship had just come, we would have a good supply of fresh fruit and vegetables but if it was the end of the month, we had almost nothing to cook with. It was always a challenge to find new things to cook'. However, these women improvised and adapted the locally available resources to make staple Gujarati dishes. Shanti Behn explained the times when they would, in the absence of onions and potatoes, take small pebbles from the beaches outside their homes and wash them to put inside the chickpea flour to make traditional pakodas, taking out the pebbles once they were fried. She also talked about the way they learnt to use the date palm stems to make vegetable dishes out of them and how many of their recipes increasingly used date juice as a natural sweetener. Life, these women said, often revolved around waiting for the monthly steamer which would bring fresh produce for their families as well as letters from home. It would also bring the *panchang* (the traditional Hindu calendar), which would be used to observe religious festivals. All the women agreed that it was primarily difficult, as a vegetarian community, to reproduce dishes from their homeland in the desert kingdom and that it was also difficult to observe festivals and rituals as they did when they were children in the absence of such necessities as fresh flowers, beetle leaves and other religious requirements.

Entertainment was, of course, limited and very occasional for these women. By 1950, the British club had begun to be operational in Muttrah and the men of the community made good use of it to play tennis and chess, read newspapers as well as to meet one another. The women had no such facility and whatever socialisation took place had to be within the closed quarters of their homes. Both Bhanu and Neeru remembered the way in which they would all pile into the only Land Cruiser in Muscat and travel all the way to Seeb, a small town about 30 km from Muscat, in order to finish their washing in fresh water, as well as to make a picnic of that day. This would be a day for which preparations would begin at least a week in advance with the women making savouries, sweets, packing, as well as, of course, getting the washing pile ready. Photographs of these outings suggest that these women took this opportunity to be outside their homes as one of escape, relief and enjoyment, a time which could be used to dress up and break free from cooking and other household tasks. Other than these occasions, there does not seem to have been any other opportunity for entertainment. In fact, all these women said that they never ventured out of their homes until their husbands came back to take them to the local shops to buy pieces of cloth or any other domestic item which would be available. For most of these women, life revolved around the community temple, observing various rituals such as fasts, and dancing and singing, which were part of the religious rituals.

That women had very few opportunities was a given, but more interesting was also the fact that public perceptions limited the opportunities available even to women who were capable of being more useful to their society. Bhanu Behn, presently 65 years old, said that she had earned a bachelor's degree in commerce before she came and settled in Muscat around 1958. When the small Indian school, housing about 400 students and situated inside the community complex, ran short of teachers, Bhanu was asked to come and help out. She says that she was stopped from going to the school by her father-in-law who suggested that she should ask students to come home to meet her in the evenings rather than go out to the school to teach. Similarly, when the Indian consulate needed an extra hand in their office to help with additional work, Bhanu was told to ask the officials to bring home the files which needed to be worked on rather than go to the consulate herself. Bhanu was, by far, the most educated woman in the community at that time, but she felt that her education and skills had not been adequately used at a time when she could have more usefully contributed to her community.

When asked about how their relationship with Oman had changed, all the women who were interviewed said that they had developed a close affinity with the country and that they all had fond memories of their youth here. In fact, most of them were nostalgic about life here. Neeru said, 'Earlier, our husbands would come home and be with us once the day at the shop was over. Now, however, because they are so busy in their shops and have to travel so much more, they hardly have any time for us. In addition, all this technology also means that they are always on the internet. Life was difficult before, but we were all a close-knit community'. Most of these women, however, do not really see their children taking up their father's businesses in Oman, although one of the sons did say that he was a businessman at heart and would never give up the family stores. Most women, however, also rued about the fact that they felt they had had a more important role in the country earlier and that, over the years, the changing political and social realities meant that they did not receive as much recognition as families who had helped to establish a new country in 1970. Most of them talked about how they would have Omani servants in their house earlier and how their relations with the local Omani neighbours had been closer and more immediate than it would ever be possible today.

The women who were part of these interviews were all well-established members of the Gujarati community as they were all married to prosperous businessmen in Muscat. In fact, demographically, the Gujarati community in Oman is largely of this class and most of the other labour force which has followed the early traders has been from other parts of India, such as Kerala and Andhra Pradesh. In fact, presently, most of the single women who come as nurses and maids are from these two Indian states. The Gujarati women still run large households, often with three generations of families living in one household, returning to Gujarat more often with increased mobility and communication, thus creating a home away from home even more easily than it had been hitherto possible.

The Gujarati diaspora in the Persian Gulf, particularly in Oman, is thus rooted in the history of the country and forms an inextricable link to its politics and economy. There is no doubt, therefore, that future studies on diaspora must focus in a more concentrated manner on this group of people who had ventured out of their homes and created successful lives against all odds. However, it is the women of this diaspora whose narratives need to be centred, for theirs is an experience which remains silent and untold. In the process of this research, what emerged was the way in which simply the telling of the tale seemed to empower these women, almost as if the realisation that their story was worth the telling, that their experiences counted equally and that their histories needed to be recounted was a revealing truth. Oral narratives thus give voice, agency and history to its participants while adding to and often reflecting on the meta-narrative of diaspora privileged by patriarchal assumptions. In this way, oral narratives seem to not only recount, but, more importantly, create identities.

REFERENCES

Allen, Calvin Jr. 'Sayyids, Shets and Sultans: Politics and Trade in Masqat under the Al Bu Sai'id 1785–1914', Unpublished PhD Thesis, University of Washington, 1978.

Alemu, Abreham. 'Oral Narratives as Ideological Weapon for Subordinating Women: The Case of Jimma Oromo', *Journal of African Cultural Studies*, Vol. 19, No. 1 (2007): 55–79.

Ahmed, Aftab. 'Continuity and Change in Indo-Arab Cultural Relations: A Survey with Special Reference Oman', Paper presented at Oman and India, Prospects and Civilization, Muscat, 3–5 February 2011.

Brah, Avtar. *Cartographies of Diaspora: Contesting Identities*, London: Routledge, 1996.

Cohen, Robin. *Global Diasporas*, London: Taylor & Francis, 1997.

Deffner, Veronika and Carmella Pfaffenbach. 'Zones of Contact and Spaces of Negotiation: The Indian Diaspora in Muscat (Sultanate of Oman)', Paper presented at the International RC21 Conference, Amsterdam, 2011, <http://www.Rc21.org/conferences/amsterdam 201/edocs/Session%2028/28-DP-Defner.pdf> (4 December 2012).

Gardner, Andrew M. 'Strategic Transnationalism: The Indian Diasporic Elite in Contemporary Bahrain', *City and Society*, Vol. 20, No. 1 (2008): 54–78.

Hua, Anh. 'Diasporic Asian Feminism: Bridging Ties', *Politics and Culture*, Vol. 2 (2010), <http://www.politicsandculture.org/2010/08/10/anh-hua-diasporic-asian-feminism-bridging-ties-2/> (4 January 2013).

Hussein, Ilias. 'Oman and the Life Histories of Cheraman Perumal and Saiyyid Fadl Moplah', Paper presented at Oman and India: Prospects and Civilization, Muscat, 3–5 February 2011.

Hussein, Yasmin. *Writing Diaspora: South Asian Women, Culture and Ethnicity*, London: Ashgate, 2005.

Jain, Shobha. 'Women's Agency in the Context of Family Networks in the Indian Diaspora', *Economic and Political Weekly*, Vol. 12, No. 23 (2006).

Karayil, Sajitha. 'Does Migration Matter in Trade? A Study of India's Exports to GCC Countries', *South Asia Economic Journal*, Vol. 8, No. 1 (2007): 14–19, <sae.sagepub.com/content/8/1.toc> (4 December 2012).

Labov, William. 'Oral Narratives of Personal Experience', *Cambridge Encyclopedia of Language Sciences*, 2001, <www.ling.upenn.edu/~wlabov/Papers/FebOralNarPEpdf> (8 December 2012).

Nelson, Linda Williamson. 'Code Switching in the Oral Life Narratives of African-American Women: Challenges to Linguistic Hegemony', *Journal of Education*, Vol. 172, No. 3 (1990): 142–55.

Niles, John. *Homo Narrans: The Poetics and Anthropology of Oral Literature*, Philadelphia: Pennsylvania University Press, 1999.

Norrick, Neil R. *Conversational Narrative: Storytelling in Everyday Talk*, New York: John Benjamins Publishing Company, 2000.

Parker, Emma. 'Introduction: Unsettling Women', *Contemporary Women's Writing*, Vol. 3, No. 1 (2009): 1–5.

Pradhan, N.S. 'Indian and the GCC: An Economic and Political Perspective', *Strategic Analysis*, Vol. 34, No. 1 (2010): 93–103.

Rahman, Anisur. 'The Socio-Cultural Dimensions of Indo-Omani Relations', *International Politics*, Vol. 2, No. 3 (Winter/Spring 2009): 99–113.

Resenhoeft, Annette C. 'Remembering You: Effects of Gender Identity and Narrative Recall Mode on Autobiographical Narratives', Unpublished PhD Thesis, University of Seton Hall, 2011, <http://scholarship.shu.edu/theses/23 > (28 May 2012).

Safran, William. 'Diasporas in the Modern Societies: Myths of the Homeland and Return', *Diaspora: A Journal of Transnational Studies*, Vol. 1, No. 2 (Spring 1991): 83–99.

Spivak, Gayatri. 'Can the Subarltern Speak?', in *Marxism and the Interpretation of Culture*, edited by Cary Nelson and Laurence Grossberg, London: Macmillan, 1988, pp. 24–28.

Tololyan, Khachig. 'The Contemporary Discourse of Diaspora Studies', *Comparative Studies of South Asia, Africa and the Middle East*, Vol. 27, No. 3 (2007): 647–55.

Vohra, Neha. 'The Precarious Existence of Dubai's Middle Class', *Middle East Report*, Vol. 252 (Fall 2009): 18–21.

CHAPTER 3

Being Ismaili in the Democratic Republic of the Congo

Identity Maintenance among Gujarati Ismailis in Kinshasa

Sahir Dewji

This chapter aims to shed light on the recent migration of Gujarati Ismailis to the Democratic Republic of the Congo (DRC). The findings of this study are based on qualitative data collected in the field and through interviews held with Ismaili families within the DRC. As in previous studies concerning the emigration of South Asians to East Africa beginning in the late nineteenth century, this study identifies similar patterns of migration and provides data on the demographics of the Gujarati Ismaili community in the capital city, Kinshasa. To date, no studies exist that examine the migration patterns of South Asians, particularly Gujaratis, to the DRC in the last decade. Therefore, this work provides significant information on the reasons for migration and its impact on the community's and individuals' sense of self. An important theme in this case study concerns the construction of identity and how individuals choose to self-identify. This research shows that the most important marker of identity among the individuals interviewed is religion. The practice of their religion, which itself is fused with elements of Gujarati culture, allows for a sense of communal belonging as well as a means of preserving their Gujarati cultural identity. The interviews conducted illustrate the multitude of meanings ascribed to religion, with a particular emphasis on the use of religion as a means to preserve the socio-cultural identity of this community. This phenomenon acts as an ethno-cultural and linguistic link to their ancestral home. As such, religion is found to be an important aspect of their Gujarati ethnic identity, which acts to unify and solidify the community. This study demonstrates how the maintenance of religious customs within these families proves to be a driver in preserving the families' cultural and ethnic traditions. As a result, religion acts as a binding force for the community to the extent that for the respondents their Gujarati identity is intertwined with their Ismaili identity.

MIGRATION TO EAST AFRICA

Much has been written about the Khoja Nizari Ismailis[1] of East Africa (Nanji 1974; Walji 1974, 1995; Thomson 1975). Migration to East Africa by members of this community, alongside other Gujaratis, began from coastal trading centres situated in western India. The initial route of migration was set towards Zanzibar and dates back to the first half of the nineteenth century. This was attributed to the early move of Seyyid Said[2] from Oman who was accompanied by many South Asian Muslims (Gregory 1993). More migrations occurred from 1890 when European powers began establishing colonial rule in East Africa. This period of migration was triggered by the British establishment in East Africa. Between 1895 and 1914, the British imported around 37,747 South Asians (ibid.). It is reported that missionaries from Bombay arrived in Africa from 1925 onwards. With the British in East Africa, economic opportunities opened new gates for success. However, it should be noted that this project could not have been successful without the willingness of certain communities of Western India (Dobbin 1996): 'The Shah, Patel, or Ismaili businessman has been perceived as the latest in a line of businessmen extending back through many centuries who have been specially endowed with remarkable commercial skills' (Gregory 1993: 9). Among these communities, in particular the Indian Muslim community, the most prominent were the Ismailis from Kutch in Gujarat who were to succeed economically in East Africa because they developed communal strategies to adapt to new commercial situations (Dobbin 1996).

MIGRATION TO BELGIUM CONGO[3]

While in East Africa, Ismaili traders took the initiative to expand their success into the interior of Africa. Dobbin (ibid.) mentions that another phase of successful trade came through the involvement of Ismailis and other Indians in caravan trade within the interior. There were two sets of long distance trade routes, from Zanzibar to Uganda in the north-east, and the eastern border of Belgium Congo in the west. By 1873, the eastern part of Belgium Congo was yielding ivory (ibid.). The first phase of emigration to Belgium Congo is known to have taken place around 1905. There are two recorded instances of Ismaili arrival in Belgium Congo. The first is based on the life of Ladha Ibrahim who initially arrived in Zanzibar from India with the early Ismaili emigrants, and later migrated to Belgium Congo. The second is tied to the migration of the Allidina Visram Group which extended its commercial interests from Uganda to Zaire, primarily in the city of Kisangani (Esmail 2010).

The second phase of migration to Belgium Congo occurred between 1937 and 1960, when Sultan Mahomed Shah (Aga Khan III), the Ismaili *Imam* (spiritual leader) at the time, encouraged Ismailis to settle in this region. By 1952, Ismailis pushed further reaching the western side of Zaire, near the Atlantic Ocean. The first Ismaili to settle in Kinshasa, the capital, was Pyarali Shariff who arrived in 1946 followed by additional Ismaili settlers in the 1950s. The Ismaili settlement continued following the independence of Belgium Congo in 1960 (ibid.). A Recreation Club Institute for Ismailis was formed to look after *waezeen* (Ismaili missionaries) and religious activities in Africa. This club then took on a new name – The Ismailia Association for Africa – established by Sultan Mahomed Shah after the conclusion of a conference held in Dar-es-Salaam on 20 July 1945. In 1951, six separate Ismailia Associations were established in Africa, Belgium Congo being one of them (Boulter and Nanji 1983). Rwanda and Burundi were included under the jurisdiction of the Ismailia Association for Belgium Congo. The headquarters for this Association was in Usumbura as the majority of the Ismailis resided in this region at the time. In 1960 Belgium Congo acquired Independence and was renamed Zaire. Soon after, in 1962, the Ismailia Association for

Belgium Congo dissolved, and in its place, Prince Karim, Aga Khan IV, appointed the first Ismaili council in Zaire.

From 1962 to 1973, the *jamat* (community) in Kinshasa increased significantly, reaching 700 members (ibid.). However, in 1972, the expulsion of South Asians from Uganda, forced many Ismailis to find new homes in Britain, Canada and the USA, while others returned to Pakistan and India (Nanji 1974; Walji 1974; Asani 2001; Mukadam 2003; Mawani 2006). This event marked a new wave of Ismaili migrations to Europe and North America (Daftary 1998). The aftershock of the expulsion of South Asians from Uganda affected other African countries, including Zaire. In 1973, the government of Zaire nationalised businesses causing many Ismailis to flee Zaire for Canada leaving behind a mere 135 individuals. Yet, in 1976, Zaire saw the return of these Ismailis as Mobutu Sese Seko, the then President of Zaire, began to invite foreign investors back. And, by 1983, the Ismailis in Zaire numbered 698 (Boulter and Nanji 1983).

Interestingly, during the early nineties, Zaire was home to a vibrant South Asian community, including a large number of Ismailis.[4] Unfortunately, many of these individuals were displaced by a civil war that began in 1997 by Laurent Kabila who aimed to overthrow Mobutu. Once successful, Kabila renamed the country, the Democratic Republic of the Congo (DRC). Nevertheless, fighting continued within the country's interior leading to Kabila's assassination in 2001. His son Joseph Kabila was then named head of state and through various negotiations, a transitional government was set up in 2003. This government was successful in setting up the first democratic elections in the DRC since the time of Mobutu. Joseph Kabila was then inaugurated president in December 2006 (CIA 2007). As a result of these events, many Ismailis left the DRC to join their extended families in Canada, Europe and India. However, at present, one can find an established Ismaili community in Kinshasa that is growing in number, as this chapter will demonstrate.

The DRC is considered one of the largest countries in Africa and is presently home to approximately sixty-five million people (BBC 2011). Kinshasa, the capital city, has a population of eight million (US Department of State 2009). Although the vast majority of DRC inhabitants are Congolese from various tribes, there are a number of expatriates from different parts of the world, the main communities being French, Belgian, Lebanese, American and Indian. With regard to religious communities, the majority in Kinshasa are Christian; however there are a number of Muslim and Hindu communities, made up largely of South Asians, living in the country (MAP 2010). Presently, there are no studies discussing recent migrations to the DRC. This chapter, therefore, will shed light on this under-researched area and focus on the migration and settlement of Ismailis to a region of the world that is still considered to be of high risk (US Department of State 2009).

A large proportion of Ismailis currently settled in the capital city of Kinshasa are originally from Gujarat. According to a 2009 survey carried out by the Aga Khan Council for Kinshasa, the majority of the *jamat* are between the ages of 19 and 40. The data demonstrates the presence of a large number of bachelors, employed under contracts, and just following that percentage are married couples. Moreover, the numbers show an increase in the number of Ismailis over the past few years. The total number of Ismailis in Kinshasa, according to the October 2009 statistics, was approximately 1,720. However, it is predicted that this number would have reached approximately 2,000 at the time of this study, and is estimated to increase as time progresses.

THE STRUGGLE FOR IDENTITY

Prior research (Nanji 1974; Walji 1974; Asani 2001; Mukadam, 2003; Mawani 2006) has demonstrated that migration to East Africa encouraged the Ismailis to understand and construct a clear identity vis-à-vis others in the new homeland. The question of identity is one of the most central questions individuals engage with during their lives. However, scholars continue to ask whether there is a definite method to answer such a question. Mukadam (2007) has described identity as a word which symbolises our need to understand who we are, where we come from and how we are linked to our ancestors. Dillon (1999) has explained that identity is most often described as an individual's sense of self, in addition to various group affiliation, which results from internal subjective perceptions and external characterisations.

According to Smith (1995), humans have access to a variety of collective affiliations and due to this overwhelming variety, individuals are capable of identifying with more than one affiliation depending on the circumstances. A subtype of collective cultural identities is categorised as 'the ethnic' or ethnic group. Ethnies is a subtype characterised by a sense of origin, a sense of distinctiveness and a sense of place. In essence, 'they are more than categories; they are communities' (ibid.: 132). As a result, an ethnie can be defined as a 'a named culture community whose members have a myth of common origins, shared memories and cultural characteristics, a link with a homeland and a measure of solidarity' (ibid.: 133). The term ethnicity is a concept that takes into account both the individual and the group. At present, ethnicity is understood to be a factor that provides a sense of belonging within a particular group (Mawani 2006). There is a close link between religion and ethnicity, and this is strongest when the sense of primordial attachment to an ancestral group and its traditions is most deeply felt (Yinger 1994).

Scholars have argued that immigrants and their descendants are more likely to maintain their religion as an integral part of their ethnicity. Mawani (2007) mentions that Hammond and Warner (1993) have indicated a mutual relationship between ethnicity and religion. They identify three types of relationships between ethnicity and religion, which include ethnic fusion, ethnic religion and religious ethnicity. The third relationship is perhaps crucial in the study of Ismailis, as this occurs when more than one ethnic group identifies with the same religion. Looking at communities of South Asian ancestry, the influence of religion as a construct of identity is evident. Such theories show a connection between religion and family, and more generally among a collective of individuals. Thus religion can be seen as an important aspect of an ethnic group which gives it unity and solidarity. 'According to Williams [1988: 12–13], although religion is often a significant aspect of ethnic culture, it is difficult to establish the exact relation between the two – either religious affiliation is essential to the ethnic community or if religious orientation is ancillary to ethnic identity' (Peek 2005: 218). It has been noted that the Ismailis evolved institutionally in a manner that provided them with a great advantage over other communities in the African enterprise (Dobbin 1996). This plays an important role, especially with respect to migration. Newly settled individuals must focus their efforts on adjusting to new surroundings and finding stability. Due to the intertwining nature of religion and ethnicity, the preservation of religious customs within a group will evidently also preserve the group's cultural elements which are seen as symbols of ethnic identity.

METHODS

The fieldwork for this study was carried out over six weeks in Kinshasa, DRC. It consisted of participant observation and in-depth interviews with three married couples.[5] In addition, a total of 54 individuals were approached to complete questionnaires. The paradigm used to frame this research was post-positivism. This methodological tradition is about a reality that is socially constructed rather than objectively determined. This approach helped gain an appreciation for the different constructions and meanings that people place upon their experience in relation to their identity (Easterby-Smith et al. 1991). With such a paradigm, a qualitative approach was used based on the case study model, focusing on a small handful of Ismailis in Kinshasa.

Both quantitative and qualitative research tools were employed. A two-page questionnaire, designed to be simple and easy to complete, was used to gain a broader picture of the reasons for migrating and the importance of the *jamatkhana* (place of worship) among the segment of the community being studied. It also allowed monitoring of the participants' initial response to specific questions that were later explored in depth during the interview phase. The data collected from the questionnaires provided valuable information about the main factors of migration and attempted to generally display the importance of *jamatkhana*. The interview process provided a great opportunity for reflexivity as well as dialogue (Fonow and Cook 1991). The interview format was semi-structured, offering sufficient flexibility while still allowing for in-depth interviews with the participants. The interviews took an ethnographic approach, allowing genuine communication both in subtle and direct ways, so as to learn more about the informant (Heyl 2001). All interviews took place at the couples' homes as this was where they felt the most comfortable. In addition, this proved a perfect opportunity to observe their homes and the interaction with their children in a natural environment. In part, the interview stage was determined by access to appropriate individuals and through prior conversations among individuals in the *jamat*. The casual conversations held with certain couples facilitated an open line of communication that would foster a deeper initiative for formal interviews. An important theme that ran through these conversations and interviews was the need for careful listening: 'When researchers listen carefully to the actual talk, they can hear these moments of translation, which can sensitize the analysis' (ibid.: 374). In all three interviews with the couples, the male interviewees were of a middle class background and either owned a small-scale business or were employed, while their female counterparts identified themselves as housewives.

MIGRATION

From the information gathered in the questionnaires and among the couples interviewed, the major motivating factor for moving to Kinshasa, among the men, was better economic opportunities. The women primarily migrated because their husbands were doing so (see Mehta's chapter in this volume). It appears that moving to Kinshasa was not really an option for these women. One female respondent, Inaara, that I spoke with in *jamatkhana* mentioned that she had no idea what and where Kinshasa was. She said, 'if it wasn't for my husband, I would have never come to Kinshasa'.

Salman, a male respondent, moved to Kinshasa from Rajkot in 2004. Salman was determined to look outside India for opportunities in Africa, and was influenced by *firmans* (edicts) of the present *Imam* (Aga Khan IV) in reference to globalisation and meritocracy. Like Salman, Rashid, who arrived in Kinshasa in 2003, did so with the aim of improving his employment prospects. As a result of settling in Kinshasa, his line of profession also changed from an employee in a small shop to a managerial position in the publicity sector. Like Salman, Rashid had also dreamt of going abroad, but unlike Salman, for Rashid Kinshasa did not fit into his category of 'abroad'. Nevertheless, a friend of his convinced him to come to Kinshasa:

> I had never really decided to come to Kinshasa. I initially just wanted to get out of India. I was looking for better option in life, better opportunities. Indian life wasn't so good. I had a friend here in Kinshasa, so he influenced me in coming here to look for job opportunities. I had come with a motivation to do something. Kinshasa didn't really fit into my description of what 'abroad' meant, however it didn't really matter because I was determined to do something.

Rashid later conveyed to me that, in his mind, 'abroad' was equated with a Western country, like America or Canada. Alykhan, another male respondent, arrived in Kinshasa in 1981 in search of better employment opportunities. His younger brother, who had already migrated to Kinshasa, encouraged Alykhan to join him. Alykhan explained that some of his family members had migrated to East Africa at the time of Aga Khan II (1881–1885). Along with encouragement from his brother, these stories about his family's history of migration also influenced his decision to move to Kinshasa.

At present, there is much growth in the DRC, and particularly in the capital city. Through observations and conversations with local Congolese and expats, all were in agreement that due to the increasing economic and political stability in Africa, the opportunities in Kinshasa are also increasing. Much like the South Asians who migrated to East Africa (Hollingsworth 1960; Gregory 1993; Dobbin 1996; Asani 2001), the motive to migrate to Kinshasa is similar – the promise of economic opportunity. Another similarity between those who migrated to East Africa and those undertaking migrations to Kinshasa is the religious motivation to follow the advice and guidance of the *Imam* (Mukadam and Mawani 2009). However, during the late nineteenth and early twentieth centuries in East Africa, society was heavily divided along racial lines (Asani 2001) and this defined the individual's economic status. In comparison, the present circumstances of the government's outlook in Kinshasa provides for a free market economy, free of a nationalist agenda.

WHAT TO PRESERVE? THE EXPERIENCE OF LIVING IN KINSHASA AND THE ROLE OF RELIGION

The findings of this study reveal that the majority of respondents identified themselves as ethnically Indian. The explanation given for this association was that identifying themselves as ethnically Gujarati (following the 2002 riots) had a political connotation and was reserved for Hindu groups. Moreover, further conversations revealed that many saw themselves as being 'Indian Ismaili'. They expressed that this construction allowed them to connect with other Ismailis in India, as well as, the global Ismaili community. Anthias (2001), who discusses hybrid identity formations, recognises this construction as a reconfiguration in ethnicity, related to the homeland and the new society of settlement. Such a re-arrangement is depicted through hybridity and opens up the formation of more trans-ethnic connections with the global Ismaili community. Moreover, the respondents expressed that they had to get accustomed to the norms of society in Kinshasa and learn two languages – Lingala and French. On the other hand, Gujarati was reported to be the *lingua franca* among family members and other Ismailis, which is not surprising, given that they are recent migrants. Despite these adjustments, the respondents expressed a deep gratitude for their religion and the community's organisational structure, which made a significant contribution to their settlement in Kinshasa.

All the women interviewed and surveyed conveyed that their only place to meet new people and share stories with other women was within the *jamatkhana* premises. However, all of them also expressed that the spiritual dimension offered by the *jamatkhana* was just as important to them, which confirms the findings of Mawani (2006), where she has pointed out that religion is an important basis for identity because of its role in society. Through information obtained from the interviews it was clear that regular participation in the liturgy and other events in the *jamatkhana* offered more than spiritual benefits. Therefore, as the other benefits, such as community networking and educational resources increase, the members of a community will choose to affiliate themselves to a religious group.

All three couples that were interviewed explained that they could identify more with the Ismaili community while residing in the DRC, than when they were in India. 'It is only natural', exclaimed Salimah, Rashid's wife. 'There is [an] instant connection because of the *jamatkhana*. We go there to pray but also to feel good, to meet others and share [experiences], to release tension … *jamatkhana* provides a sense of unity for us'. However, they did mention that in India most of their friends were non–Ismaili. Moreover, Salman explained that while in India he did not have time to attend *jamatkhana* regularly and that the neighbourhood in which he lived consisted of very few Ismaili households. It was only in Kinshasa that he found himself immersed in the Ismaili community to a greater extent. The women also expressed that they had much more interaction in Kinshasa with other Ismaili couples due to their regular attendance at *jamatkhana*. They all explained that in India they lived with extended families, thereby reducing the need for friends outside the family. This is highlighted very clearly by Salman's wife, Begum, who said, '[In India, there is] no need for friends outside. [We] lived in [a] joint family so had good company, so I never felt like going outside. But here in Kinshasa, I have lots of Ismaili friends. [We] meet and talk in *jamatkhana*'.

Although the Ismailis of the DRC are loyal to their new country of residence, they continue to think of themselves as Indian, as do the East African majority (Nanji 1974; Asani 2001). Conversations with Ismailis and following interviews with my respondents it became clear that the Ismailis of Kinshasa increasingly make it a point to project their Ismaili identity over their Indian identity. Salman, for example, explained that the Congolese see him as Indian. Nonetheless, he feels strongly about educating them about the Ismaili community. When someone asks who he is, his first response is that he is an Ismaili. This, he added, was more of a typical response in Kinshasa than in India:

> When locals ask us, we say first Ismaili. However, when they come they first think we are Indian. Then we have to explain. It is here that we have realised importance of [being] Ismaili. Mostly in Kinshasa. Feeling we are the Ismailis. First impression, if someone asks us 'Who are you?', we say we are

> Ismaili. After that we say that we are the Indian. Coming to African country [we] see the importance of being Ismaili. We recognise this over here. In India we ... held many positions in [Ismaili] Tariqah [and Religious Education] Board and I was also *mukhi* (male religious official) but [the] feeling of [being] Ismaili didn't come too much. But here it came that we are Ismaili. What is good here, we go to *jamatkhana* every day, see programs that are happening. Due to this, we know it. I also attend parent-student programme, but [I] never attended [the] programme in India.

Throughout the interview process, it became apparent that relationships with family, friends and partners were a significant force in preserving their Ismaili identity. This finding contradicts Bibby's (1997) study that avers the gradual weakening of immigrants' religious identity upon arrival to the new home. Another aspect that was equally important was language and Indian culture. With this observation in mind, determining what parents wanted to pass on to their children became imperative. It was clear that the couples interviewed did not discard their culture and traditions. They maintained links with Gujarat through different avenues such as language, food, dress, etc. Due to the intertwining nature of religion and ethnicity, the preservation of religious customs within these families proved to be a driver in preserving the families' cultural traditions. Mukadam and Mawani (2009) also reported a similar strategy used by parents of Ismaili children brought up in Britain who chose to use Gujarati/Kutchi as a medium of communication at home and English at school.

The comments from informants illustrated the role of parents in providing an understanding of their culture, language, relations, and also a bright future for their children through education. All respondents expressed the importance of their Indian culture as well as Ismailism; for them these two aspects went hand-in-hand. One way of preserving their culture was through the lived experiences of the Ismaili community. Another important aspect of preservation came through education, both at school and religious education classes at the *jamatkhana*. Begum conveyed the importance of religious education: 'Sending my children to religious education classes, they can learn about the *Imam* and get discipline.

Without religion there's no way to go ahead in life. Also they can learn how to be active members of society by interacting with other Ismailis. Religious education classes are fundamental to [the] Ismaili core, to learn about what it is to be a Muslim, to be Ismaili'. In general, the parents in this study insisted that secular education would provide their children with the best of opportunities. They connected this with guidance from the *Imam* and his emphasis on higher education. For these parents education was very important; any career choice, or relocation made by their children would be supported as long as their children were gaining from that decision. The parents in this study did, however, mention that they would be much happier knowing that the city in which their children lived had an Ismaili community and a *jamatkhana*.

The Ismailis currently residing in the DRC do not construct their identity in the same manner as those who had migrated and settled in East Africa during the late nineteenth and early twentieth centuries. Walji (1995) and Mawani (2006) noted that of those individuals a tri-polar identity was constructed, Ismaili-British (colonial)-African. However, the Ismailis of the DRC self-identify in terms of a dual identity, as Indian Ismailis.[6]

TRANSLOCALITY AND ITS SIGNIFICANCE TO ISMAILI IDENTITY

Another salient theme in this study is the notion of 'home'. How 'home' is interpreted and where the 'home' is situated affects an individual's identity formation. The articulation of home impacts how families evaluate what they perceive as important markers of identity that need to be passed on to their children. Among some respondents there is a sense of an 'imagined home' that is located in a specific area of Gujarat. Others see their new abode as one of many homes. Such a layered construction adds yet another element to their identity construction (Mawani and Mukadam 2012).

Salman and Begum articulated very clearly that they had two homes – Kinshasa and their respective cities in India. They expressed that eventually moving back to India was a priority. For them, India was their home and would remain so forever, while Kinshasa was more of a temporary home. From informal conversations in the *jamatkhana*, it is clear that there are many other individuals in the *jamat* that share this view. For these couples, Kinshasa was a chance at success, an avenue for economic growth and new experiences, but ultimately the aim is to leave their temporary home, Kinshasa, for their permanent homes, in India. As with many immigrant communities, in time the dream of going back 'home' becomes a 'myth of return' (Anwar 1979); time will tell if this too becomes the reality for many of these individuals.

Salimah and Rashid presented a similar view about their home but with a slight variation. Rashid, the head of the family, understood Kinshasa as a permanent home (for now), until another opportunity arises: 'For the moment Mumbai and Kinshasa is home for us. But I don't see myself moving back to India. I would prefer to go for an even better opportunity. If I have a better chance, I would move to another country, possibly a western country'. It was clear through this conversation that the incentive for Rashid to move lies in the manifestation of a greater opportunity, and that his dream would be to relocate to the Western world. Returning to India was not of interest nor a priority.

Another couple interviewed, Alykhan and Sitara, also expressed that Kinshasa was their permanent home. This couple articulated that although India was considered their home due to family ties, Kinshasa was their overall place of permanent living. They did mention that they frequently visit India with their children. The luxury of travel is something this family can afford. Nevertheless, moving back to India was not of immediate importance. To them Kinshasa was 'home', as they have been in Kinshasa for most of their lives and did not want to leave. They are happy in Kinshasa.

It became apparent that the respondents' age at which they arrived to Kinshasa and the length of time they spent in Kinshasa had an influence on their understanding of home.[7] In Tweed's ethnographic work, *Our Lady of the Exile* (1997), he suggests that the length of displacement has an effect not only on the individual's identity but also on their religion. Although some of the informants had been in Kinshasa for several years, none of them expressed themselves in terms of an African identity, nor did they construct a tri-polar identity. For my respondents, a dual identity – Indian and

Ismaili – was a salient marker for the couples' collective and individual identities. In addition, the attachment to their birthplace and where they currently reside also affected their perception of who they are. Anthias (1999) suggests understanding this hybrid identity through 'translocational' positionality. This approach allows one to acknowledge identity through the role of the local and the contextual rather than focusing on permanence. 'Narratives of belonging may then be seen as forms of social action that is, actively participating in the very construction of subject positionalities' (Anthias 2001: 633). Therefore, their homes provide them with a hybrid understanding of themselves and their environment within both a physical and psychological space. Moreover, Tweed (1997) suggests that such a religious group should be understood as translocative (moving symbolically between the homeland and the new land).

CONCLUSION

The issues of identity play an important part in the relationship between a group and society. One way such a relationship can be studied is through religion. The Ismaili experience in the Democratic Republic of the Congo (DRC) is one in which religion is a crucial marker of the community's identity. This is similar to the experiences faced by the Ismailis who migrated to East Africa. The *jamatkhana* was a place of worship and a centre for many social focal points. This setting continues to be a base, in East Africa and in the DRC, for many aspects, both social and religious. The *jamatkhana* becomes a significant factor for my informants in their decision to move. This is echoed in a statement by Rashid: 'I inquired about jamatkhana before coming to Kinshasa. It makes a difference to know there is a *jamatkhana*. Without it you feel lost'. In effect, this statement was echoed by all the respondents indicating that this is clearly an important space in the lives of these Ismailis. This physical space fosters an emotional connection with the members who attend it and stands as a pillar for the community's strength, social network, culture and practices.

These individuals are not migrating to the DRC because of economic hardship in their original home country, India, as was the case in the early nineteenth century. Nevertheless, they are in search of a better life, and are interested in being part of a global network. The notions of globalisation and meritocracy echoed in the *firmans* of the *Imam* contribute to motivating the Ismailis to explore new opportunities outside India. This mindset provides a whole different outlook in the way these Ismailis self-identify. At this point it is worth stressing that all three couples interviewed expressed that the DRC and India were their homes. This is in line with Wise's (2006) theory of translocality, in which a social network can extend over different places, creating a community that exists based on its relationships. However, another element still remains a factor, to some degree, in the issues of identity through translocality; that is the building of a strong connection with the physical space itself, as is evident in the interviews conducted for this study.

Through the number of discussions held with the respondents in this study, it is clear that Ismailism, as an ideology, has become a sort of communal citizenship that allows Ismailis to move from one place to another. It is a global citizenship that fosters much more than a religious purpose. This research portrays the continuing importance of religion in the lives of Ismailis in the DRC and also shows the importance the community takes in preserving their ethnic and cultural traditions. This is in line with the works of Herberg (1960) and Lenski (1961) who also noted the strengthening of religio-cultural identity post-migration. It should, however, be noted that it is difficult to make a clear distinction between religious traditions and cultural or ethnic traditions as, in many cases, they are interconnected. Thus, the community's effort in preserving many of these traditions subconsciously becomes religiously affiliated. Moreover, this research brings to light the adjustments that these immigrants make in their new host society and provides insight as to the identity that becomes important for them to preserve for their children. In sum, the expression of identity is always in motion, as there is a continuous process of construction and reconstruction, showing yet again that identity is never fixed but fluid.

NOTES

1. The term 'Ismaili' will be used throughout this chapter to refer to the Khoja Nizari Ismailis.
2. A census of the Sultan's domain in 1887 revealed that Muslims formed the largest community of around 4,866 (Gregory 1993).
3. The name of Zaire before it gained its independence from the Belgium kingdom.
4. This is based on my knowledge while growing up in Zaire. As far as I know, there has not been any study conducted on the Ismailis of Zaire. Moreover, during the civil war (1997–2003), many Ismaili families moved away and some remained. There are no recorded details about how this affected the Ismaili *jamat* in Zaire (now DRC).
5. Pseudonyms have been used throughout this chapter to protect the identity of the respondents.
6. On the other hand, the children of these migrants will have a new component in their experience, African culture and attitudes, which are not yet a significant part of their parents' identities.
7. Salman moved to Kinshasa in 2004, Rashid moved in 2003, and Alykhan was a long-time resident since 1981.

REFERENCES

Anthias, Floya. 'Beyond Unities of Identity in High Modernity', *Identities*, Vol. 6, No.1 (1999): 121–44.

——. 'New Hybridities, Old Concepts: The Limits of Culture', *Ethnic and Racial Studies*, Vol. 24, No. 4 (2001): 619–41.

Anwar, Muhammad. *The Myth of Return: Pakistanis in Britain*, London: Heinemann Educational Books, 1979.

Asani, Ali S. 'The Khojas of South Asia: Defining a Space of their Own', *Cultural Dynamics*, Vol. 13, No. 2 (2001): 155–68.

BBC. 'Democratic Republic of Congo Profile', *BBC News Africa*, 2011, <http://www.bbc.co.uk/news/world-africa-13285761> (30 June 2013).

Bibby, Reginald W. 'Going, Going, Gone: The Impact of Geographical Mobility on Religious Involvement', *Review of Religious Research*, Vol. 38, No. 4 (June 1997): 289–307.

Boulter, Razia-Begum and Sadrudin Nanji. *Al-Hidayat: Imamat Day Issue*, Aga Khan Council for Zaire, 1983.

CIA. 'The Democratic Republic of Congo', *The World Factbook*, 2007, <https://www.cia.gov/library/publications/the-world-factbook/geos/cg.html> (15 February 2010).

Daftary, Farhad. *A Short History of the Ismailis*, Edinburgh: Edinburgh University Press, 1998.

Dillon, Michele. *Catholic Identity: Balancing Reason, Faith, and Power*, New York: Cambridge University Press, 1999.

Dobbin, Christine. *Asian Entrepreneurial Minorities: Conjoint Communities in the Making of the World Economy, 1570–1940*, London: Routledge, 1996.

Esmail, Ally. *Ismaili Settlement in Zaire*, Ismaili Heritage website, <http://www.ismaili.net/Source/0379a.html> (1 February 2010).

Easterby-Smith, Mark, Richard Thorpe and Andy Lowe. *Management Research: An Introduction*, London: Sage Publications, 1991.

Fonow, Mary M. and Judith A. Cook. *Beyond Methodology: Feminist Scholarship as Lived Research*, Bloomington: Indiana University Press, 1991.

Gregory, Robert G. *South Asians in East Africa: An Economic and Social History, 1890–1980*, London: Westview Press, 1993.

Hammond, Philip E. and Kee Warner. 'Religion and Ethnicity in Late-Twentieth Century America', *Annals of the American Academy of Political and Social Science*, Vol. 527, No. 1 (May 1993): 55–66.

Herberg, William. *Protestant-Catholic-Jew: An Essay in American Religious Sociology*, Garden City, NY: Anchor Books, 1960.

Heyl, Barbara S. 'Ethnographic Interviewing', in *Handbook of Ethnography*, edited by Paul Atkinson, Amanda Coffey, Sara Delamont, John and Lyn Loflkand, London: Sage Publications, 2001, pp. 369–83.

Hollingsworth, Lawrence W. *The Asians of East Africa*, London: Macmillan, 1960.

Lenski, Gerhard. *The Religious Factor*, Garden City, NY: Doubleday, 1961.

MAP. 'Basic Facts of Democratic Republic of Congo', Missionary Atlas Project, Africa, <http://worldmap.org/maps/other/profiles/democratic%20republic%20of%20the%20congo/Republic%20of%20the%20Congo.pdf> (21 May 2010).

Mawani, Sharmina. 'Aapun Aap Pichano: The Ginanic Tradition of the Nizari Ismaili Muslims of Gujarati Ancestry', in *Gujaratis in the West: Evolving Identities in Contemporary Society*, edited by Anjoom A. Mukadam and Sharmina Mawani, Newcastle: Cambridge Scholars Publishing, 2007, pp. 25–41.

——. 'The Construction of Identities amongst Young Adult Nizari Ismaili Muslims in Toronto and Mumbai', Unpublished PhD Thesis, SOAS, University of London, 2006.

Mawani, Sharmina and Anjoom A. Mukadam. 'Introduction', in *Gujarati Communities across the Globe: Memory, Identity and Continuity*, edited by Sharmina Mawani and Anjoom A. Mukadam, Stoke-on-Trent: Trentham, 2012, pp. xxvi-xxvii.

Mukadam, Anjoom A. 'Shattering Stereotypes: Post-Diasporic Swaminarayan Gujaratis in London', in *Gujaratis in the West: Evolving Identities in Contemporary Society*, edited by Anjoom A. Mukadam and Sharmina Mawani, Newcastle: Cambridge Scholars Publishing, 2007, pp. 106–26.

——. 'Gujarati Speakers in London: Age, Gender and Religion in the Construction of Identity', Unpublished PhD Thesis, University of Reading, 2003.

Mukadam, Anjoom A. and Sharmina Mawani. 'Excess Baggage or Precious Gems? The Migration of Cultural Commodities', in *Muslims in Britain: Race, Place and Identities*, edited by Peter Hopkins and Richard Gale, Edinburgh: Edinburgh University Press, 2009, pp. 150–68.

Nanji, Azim. 'Modernization and Change in the Nizari Ismaili Community in East Africa: A Perspective', *Journal of Religion in Africa*, Vol. 6, No. 2 (1974): 123–39, <http://www.jstor.org/stable/1594884> (17 January 2010).

Peek, Laura. 'Becoming Muslim: The Development of a Religious Identity', *Sociology of Religion*, Vol. 66, No. 3 (2005): 215–42.

Smith, Anthony D. 'The Formation of National Identity', in *Identity: Essay Based on Herbert Spencer Lectures Given in the University of Oxford*, edited by Henry Harris, Oxford: Clarendon Press, 1995, pp. 129–53.

Thomson, Gardner. 'The Ismailis in Uganda', in *Expulsion of a Minority: Essays on Uganda Asians*, edited by Michael Twaddle, London: Athlone Press, 1975, pp. 30–52.

Tweed, Thomas A. *Our Lady of the Exile: Diasporic Religions at a Cuban Catholic Shrine in Miami*, New York: Oxford University Press, 1997.

US Department of State. 'Travel Warning', *Bureau of Consular Affairs*, 2009, <http://travel.state.gov/travel/cis_pa_tw/tw/tw_2198.html> (21 February 2010).

Walji, Shirin. 'A History of the Ismaili Community in Tanzania', PhD Dissertation, University of Wisconsin, Madison, 1974.

——. 'Ismailis in Kenya: Some Perspectives on Continuity and Change', in *Islam in Kenya: Proceedings of the National Seminar on Contemporary Islam in Kenya,* edited by Mohamed Bukari and Saad S. Yahya, Kenya: Mewa Publications, 1995, pp. 1–17.

Williams, Raymond B. *Religions of Immigrants from India and Pakistan: New Threads in the American Tapestry,* NY: Cambridge University Press, 1988.

Wise, Amanda. *Exile and Return among the East Timorese,* Philadelphia: University of Pennsylvania Press, 2006.

Yinger, John M. *Ethnicity: Source of Strength? Source of Conflict?,* Albany: State University of New York Press, 1994.

CHAPTER 4

Buying and Selling an Illusion

Multinational Corporations and Young Gujaratis in Mumbai

Sharmina Mawani

This chapter examines how the process of globalisation[1] has brought Western goods to India, particularly Mumbai, and the effect that this has had on the identities of young adult Nizari Ismaili Muslims of Gujarati ancestry.[2] Drawing on examples from multinational corporations that have established their brands in Mumbai, the chapter questions whether the products these multinationals are selling to the Indian consumer can be labelled as 'Western'. An analysis of how these products are being glocalised to incorporate a local flavour in an attempt to appeal to the tastes of young middle- and upper-class Indians, will further elucidate the extent to which these young adults can be said to possess a Western identity. In addition, an analysis of empirical data in relation to the respondents' preferred cuisine, as well as the extent to which they use English and Hindi (or sometimes Gujarati) in the form of code-mixing, will shed light on whether these young people truly possess a hybrid identity.

GLOBALISATION

From its economy to its popular culture there is ample evidence to suggest that India is being affected by globalisation. The phenomenon of globalisation has been defined as many times as it has been written about in academic journals and the media. And, while this phenomenon is seen to be somewhat of a recent development, some may argue that globalisation is nothing new and that its processes were underway hundreds of years ago on the trade routes where peoples from different communities encountered and exchanged goods, as well as cultures. What can be said about globalisation is that it has recently taken on a rate of acceleration that is faster than at any other time in history. Inda and Rosaldo (2002: 2) have defined globalisation as 'the intensification of global interconnectedness, suggesting a world full of movement and mixture, contact and linkages, and persistent cultural interaction and exchange'. Speaking about religions in a global world, Warburg (2001, original emphasis) classified globalisation as 'the standard term for describing how humanity in these years experiences a historically unique *increase of scale* to a global interdependency among people and nations .... Globalisation is a *process of change* that affects nation states, local communities, industrial companies and individuals all around the globe'. Pieterse (2000: 101), writing about the way in which globalisation has led to hybridisation, defines globalisation as 'the intensification of worldwide social relations which link distant localities in such a way that local happenings are shaped by events occurring many miles away and vice versa'. Tomlinson (1999: 25), like Inda and Rosaldo (2002), has identified globalisation as 'the complex pattern of interconnections and interdependencies that have arisen in the late-modern world'. It appears that there is a definite common thread among all these definitions, which leads one to infer that globalisation is a relationship in which societies mutually exchange political, cultural, economic and social information across the globe. Albrow (1990: 9) raises another important point about globalisation, suggesting that it 'refers to all those processes by which the peoples of the world are incorporated into a single world society, global society'. As these processes are plural, globalisation itself may be viewed in the plural, as globalisations. With this perspective one may say then that this process consists of many, fluid dimensions, which are taking place concurrently in different regions. This also highlights another significant point: globalisations are not processes of standardisation (Pieterse 2000). So, these processes, in which information is exchanged across the globe, do not result in a world that begins to look the same, rather, local cultures, norms and practices affect the ways in which this information is localised.

Lord Meghnad Desai, Professor Emeritus at the London School of Economics and an international authority on globalisation, in an address to the participants of the *Pravasi Bharatiya Divas* (Diaspora Day) celebrations in New Delhi on 10 January 2004 spoke about the process of globalisation in India:

> One good thing with India is that now the process of globalisation is persistent here, thanks to the leadership ... . India started on the path to liberalisation and globalisation under duress in the early 1990s, but now it is clear that it has persisted with globalisation, even if reluctantly ... . A corner was turned around the turn of the century, making India an integral part of the world economy. The credit for that goes to the leadership. (*Asian Voice* 2004: 18)

It is evident, therefore, that the process of globalisation is not one way. India and its various cultures are finding their way into the West just as rapidly as the West and its cultures are finding their way into India. This chapter will examine the way in which Western cultures are successfully penetrating Indian society and the ways in which this is affecting the identities of young adults in Mumbai.

GLOCALISATION

It has now become a well-known fact that multinational companies, lured by the lower wages of skilled and semi-skilled labour, India's strategic location as a manufacturing and exporting base and the rapidly increasing middle class, have established offices and industries in India. However, the invasion of multinationals is not only limited to offshore outsourcing. Recognising the growing number of young middle- and upper-class Indians with a disposable income, multinationals are marketing their products to this small minority in India by the strategic use of glocalisation (Mukadam and Mawani 2004).

A term that has been around since the late 1980s, glocalisation refers to 'the interpenetration of the global and the local resulting in unique outcomes in different geographic areas' (Ritzer 2010: 255). In other words, creating products or services intended for the global market, but customised to suit the local culture. According to some, glocalisation is a means by which aspects of the dominant culture can be absorbed without losing elements from the local: 'I define healthy glocalization as the ability of a culture, when it encounters other strong cultures, to absorb influences that naturally fit into and can enrich that culture, to resist those things that, while different, can nevertheless be enjoyed and celebrated as different' (Friedman 1999: 295). In most cases, this is not the process of glocalisation evident in India. It is primarily non-local businesses that are capitalising on aspects of local Indian culture to make their products more marketable in this region of the world.[3]

Various forms of glocalisation are readily visible on the streets of Mumbai. One of the most radical examples of glocalisation may be seen at the local McDonald's where the main food items that one would find in a McDonald's in the West are absent, with new culinary innovations having taken their place. The Big Mac has been replaced by the Maharaja Mac, a burger made of chicken rather than the original beef patties. Although at one point McDonald's in India did sell lamb burgers in place of the beef burgers, the manager at the Linking Road branch informed me that McDonald's had stopped selling lamb since 2002, as it was not very popular with the Indian consumer. The Spicy Paneer Wrap and the McAloo Tikki (vegetable and potato patty) with mint sauce, the highest-selling burger, created only for the Indian market, are targeted specifically at vegetarians (Tripathi 2003). Unlike in other McDonald's, in India, one has the choice of indulging in authentic Indian chai (boiled tea with milk and spices) or English tea (boiled water and a tea bag). Other examples of glocalisation in India include, Subway's Veg Shammi (lentil kebabs) and Chicken Achari (spicy chicken combined with traditional Indian pickle) subs; Pizza Hut's Paneer El Rancho, Tandoori Paneer and Paneer Makhani pizzas; and Frito-Lay's Masala Balls and Magic Masala flavoured crisps. The glocalisation strategy is proving to be a successful way of attracting consumers out of their homes and into fast food restaurants:

> Fuelled by a younger audience that considers cooking to be another word for tedium, the out-of-home consumption of food has grown to a ₹ 35,000-crore market … . Long pilloried

> as 'not-Indian', the market for global fast food has come a long way .... ' A majority of the population is less than 50 years old,' says Arvind Singhal, chairman of KSA Technopak, who feels the best strategy for global food chains remains a pan-Indian menu to begin with and a gradual movement towards a global one .... A KSA study says that an Indian consumer spent 11 per cent of his total discretionary income on eating out in 2002 compared to 9 per cent in 2001. The ratio of eating-in to eating-out has changed to 80:20 from 90:10 two years back. (Tripathi 2003)

In July 2013 PepsiCo launched its Tropicana Coconut Fruit Blends, a product which blends fruit juice (orange or lychee) with coconut water. Homi Battiwalla, PepsiCo India's Senior Director of Marketing for Colas, Juices and Hydration, explains why this product was launched: 'With this new and innovative launch of Tropicana Coconut Fruit Blends, we are looking at expanding and diversifying our portfolio with offerings tailor made for the evolving consumer tastes and preferences' (PepsiCo 2013). Through the use of glocalisation, multinational companies in India have found a creative way to market their products and make them appealing without diminishing the place of local cuisines.

FOOD AND IDENTITY

Food and consumption practices are significant indicators of cultural and other identities. Examining eating habits and cuisines enables one to build 'a significant knowledge of the unconscious attitudes of the society or societies under consideration' (Lévi-Strauss 1968: 87). It is not only the consumption of food, but also a range of associated processes, from preparation to taboos, from which we can understand a group's notion of belonging. It is another means, like ethnicity, of creating boundaries and identifying with those who eat similar food, thereby creating a sense of communal identity. These boundaries are drawn based on classifications of that which can or cannot be eaten, often due to religious restrictions. Taking the example of McDonald's in Mumbai, those consuming the Maharaja Mac (which consists of a chicken patty), may feel that they are identifying themselves with others in the West who are also consuming food from the same food outlet.

However, in reality, they are actually identifying with other affluent middle- and upper-class Indians who, like them, are also consuming a chicken burger, and not with Americans, who are consuming Big Macs and the like (which consist of beef patties). So, while it cannot be said that it is by consuming the same food as their counterparts in the West that young adults in Mumbai are participating in a global culture, what can be argued is that consuming the brand of McDonald's helps them to identify with those in the West, while consuming the goods produced by a Mumbai branch shows that they are identifying with other young people in India. McDonald's, therefore, like other Western brands, is selling more than food. It is a means by which these young Indians are connecting to the West, and more specifically, to America. McDonald's, says James Cantalupo, the former president of the company, 'is not just a hamburger. It's an experience ... that people want all over the world' (Pendleton 1991). Sherman (2010: 3) in his book on intercultural communication through the case studies of China and India writes, Americans 'are a people to be emulated ... . If the American people were not admired around the world, and the American identity was not one that everyone desires to take on, why would American television programming be as popular as it is'. While Sherman has taken on a satirical voice, his words ring true for young people in India, who aspire to take on American cultural elements and become more like their counterparts in America. What it means to be American, as defined by Indians, may differ greatly from the sense of how Americans see themselves, but this does not diminish the desire to be more American. By consuming what are seen to be American products, these young people are participating in a global popular culture, which is symbolic of an imagined American lifestyle.

Not all scholars agree with the notion of food being a key feature of identity creation. Warde (1997: 199–200) argues that food is a 'marginal way of expressing personal identity,' as he feels that 'there are limits to the capacity of food to express personal identity.' For Warde, the connection between food consumption and an individual's identity is superficial. While, this may be partly the case for the Ismailis in this study, as they are partaking in food that is branded under a global banner, after a more detailed examination of what is being consumed at these eateries, glocalised versions of what is served in the same chain in the West, it becomes evident that for this group eating is closely tied to their sense of who they are. However, if one looks at the concerted efforts made by certain communities, such as migrants, to preserve cultural food habits, with less attention given to other cultural elements, such as language, which are often lost, it soon becomes quite apparent that 'food is central to our sense of identity' (Fischler 1988: 275). In her study on changing diets of Gujaratis in Britain, Kalka (1998) indicates that preserving traditional forms of consumption are key factors in maintaining a sense of stability and cohesion, in other words, a sense of a collective Gujarati identity. When one consumes food, then, it is not simply the nutritional properties that are absorbed, but also the ideological elements imbued in the food (Fischler 1988). So, in effect, 'we become what we eat' (ibid.: 279). Food, therefore, is never just food. It embodies concepts, carries with it memories and associations and provides an insight into a community's understanding of and approach to the world. If we take this discussion into account, the decisions made by multinational companies, like McDonald's and PepsiCo, to incorporate local flavours into their products, are almost to be expected.

LANGUAGE AND IDENTITY

Language is key to our everyday lives as it is a means by which we communicate with one another, distinguish how others are related to us through the use of kinship terms, as well as classify individuals based on the way they speak. As with individuals' identities, which are fluid and constantly shifting, language, too, is not fixed, and changes based on the varying contexts in which individuals find themselves. While language use may be unique to each individual, it is the language itself, as well as the variations in vocabulary, intonation, accent, etc., that establishes our place within specific social groups with which we share linguistic behaviour. Individuals also have agency in the languages they use, how they use them and where they use them, which in turn signals the identity that they wish to highlight at a certain point in time. Language 'allows you to say a great deal about yourself, your likes and dislikes, the kind of person you are; it also allows you to convey in numerous subtle ways something about your reliability as an ally or friend' (Dunbar 1996: 78). Language use, therefore, is significant in two ways: first, it is an indication of the individual's own identity; second, it determines belonging to a particular social group. Rehana's comments are representative of the remarks made by the respondents in this study, which indicates the value they place on language, in this case, English, as an element that connects them to the wider global community, to which they desire to belong: 'I can communicate with people as English is a common language in the world'.[4]

For students in Mumbai schools, Hindi and Marathi are compulsory subjects and, according to some of the respondents, French was an optional language offered at their schools. When asked which languages they would prefer to study at school, the majority of respondents (45%) indicated that French would be their preferred choice, with Arabic selected by 25 per cent of the respondents and Gujarati coming in third at 9 per cent. The primary reasons for the popularity of French was that the respondents felt it was a global language, second only to English:

> Suraiya: It [French] is the second most spoken language in the world after English.
>
> Armaan: Because it [French] is an upcoming language and the popularity of French is being quite high as compared to any other language. So, it's almost a universal language now after English.

These responses illustrate that individuals want to belong to a global community, and they feel that this can be achieved by communicating with others in, what they consider to be, global languages. For others, like Sheliza, Arabic was the language of choice, and her rationale for the selection of Arabic, was typical of others in this study: 'The Quran is in Arabic and I would personally like reading the Quran and having more knowledge about my own religion. So I would like to know that language so that I can have my own interpretations.' Such motivations are not surprising, and were in fact expected, as choosing Arabic as a language individuals desire to learn, shows that there is a clear identification between a specific language and their religion, and their longing to belong to the larger Muslim *ummah* (community). Only four respondents chose Gujarati as the language they would have preferred to learn in school, primarily because it is a language spoken by Ismailis in Mumbai, and used in the liturgy in *jamatkhana* (place of worship):

> Aliya: Because my family speaks in Gujarati and also most of the *firmans* [edicts] of Sultan Mahomed Shah [Aga Khan III] are in Gujarati. In Bandra [*jamatkhana*] ... the announcements are made in Gujarati.
>
> Soheil: This [Gujarati] is the language which all Ismailis in JK [*jamatkhana*] speak and I would really like to learn it.

The poor motivation of individuals to learn Gujarati may stem from the neo-colonial negative attitude towards languages of the developing world (Ghuman 2003). While conducting his study among South Asian adolescents in the West, Ghuman (ibid.: 200) had difficulty in locating adolescents interested in learning their heritage language: 'During my fieldwork, I met students who are quite content to learn one of the European languages in preference to their own community language. An often-repeated response was: "What's the use of learning Punjabi?"' Interestingly, the majority of the respondents in this study claimed high levels of Gujarati/Kutchi comprehension, but low levels in speaking, reading and writing Gujarati/Kutchi. An analysis of the data reveals that all of the respondents are claiming a high level of proficiency in spoken Hindi and Hindi comprehension and high levels of proficiency in reading and writing English. These claims may be reflective of the use of Hindi in everyday communication, whereas, it is highly likely that due to their education in English-medium schools they are more comfortable reading and writing in English. The respondents' preferred language, whether English, French, Arabic, or Gujarati, portrays their need to belong to a community – be it a global one, the *ummah* or the local Ismaili community.

The majority of respondents also indicated that Gujarati/Kutchi was a language that their mothers and grandmothers used to communicate with them and that even though their productive skills in Gujarati/Kutchi were not very high, they would encourage their children to speak Gujarati/Kutchi. Zakira went so far as to say that she would 'make it compulsory' for her children to learn these languages because it is a means by which they 'can be bonded with their roots. Most of our scripts are in Gujarati, we have *ginans* [devotional songs], we have old *firmans* ... which are all in Gujarati. So it's better that they should have a sound knowledge of Gujarati'. Salim highlighted how speaking these languages would enable his children to 'converse with my mom and dad and my grandparents'. Salim went on to illustrate why he felt it was important to speak Gujarati: 'Because ... many people converse in Gujarati, like elderly people, and you can't speak with them properly. You can understand them but they can't understand you.' These responses suggest the need for a sense of belonging within the family unit and the local Ismaili community through the use of language. As Giles and Noels (1988) have pointed out, language is an important element of one's cultural identity as it provides a sense of solidarity for an ethnic group and helps to create boundaries between the in-group and out-group.

CODE-MIXING

Shifting from one language to another may be seen as an element of shifting identities, and a more permanent shift may result in language loss and therefore indicate the desire to associate oneself more with one identity rather than another. Some individuals may choose to alter the way in which they use language, by code-mixing, where two languages are combined in the same conversation, and even in the same sentence. Code-mixing, as with language shift, may also result in language loss, or partial language loss, as words from one language begin to replace that of another. Individual agency, again, plays a crucial role when code-mixing is selected, as it signals a hybrid identity (see Mukadam's chapter in this volume). One such example is the use of Hinglish among young adults in Mumbai. The majority of female respondents in this study indicated that they code-mix Hindi and English at home, while an equal majority of male respondents claim to primarily code-mix Hindi and English or speak only Hindi at home. Interestingly, in the *jamatkhana* domain, where there is a greater use of Gujarati/Kutchi in the liturgy, none of the respondents use Gujarati/Kutchi as a means of communication, rather, the majority of respondents code-mix Hindi and English when communicating with others in this space. It is significant to note that none of the respondents use Gujarati/Kutchi as the primary means of communication in any domain, ranging from the home to school to *jamatkhana*.

As discussed earlier, the spending power of the ever-increasing Indian middle class is allowing them to buy Western brands, albeit altered to cater to the tastes of local consumers, thereby giving them the feeling that they are partaking in a global culture. The influence of cable television and the desire for all things Western has transformed the mode of communication among young Indians, which has resulted in the emergence of Hinglish – a unique form of code-mixing (Dwyer 2000; Mukadam and Mawani 2004). 'Most commonly seen in the urban and semi-urban locations of India [Hinglish] is a tendency of combining English and Hindi words in a sentence' (Majumdar 2010: 137). Although Hinglish has gained popularity across India, it is seen to be trendy in Mumbai and other North Indian cities (Dwyer 2000; Ghosh 2002). One primary reason for the widespread popularity of Hinglish may be the 'pressure for a new identity which combines various Indian identities with global trends' (Ghosh 2002). A survey found that more people in India are speaking Hinglish than just English (Majumdar 2010). English is also being mixed with other Indian languages, and the use of Gujlish (a mix of Gujarati and English) was evident during interviews with the respondents in this study: 'Passport clearance *mate kaam karu chhu.*'

Since the mid-1990s, Hinglish has also become the norm in television soaps, chat shows and game shows, and is also evident in Hindi films. Multinational corporations, as well as local companies, are using this new vernacular in advertisements in an attempt to target their niche market and make their products more appealing. Some companies, like Frito-Lay, are simply translating their English slogan (Betcha can't eat just one!) into Hinglish (No One Can Eat Just One ... *Lagi* Bet?). While others, like Domino's Pizza (Hungry *kya?* – Are you hungry?) and Kellogg's (Iron *Shakti*[5] – Strength from iron) are developing original Hinglish slogans to promote their products (Mukadam and Mawani 2004). The Hungry *kya?* tagline, introduced by Domino's Pizza in 2001, focused on an individual's need to satisfy their hunger. Domino's' new tagline, *Yeh hain rishton ka* time, introduced in 2012, can be viewed in two ways. Domino's can be seen to be the place where families and friends can spend time together and strengthen their relationships. Seen from a different angle, this tagline can also be perceived to be encouraging the individual to create a relationship with Domino's, thereby creating a link between the individual and America, again, selling the consumer a Western identity and the notion that by consuming this brand's products, the consumer belongs to a larger Western community. Harmeet Singh Rajpal, Vice-President of Marketing of Domino's India, indicated the significance of their new tagline: 'The new positioning *Yeh Hai Rishton ka* Time would take us to a new level of emotional connect so that the engagement with the consumer is deeper and more enduring' (Domino's 2012). It is important to note that in writing Hinglish the Hindi words are transliterated into English. If, as mentioned above, the high levels of reading comprehension in English claimed by the respondents in this study can be presumed to be similar to other young adults in Mumbai, then the use of transliterated English is a strategic move on the part of the multinationals, as utilising Hindi script may not be as attractive to this sector of Mumbai society. While a combination of English and Hindi is being used in slogans and taglines, the main text is in English with Hindi words and phrases being transliterated, again creating the illusion of being Western.

CULTURAL IDENTITY

More often than not, research on the effects of the majority culture focuses on diasporic and post-diasporic ethnic minority communities. While the Ismailis of Gujarati ancestry in Mumbai can be classified as such, the primary focus here will be the infiltration of an outside culture, namely, Western cultural traits which, as we have seen above, over the last few decades, have become part of Indian society more rapidly than ever before, albeit sometimes in more glocalised forms. In this sense, one can say that the culture of Indians in general, and for the purposes of this chapter, the Ismailis of Mumbai, is at risk of being marginalised. Globalisation has resulted in many positive outcomes, nevertheless the threat of homogenisation, and in some instances, Westernisation, is still very valid: 'Considering our own society, we cannot deny that the country's linguistic and cultural diversity is endangered by the forces of globalization, which work to homogenize and standardize even as they segregate and marginalize' (Dutta and Bhadra 2012: 85).

Culture and Ethnic Identity

Kroeber and Kluckhohn (1952) identified 164 definitions of culture thus demonstrating the complexity of the term. To further complicate matters 'the terms ethnic and culture are often confused .... By ethnicity we refer to a belief in putative descent .... Culture is instead an open project .... [but] since culture is necessarily based on tradition and continuity, it is often confused with ethnicity' (Conversi 2000: 134–35). The earliest definition of culture was proposed by Tylor in 1873 who classified it as 'that complex whole which includes knowledge, belief, art, law, morals, custom, and any other capabilities acquired (learned) by man as a member of society' (Tylor 1920: 1). In the 1960s and 1970s, definitions of the term broadened so it is regarded as one of the pivotal forces in history, alongside politics and the economy. Perhaps Agger's (1992: 6) definition, though succinct, captures the notion of the term in three words: 'Culture is us.' A more recent definition is that of Fenton (2003: 21) who has identified culture as 'custom and practice often with reference to a particular group'. However, culture is not fixed and does not simply consist of customs that have been passed down from one generation to the next in a preserved state. Unlike one's ethnic group which is indicative of one's ancestry, one's culture is not evident of a former cultural presence: 'when one traces the history of an ethnic group through time, one is *not* simultaneously ... tracing the history of 'a culture': the elements of the present culture of that group have not sprung from the particular set that constituted the group's culture at a previous time' (Barth 1969: 38, original emphasis). Rather, like one's identity one's culture is also constantly changing: 'cultures change; they are borrowed, blended, rediscovered, and reinterpreted' (Nagel 1994: 162). Therefore culture is formulated by selecting certain aspects from the past and the present and an individual's cultural identity is negotiated based on past and present elements in which one decides to participate.

Nagel (ibid.) has identified two primary cultural reconstruction techniques. The first, cultural revivals and restorations, takes place when 'lost or forgotten cultural forms or practices are excavated and reintroduced, or when lapsed or occasional cultural forms or practices are refurbished and reintegrated into contemporary culture' (ibid.: 162). An example of this technique is language documentation projects, which aim to revive and preserve dying languages. The second, cultural revisions and innovations, takes place when 'current cultural elements are changed or when new cultural forms or practices are created' (ibid.: 163). An example of this technique can be found in the popular use of Hinglish by young adults in India, as well as in the manner in which Gujarati and Hindi film songs were adapted to form Ismaili *gits* (songs of praise) (Mawani 2012). The main purpose of these two cultural reconstruction techniques is to support the construction of a community in terms of defining group boundaries and nurture collective mobilisation as a foundation for group solidarity (Nagel 1994). Therefore, it is through participation in cultural activities, even mundane ones, such as celebrations and music, that one is able to express one's cultural identity. It is such activities, which serve individuals' need for meaning. The maintenance or reconstruction of one's culture makes it possible for the Ismailis to preserve their collective identity despite the continuous influence of Western culture. The desire for meaning is an elementary human need, for humans as 'creatures who "make" sense could not live in a world without meaning' (Hannerz 1992: 3). Culture is passed on, not in a calcified form, but in a fluid state so it takes on new elements and discards others, thereby creating a collective cultural identity, in which the meanings behind the symbols of a culture are agreed on by the group. This is also a means by which individuals can demonstrate their preferred cultural adaptation strategy – be it acculturation, assimilation, dissociation or marginalisation (Hutnik 1991; Mukadam 2003; Mawani 2006).

Cultural Expressions of Ethnic Identity

Many scholars (Smolicz 1984; Fenton 1988; Ghuman 1994; Baumann 1995; Modood 1997; Mukadam 2003) have identified various cultural aspects of minority ethnic communities, including attitudes towards dating and arranged marriages, preference of music and language skill. In their studies these scholars have analysed the responses of the participants in order to ascertain whether or not they have acculturated into the dominant society. Mukadam (2003) highlighted seven cultural aspects that she felt would reflect the individuals' own cultural preference, rather than that preferred or promoted by their family or community. In her study Mukadam (ibid.) asked the participants to respond to the following statements:

My favourite food is ...

At home we celebrate ...

On special occasions I like wearing ...

My favourite singer is ...

My favourite movie is ...

Two further cultural aspects were drawn from the participants' responses for their religious affiliation as well as their ability to speak/understand Gujarati/Kutchi. Mukadam (ibid.) introduced the Post-Diasporic Acculturative Model (PAM) to assess the level of acculturation of the respondents. The model consists of five main types of acculturated individuals:

1. Western – individuals who are highly integrated into the culture of the ethnic majority.
2. Symbolic *'Desi'** – individuals who show a greater affinity with the culture of the ethnic majority, but who have maintained certain aspects of their ethnic minority culture.
3. Balanced Acculturated – individuals who have maintained equal aspects of their ethnic minority culture and that of the ethnic majority.
4. Symbolic Western – individuals who show a greater affinity with the culture of the ethnic minority, but who have integrated to some degree.
5. *'Desi'* – individuals who show very little integration (ibid.: 262).

Drawing on Mukadam's study, which was conducted in the UK, the Western Culture Adoption Model was developed to

* *Desi* is a Hindi word meaning 'of the homeland'.

determine the level of Westernisation of the respondents in Mumbai, which consists of seven main types of strategy adopted by individuals:

1. *Pukka*** Western – individuals who exhibit adoption of all aspects of Western culture
2. Western – individuals who exhibit a high preference for some aspects of Western culture
3. Symbolic *Desi* – individuals who exhibit a preference for aspects of Western culture, but who have maintained certain aspects of their Indian culture
4. Westernised *Desi* – individuals who exhibit an equal preference for aspects of Western culture and Indian culture
5. Symbolic Western – individuals who exhibit a preference for aspects of their Indian culture, but who have integrated certain aspects of Western culture
6. Desi – individuals who exhibit a high preference for some aspects of Indian culture
7. *Pukka Desi* – individuals who exhibit maintenance of all aspects of their Indian culture (Mawani 2006: 372)

Like those in Mukadam's study, the respondents in this study were asked to indicate their favourite food, music and movies, as well as the clothes they are likely to wear on special occasions and the celebrations observed at home. The results were then inserted into this model and indicate that the majority of female (53%) and male (44%) respondents can be placed in the Symbolic Western category, although they are adopting some aspects of Western culture, they are maintaining more aspects of their Indian culture (Figure 4.1). A minority of female (7%) and male (6%) respondents appear to have found a balance between Western culture and Indian culture and can be said to be Westernised *Desis*. As only 11 per cent of the male respondents were Symbolic *Desis* this shows that the respondents in this study are adopting aspects of Western culture at a very slow pace. Furthermore, these results also indicate that the female respondents appear to be adopting aspects of

** *Pukka* is a Hindi word meaning genuine or authentic and in this case can also be understood as 'wholly'.

Western culture at a slower pace than their male counterparts. As all of the respondents indicated affiliation to the Ismaili tradition as well as some proficiency in either oral or aural Gujarati/Kutchi none of the individuals were *Pukka* Western. The aspect of Western culture that is preferred by the majority of the female respondents (67%) is food. However, on closer examination, it would appear that the food choices that these individuals are referring to as Western, are in fact glocalised versions. On the other hand, the majority of male respondents (94%) indicated their preference for Western clothes on special occasions.

Figure 4.1 *Western Culture Adoption Model as Applied to Young Adult Nizari Ismailis in Mumbai*

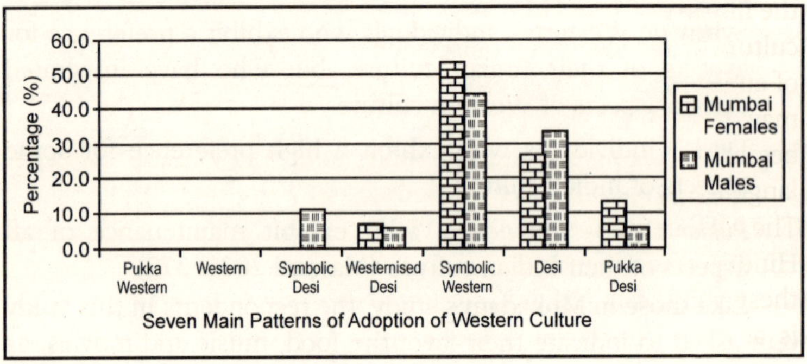

CONCLUSION

Writing about how the nation is an 'imagined community', Anderson (2006: 6) states: 'It is imagined because members of even the smallest nation will never know most of their fellow-members, meet them, or even hear of them, yet in the minds of each lives the image of their communion.' It would appear that this definition of an 'imagined community' is applicable to these young Ismailis in Mumbai. While globalisation has brought Western brands to India and with it the desire among young middle- and upper-class Indians to be Western, which is evident in their consumption patterns, the glocalisation of many Western products limits the extent to which these individuals can truly classify themselves as Western. Multinational corporations are presenting young Indians with the illusion that they are consuming Western products, the majority of which cannot be found in

Western chains as they have been created specifically for the local market, and, apart from the brand, they are not Western in any other aspect. Therefore, this creates a false impression among the young that by consuming Western branded goods, they are demonstrating a Western identity and belong to the larger community in the West that consumes the same brands. In reality, young Indians are participating in a culture that is presented as Western, but at its core is still quite Indian.

While there is a sense that these multinational companies are showing respect for the local culture by producing products that maintain a mix of the local with the Western, this too is the genius of marketing, it brings the product closer to home thus giving one the illusion of familiarity while changing the purchasing habits and culture of a whole group of individuals. For some this may be a way of engaging with a Western identity, albeit a false one, for others it may have more damaging consequences, as the illusion which begins with simple changes in food habits, then moves to clothes, language, values and over time erodes their Indian cultural identity. The consumption of so-called Western food products, code-mixing Hindi (or sometimes Gujarati) and English, are examples of how these young Ismailis are aspiring to create a hybrid identity, which is at once Western and Indian. The food habits of these young people, as well as their preference for clothes, music and movies may appear to be a pick and mix approach in everyday life. Nevertheless, this hybrid identity is somewhat of an illusion, as a closer examination of the preferences of these individuals demonstrates that ultimately the favourite, on all occasions, for young adult Nizari Ismaili Muslims of Gujarati ancestry in Mumbai is that which can be identified with Indian cultural elements.

NOTES

1. It is important to point out from the outset that while this section will provide a brief overview of the ways in which globalisation is affecting Indian society; this is by no means a thorough investigation of globalisation.
2. The data presented in this chapter are not representative of all Ismailis living in Mumbai, but are specific to the respondents who

participated in this study and who reside in Bandra, an affluent suburb in West Mumbai.

3. An example of glocalisation being applied to a non-Indian cultural element by Indians themselves is Chinese cuisine, which has been altered to suit the tastes of locals, resulting in Indo-Chinese dishes like hakka noodles and chicken manchurian.
4. It is important to note that all the respondents in this study claimed high levels of proficiency in productive and receptive English skills.
5. Kellogg's Iron *Shakti* tagline was discontinued in 1999 due to little increase in sales (Sangameshwaran 2004).

REFERENCES

Agger, Ben. *Cultural Studies as Critical Theory*, London: Routledge, 1992.

Albrow, Martin. 'Introduction', in *Globalization, Knowledge and Society*, edited by Martin Albrow and Elizabeth King, London: Sage Publications, 1990, pp. 3–13.

Anderson, Benedict. *Imagined Communities*, London: Verso, 2006.

Asian Voice. 'India Firmly on Globalisation Path: Lord Meghnad Desai', 17 January 2004.

Barth, Fredrik. 'Introduction', in *Ethnic Groups and Boundaries: The Social Organization of Culture Difference*, edited by Fredrik Barth, London: George Allen & Unwin, 1969, pp. 9–38.

Baumann, Martin. 'Conceptualizing Diaspora: The Preservation of Religious Identity in Foreign Parts, Exemplified by Hindu Communities Outside India', *Temenos*, Vol. 31 (1995): 19–35.

Conversi, Daniele. 'Autonomous Communities and the Ethnic Settlement in Spain', in *Autonomy and Ethnicity: Negotiating Competing Claims in Multi-ethnic States*, edited by Yash Ghai, Cambridge: Cambridge University Press, 2000, pp. 122–44.

Domino's. 'Domino's Pizza India Unveils New Brand Positioning 'Yeh Hai Rishton Ka Time', 30 October 2012, <www.dominos.co.in/blog/domino%E2%80%99s-pizza-india-unveils-new-brand-positioning-%E2%80%9Cyeh-hai-rishton-ka-time%E2%80%9D/> (9 July 2013).

Dunbar, Robin. *Grooming, Gossip and the Evolution of Language*, Boston, Mass.: Harvard University Press, 1996.

Dutta, Chandrabali and Bula Bhadra. 'Youth Language(s): A Sociolinguistic Enquiry of Native Language Displacement vis-à-vis

Popular Linguistic Patterns in Contemporary Kolkata', *Journal of the Indian Sociological Society*, Vol. 1, No. 1 (July-Dec. 2012): 63–89.

Dwyer, Rachel. *All You Want is Money, All You Need is Love: Sex and Romance in Modern India*, London: Cassell, 2000.

Fenton, John Y. *Transplanting Religious Traditions: Asian Indians in America*, New York: Praeger, 1988.

Fenton, Steve. *Ethnicity*, Cambridge: Polity Press, 2003.

Fischler, Claude. 'Food, Self and Identity', *Social Science Information*, Vol. 27, No. 2 (1988): 275–92.

Friedman, Thomas. *The Lexus and the Olive Tree*, New York: HarperCollins, 1999.

Ghosh, Nirmal. '"Cool" Indian Youths Switching to Hinglish', *The Straits Times, Singapore*, 29 September 2002.

Ghuman, Paul A.S. *Double Loyalties: South Asian Adolescents in the West*, Cardiff: University of Wales Press, 2003.

——. *Coping with Two Cultures: British Asian and Indo-Canadian Adolescents*, Clevedon: Multilingual Matters, 1994.

Giles, Howard and Kimberly A. Noels. 'Communication Accommodation in Intercultural Encounters', in *Readings in Cultural Contexts*, edited by Judith N. Martin, Thomas K. Nakayama and Lisa A. Flores, Mountain View: Mayfield, 1988, pp. 139–49.

Hannerz, Ulf. *Cultural Complexity: Studies in the Social Organization of Meaning*, New York: Columbia University Press, 1992.

Hutnik, Nimmi. *Ethnic Minority Identity: A Social Psychological Perspective*, Oxford: Oxford Science Publications, 1991.

Inda, Jonathan X. and Renato Rosaldo. 'Introduction: A World in Motion', in *The Anthropology of Globalization*, edited by Jonathan X. Inda and Rosaldo Renato, Oxford: Blackwell, 2002, pp. 1–34.

Kalka, Iris. 'The Changing Food Habits of Gujaratis in Britain', *Journal of Human Nutrition and Dietetics*, Vol. 1, No. 5 (1998): 329–35.

Kroeber, A.L. and Clyde Kluckhohn. *Culture: A Critical Review of Concepts and Definitions*, New York: Vintage Books, 1952.

Lévi-Strauss, Claude. *Structural Anthropology*, Vol. I, Harmondsworth: Penguin, 1968.

Majumdar, Ramanuj. *Consumer Behaviour: Insights from Indian Market*, New Delhi: PHI Learning, 2010.

Mawani, Sharmina. 'Songs of Praise: The *Git* Tradition of the Nizari Ismaili Muslims', in *Gujarati Communities across the Globe: Memory, Identity and Continuity*, edited by Sharmina Mawani and Anjoom A. Mukadam, Stoke-on-Trent: Trentham, 2012, pp. 59–78.

——. 'The Construction of Identities amongst Young Adult Nizari Ismaili Muslims in Toronto and Mumbai', Unpublished PhD Thesis, SOAS, University of London, 2006.

Modood, Tariq. 'Culture and Identity', in *Ethnic Minorities in Britain: Diversity and Disadvantage*, edited by Tariq Modood et al., London: Policy Studies Institute, 1997, pp. 290–338.

Mukadam, Anjoom A. 'Gujarati Speakers in London: Age, Gender and Religion in the Construction of Identity', Unpublished PhD Thesis, University of Reading, 2003.

Mukadam, Anjoom A. and Sharmina Mawani. 'Code-Mixing in Indian Advertising: A Desi Twist', Paper presented at the annual meeting of the International Association for World Englishes, Syracuse, NY, 16–18 July 2004.

Nagel, Joane. 'Constructing Ethnicity: Creating and Recreating Ethnic Identity and Culture', *Social Problems*, Vol. 41, No. 1 (1994): 152–76.

Pendleton, Scott. 'Giving Golden Arches Global Span', *The Christian Science Monitor*, 1991, <http://www.csmonitor.com/1991/0521/21081.html> (20 June 2013).

PepsiCo. 'PepsiCo Launches a First Ever in the Industry: NEW 'Tropicana Coconut Fruit Blends'', 15 July 2013, <www.pepsicoindia.co.in/media/Press-Releases/release_07_15_2013.aspx> (19 July 2013).

Pieterse, Jan N. 'Globalization as Hybridization', in *The Globalization Reader*, edited by Frank J. Lechner and John Boli, Oxford: Blackwell, 2000, pp. 99–105.

Ritzer, George. *Globalization: A Basic Text*, Oxford: Blackwell, 2010.

Sangameshwaran, Prasad. 'Second Thoughts on the Indian Consumer', *Business Standard*, 7 June 2004, <www.business-standard.com/article/management/second-thoughts-on-the-indian-consumer-104060701131_1.html> (9 July 2013).

Sherman, Edward D. *America through the Eyes of China and India: Television, Identity and Intercultural Communication in a Changing World*, New York: Continuum, 2010.

Smolicz, J.J. 'Minority Languages and the Core Values of Culture: Changing Policies and Ethnic Response in Australia', *Journal of Multilingual and Multicultural Development*, Vol. 5, No. 1 (1984): 23–41.

Tomlinson, John. 'Globalized Culture: The Triumph of the West?', in *Culture and Global Change*, edited by Tracey Skelton and Tim Allen, London: Routledge, 1999, pp. 23–31.

Tripathi, Dhirendra. 'Global Food, Desi Stomachs', *The Times of India, Hyderabad,* 15 December 2003.

Tylor, Edward. *Primitive Culture,* New York: G.P. Putnam's Sons, 1920.

Warburg, Margit. *Religious Organisations in a Global World: A Comparative Perspective,* 2001, <www.cesnur.org/2001/london2001/swarburg.htm> (16 October 2002).

Warde, Alan. *Consumption, Food and Taste: Culinary Antinomies and Commodity Culture,* London: Sage Publications, 1997.

Part II
LANGUAGE AND CULTURE

CHAPTER 5

The Administrator and the Poet

Language and Globalisation in Nineteenth Century Gujarat

Arvind Bhatt

HISTORICAL CONTEXT

The region we know today as Gujarat has the longest (1,625 km) coastline of all the other modern states of India. For more than a millennia, Gujarat has had trade links with the outside world, especially with Persia, the Arab states, East Africa and even with the Roman and Byzantine empires. The ancient ports of Surat, Khambhat, Bharuch, Veraval and others were developed and protected by the Mughal emperors and by the independent sultans of Gujarat. In early modern times, these ports attracted the attention of the European trading nations and the Dutch, French, Portuguese and English fought for dominance over these trade facilities. Seafaring and trade, therefore, have been in the blood of the coastal Gujaratis and in the merchants who financed the trade. Seafaring and trade were great conduits for globalisation and for cultural and linguistic influences on the indigenous cultures and traditions. Invasions and occupation also obviously played a role in globalisation. Giddens (1993: 181) defines globalisation as 'the intensification of worldwide social relations which link distant localities in such a way that local happenings are shaped by events occurring many miles away and vice versa'. I take this definition to include the process of transformations brought about by encounters between cultures, whether by trade, invasion, occupation or colonisation. Modernity, as Giddens (ibid.) states, is inherently globalising. In this chapter, therefore, I describe the transformation of the Gujarati language and, particularly its literature, as a consequence of the encounter between cultures as represented by Alexander Kinloch Forbes (1821–1865), a Scottish administrator, and the learned Shrimali Brahmin poet Dalpatram Dayabhai (1820–1898).

Ancient trade, however, did not affect the traditions and cultures of the interior regions to a great extent until the encounters with Islam beginning in the eighth century and the arrival of the European maritime powers from the seventeenth to the nineteenth centuries. In particular, the spread of the control exercised by the East India Company,[1] beginning with Bengal in 1757 and gradually spreading to Gujarat in 1818, brought about wholesale transformations in the daily lives of those under the rule of the Company. At first the Company was primarily interested in trade, but as it had to renew its charter every 20 years, the Directors and British parliament forced it to undertake the education of the 'natives' and provide better training for its administrators in newly acquired territories. For the latter, the Company set up a college in 1806 at Haileybury, Hertford, where the future civil administrators received a 'classical' education (law, history, economics, science, etc.), as well as training in classical languages, including Sanskrit, Farsi, Bengali and Hindustani (Woodruff 1954). The political and social reforms then under way in Britain also influenced the attitudes and values of the administrators who then shaped the transformations in the cultures and languages of the areas they ruled over. It is this process of transformation that I would argue is a process of globalisation, which occurred in Gujarat in the first half of the nineteenth century. In this chapter I examine this process through the lens of the friendship between Forbes (1849, 1857, 1924) and Dalpatram (1849).

THE POET AND THE SAHIB

Alexander Forbes, a scion of Scottish landed gentry, was born in the Marylebone district of London on 7 July 1821. He was a descendent of the seventeenth century Sir John Forbes of Craigievar of Aberdeenshire (Mosley 2003). After a private education and having attended schools in Finchley, he was apprenticed to the well-known architect George Bassevi (1794–1845). However, just eight months into his apprenticeship, he was nominated (by Sir Charles Forbes) to join the East India Company's Bombay Civil Service as a grade six clerk (East India Register R10/50), and in preparation for this service he attended Haileybury College from September 1841 to December 1842 (Haileybury College 1843). After finishing his course, he arrived in Bombay in November 1843. His talents as a linguist and administrator were soon recognised and he was rapidly promoted to assistant collector in Ahmadnagar, Maharashtra, where he learnt Marathi and Hindustani. After marrying Margaret Moir in 1846, he was posted to Ahmedabad, the then capital of Gujarat, as an assistant judge.

He began to learn Gujarati but soon also began to take a keen interest in the ancient monuments, inscriptions, bardic legends and old manuscripts during his travels around the region. As he says later in the preface to his *Ras Mala* (Garland of Chronicles):

> I had not been very long in Goozerat when, in the course of my public employment, a paper was placed before me which bore the characteristic signature of two bards. My curiosity was excited; I made enquiries, and sought acquaintance of such of the class as were within my reach. Of the treasure of the bardic repertoire I thus obtained a glimpse which stimulated instead of satisfying me. (Forbes 1924: xx)

He realised, however, that he required help from local scholars to translate, classify, record and seek out further historical materials.

One must realise that at that time, such materials were widely scattered and much was lost during the lawless decades and centuries during which Gujarat was fought over by the Mughals, Marathas, petty chiefs and warlords. Brahmins and Jain monks became the usual custodians of manuscripts and interpreters of inscriptions and these custodians were reluctant to reveal their treasures to foreigners, such as Forbes, who might be seen to 'pollute' them or use them against any land grants made to them by local chiefs and feudal warlords. As Forbes (ibid.: xxi) states:

> It might perhaps amuse, but would certainly weary the reader were I to describe the numerous obstacles which we found opposed to us by ignorance, jealousy and avarice ... . I was

> sometimes believed to be employed in searching for concealed treasure, that at other times my object was supposed to be that of detecting flaws in the titles to lands with the view of their assumption by the government.

The 'we' and 'us' referred to in this passage are Forbes himself and his newly acquired assistant, Dalpatram, a Shrimali Brahmin from the town of Wadhwan, some 137 km southwest of Ahmedabad. There is an amusing story, related by Nanalal, the son of Dalpatram, of how the two future pioneers of the renaissance of the Gujarati language and its literature met in November 1848 (Kavi 2000).

As we noted earlier, Forbes was on the lookout for an able assistant and after some enquiry he was recommended the penniless but learned Brahmin poet from Wadhwan. As there was no postal system at the time, a runner was sent to request Dalpatram to attend, what we might now call, an interview in Ahmedabad. Borrowing a small sum of money, Dalpatram walked all the way to Ahmedabad and was taken to the *chanda-suraj mahel* (the moon and sun palace) where Forbes' office was located. Dalpatram was 28 and Forbes was 27 and one can imagine that this similarity in age must have facilitated a friendly conversation in Hindustani, as Dalpatram knew no English and Forbes was not yet fluent in Gujarati. After an initial conversation, during which Forbes gauged the abilities of his putative assistant, he asked how much pay Dalpatram expected. When Dalpatram said 100–125 rupees, Forbes was taken aback: 'Look, Kaveshwar (honorific title of Dalpatram), I have to pay you from my own salary of 800 rupees, I can only give you 20 rupees a month' (ibid.: 16). At this, Forbes' assistant Bholanath Sarabhai, who was also present, explained that Dalpatram meant a yearly salary, as was the custom; 20 rupees a month would be more than double what Dalpatram expected! This misunderstanding of the system of payment represented something of the new concept (to Gujaratis) of regular monthly payments. The two young men appreciated the other's sense of humour and a bond was established which was to last a lifetime: 'Good fortune brought early to my notice the name of the Kuveshwar, or poet – for with that title, Dulputram (sic) is invested by the suffrage of his countrymen, – and I secured his services in A.D.1848. From that period my valuable co-adjutor has been almost constantly by my side' (Forbes 1924: xxi).

As we have seen, Forbes' first contacts were with the Hindus, especially Brahmins, and he took a keen interest in their customs, legends and history as well as monuments, temples, forts and palaces. He also noticed the hierarchy of languages used around him. Gujarati seemed to him a 'bazaar language' used by the Baniyas (the merchant caste) to keep accounts. This hierarchy of languages was satirised in a seventeenth-century poem, caricaturing the sounds of the languages current at the time:

idher udherka solahi ana,	Hindustani is worth 16 anas, (i.e., one rupee),
utthe kattheka bar;	Marathi is worth 12 anas;
ikdum tikdum aath ana,	Marwadi is worth 8 anas,
shun sha paisa char (Yashashchandra 2003: 582).	and Gujarati is worth 4 paisa, (i.e., one ana) (my translation).

Dalpatram, himself a Sanskrit scholar and a poet, used Brij Bhasha to write his poetry, rather than Gujarati, which was his mother tongue. Brij Bhasha is a language related to Hindi and the language of medieval poets like Surdas and Amir Khusro. A living language, it is spoken by over 500,000 speakers, mainly in the Agra-Mathura areas of northern India. It is rich in vocabulary from Sanskrit and used primarily by devotees of the Hindu god Krishna. Gujarati, however, has a long history with the first Gujarati poem composed in 1169 by Vajrasen, a Jain monk (Thaker 1994; Yashashchandra 2003). And, in the eighteenth and nineteenth centuries the poet Dayaram (1777–1852) composed his popular *garbis* (folksongs, which are based on religious themes and which are used during traditional dances) in Gujarati. Up to the time of Dalpatram, almost all of the literature in Gujarati was dominated by verse form and mainly devotional in character (Pandya 1976; Nayak et al. 1989).

The establishment of the Company's rule brought a measure of stability and security to Gujarat; so much so that the universal greeting to an Englishman was: '*Atul Raj*! [May your rule last for ever!]' (Woodruff 1954: 204). The hierarchy of languages, as indicated above, was a reflection of the existing political and economic power relationships: Hindustani was the language of administration, Marathi the language of the Marattha power-brokers, and Marwadi the language of moneylenders. Gujarati was thus seen to be at the bottom of the hierarchy, reflecting its relatively low status as perceived by people in general. This perspective changed due to the new education system introduced by the Company, which, at first, emphasised the role of the vernacular in primary education. This is part of the theme of modernisation of Gujarati in the mid-nineteenth century. In recent times, it appears that the status of Gujarati is still under debate, both in Gujarat itself and among the Gujarati diaspora.

For two hours a day, Dalpatram taught Brij Bhasha and 'old' Gujarati (or, more correctly, pre-modern Gujarati, current in the seventeenth and eighteenth centuries) to Forbes and helped him translate between these and Sanskrit. Dalpatram also introduced Forbes to other scholars who brought old manuscripts, among which were references to the Solanki and Waghela dynasties going back to the eighth and ninth centuries. Forbes had already come across bardic legends referring to these histories and he began to connect these stories and documents that came his way in his work as a judge. He commissioned Dalpatram to travel around the country so that he could gather and copy further manuscripts and translate inscriptions. In essence, Dalpatram became an able co-researcher. During his furlough in March 1854, Forbes returned to London and in 1856 published his two-volume *Ras Mala,* which chronicles Gujarat from the eighth century to the arrival of the British. While the focus of these volumes was on the Hindus, and more specifically on the Rajputs, Forbes hoped his works would be of interest to British officials in India, as well as those in Britain: 'The result is now placed before the public in the hope that, unworthy as it is, it may still be of use to the local officer, and may interest some few even of my countrymen at home, in the fortunes of their fellow-subjects – the Hindus in Goozerat' (Forbes 1924: xxii).

The *Ras Mala* was an important step in the process of globalisation in that it gave a clearer definition, available to all, of Gujarat; in the first chapter of his book, he defines, for the first time, the borders of 'the province of Goozerat' (ibid.: 3). A 'sketch' map was included in the 1856 edition [see MSS EUR B78, British Library], as well as in the 1878 edition. As Simpson and Kapadia

(2010: 20) remark: 'At that time 'Goozerat' was commonly regarded by the British as an administrative zone in what is seen as central Gujarat today. Yet, in Forbes' work, Gujarat emerges as quite different: as a broad and distinct region, encompassing the peninsular portion and the mainland, and united by a common language'. It is also worth noting that Forbes (1924: xxii) included the Hindus as 'fellow-subjects' with his 'countrymen at home' signifying his view that eventually Indians would be self-governing and be seen as fellow-subjects. In this he was following his mentors such as Mountstuart Elphinstone (1779–1859, Lieutenant Governor of Bombay, 1819–1827) and John Malcolm (1769–1833, Governor of Bombay, 1827–1830). Dalpatram (1849) also remarks on the liberal attitude that governed Forbes' conduct with the 'natives', highlighting that he showed no haughtiness of a ruler, went about on foot rather than on horseback whenever possible, carried a stick, a pistol, a money bag and a map, respected the traditions and taboos of the Hindus (not much is known about his conduct with Muslims) and paid handsomely the bards and local copyists for their labour. Rawlinson (1924: xiv), in his *Memoir of Forbes,* points out that when Forbes died in 1865, 'the news of Forbes' death was received with profound grief all over the Presidency, and especially in his beloved Gujarat. The chieftains of Kathiawar ... mourned for him as if they had lost a member of their own family'. Dalpatram composed *Farbeswirah,* an innovative and well-known Gujarati elegy in memory of his dear friend, and *Farbesvilas,* his account of the gathering of bards (which Forbes presided over). Both are now considered to be a part of modern Gujarati literature. Not only was *Ras Mala* used by his countrymen and officers of the Company, it was also used later by the eminent Gujarati novelist Nandshanker Mehta who wrote the first Gujarati novel in 1866 entitled, *Karanghelo,* (based on an episode in *Ras Mala*) (Dave 1978). The critic and dramatist Navalram also based his pioneering drama *Veermati* on material in the *Ras Mala* (Pathak 1978).

Forbes inspired Dalpatram to write in Gujarati rather than in Brij Bhasha and this led to the beginning of a new age, even a renaissance, of Gujarati literature. In 1849, for the first time, Dalpatram published his *Bhoot Nibandh,* an anthropological essay on beliefs in ghosts, witches and other superstitions. This was one of the first prose writings in Gujarati to address a social issue, a considerable departure from the medieval writings on spiritual and religious matters. He went on to write *Hunnerkahanni Chadhai* (1851) on technology and *Gnati Nibandh* (1851), a critique of the caste system. Forbes used *Bhoot Nibandh* in the second volume of *Ras Mala*, which includes a lengthy treatise on customs and beliefs of the Hindus at the time. Dalpatram's contribution to the making of *Ras Mala* has led some Gujarati writers and scholars to wonder if Dalpatram should not be cited as a joint author. Forbes also inspired Dalpatram to write *Laxmi Natak* (1849), the first play in Gujarati, based on Aristophanes' *Plutus* (446–386 BCE), but using the local idiom of *bhavai*, the satirical verse-drama long used to entertain lay people in the towns and villages of Gujarat. This translation of Greek drama, adding to the burgeoning genres of modern Gujarati literature, is also an instance of globalisation of culture and literature.

All these literary activities did not happen in a vacuum, of course. Technologies of communication, printing, and transport all began to accelerate the transformation of the political, social and cultural fabric of Gujarat in the first half of the nineteenth century. A Parsi, Furdunji Marzbanji (1787–1847), started a Gujarati weekly, *Mumbai Samachar*, in 1822; a library was established in Surat in 1824; the Native Education Society under Colonel Jarvis appointed Ranchhodas Jhaveri to produce Gujarati textbooks and train Gujarati teachers; in 1844 a *Manavdharm Sabha* (Humanist Society) was founded in Surat; in the same year, Dalpatram and others started a *Pustak Prakshan Mandli* (Book Publishing Group); in 1849 a lithographic press was imported to Ahmedabad and the *Vartmanpatra* (News) was published every Wednesday (hence it was called *budhvariu* (which translates as Wednesday) by the Gujaratis), with Forbes as a nominal editor. Such technological innovations produced similar results for other vernaculars of India.

There were virtually no state organised schools in Gujarat before the British arrived. Education was confined to learning the religious scriptures and basic reading, writing and arithmetic and the state, such as it was, did not consider itself responsible for education – though, one must remember that state education did not arrive in England until the 1870s. Because Gujarat was divided up into numerous, and usually antagonistic, kingdoms and chieftainships, there was no consistent approach to education which was, in any case, available only to the higher castes and wealthy. Schools were supported by fees and donations from temples (both Jain and Hindu) and mosques (Desai 1978). According to the licence of the East India Company, it was charged by the British parliament to set aside a sum of money for the education of the 'natives'. Questions arose as to how this education was to be achieved. The Anglicists, T.B. Macaulay and Charles Trevelyan advocated English as the medium of instruction to spread Western knowledge (Macaulay 2006), whereas the Orientalists, Elphinstone and Forbes were in favour of promoting and using the vernacular to transmit Western knowledge. There is no space in this chapter to discuss the debates in great detail, but it should be noted that Macaulay's views held sway in the Calcutta and Madras Presidencies and the vernacular continued to be used in the Bombay Presidency, for a time at least. Thus primary schools began to be established in Gujarat under British rule and these acted as channels of development for the Gujarati language and its literature, as well as for spreading Western knowledge. After decades of neglect, there was an increasing demand for knowledge, and opportunities of regular employment in the new administration were keenly taken up by the emerging elites. Forbes and Dalpatram were actively involved in establishing schools for both boys and girls that were open to all castes (in theory, at least). Education, then, was another conduit for the globalisation of knowledge.

As Forbes was collecting material for *Ras Mala*, he began to develop a fondness for both the Gujarati language and Gujarati people. Hiralal Parekh (2010: 8), assistant secretary of the Gujarat Vernacular Society in 1923 writes in his history of the Society:

> While he [Forbes] collected historical materials, he began to know the soul of the people but also felt pain in his heart to observe the people in the grip of superstition, ignorance and brutish rituals; he felt the need of an organisation that would preserve the historical and literary writings and educate the people about their own (glorious) past. Inspired by this noble aim he consulted his friends and founded the Gujarat

> Vernacular Society on 26 December 1848. [My translation from Gujarati]

The aims of the organisation ranged from publishing a regular paper to commissioning new books to awarding prizes for the best publications. In its first year report, in English, it states the central aim of the organisation:

> We try to lift up the language of the province from its present ignoble condition and encourage the more gifted fancies among those to whom it is a vernacular, to enlarge, refine and regulate it by manifold application, that it may become fitter to convey from mind to mind and from generation to generation both the beautiful and the true, then too we acknowledge the same call to benefit those among whom for the present we are sojourners. (ibid.: 9)

The principal tone of this report seems patronisingly Christian and Orientalist, this is hardly surprising, as the first committee was entirely British and sought funds and approval from the government. The reference to the 'sojourners', however, indicates the uncertainty of British rule and echoes Forbes' (1857: 139) own views, expressed just after the 1857 Uprising:

> It is melancholy to think how little our conduct in India has accorded with the wise principles of Sir John Malcolm ... there is much in them which is of universal application, and which it must concern every thinking man to see disregarded. We cannot, especially regard without anxiety the rapid growth among both our military and civil officers, of a supercilious contempt for everything which relates to customs and feelings of India.

The Gujarat Vernacular Society played a central role in developing and modernising the Gujarati language and its literature and continues to do so to this day and is a monument to the memory of Forbes and Dalpatram who was its secretary for more than 25 years, until the latter went blind. Another such society was founded in Bombay with help from Forbes just before he died (1865), the Forbes Gujarati Sabha, which still continues to promote the Gujarati language. Both these societies, together with the later

Gujarat Sahitya Academy, founded in 1982, continue to act as conduits for the globalisation of the Gujarati language and its literature, especially considering the widely spread Gujarati migrations outside of Gujarat.

In the second half of the nineteenth century, an event thousands of miles away in America also had an influence on the developments in Gujarat. During the American Civil War, the export of cotton from America was disrupted and Britain had to switch to Egyptian and Indian cotton. The price of cotton shot up in Gujarat and speculators inflated the prices. Many Gujaratis, including Dalpatram, gambled on the shares and stock market and lost when the bubble burst at the end of the Civil War. Forbes, too, lost part of his property, as his bank in Bombay went under. It is important to mention this episode to illustrate how Gujarat and its people came into the global ambit of the British economy within a relatively short time after British rule was established and the first cotton mills arrived in Ahmedabad in the first half of the nineteenth century. The speculation on shares and stocks introduced the phrase '*share ane sattabaji*' (shares and playing the stockmarket) into Gujarati (Mancherji Kavasji 1869).

In August 1865, Forbes became ill and went to Pune to seek medical assistance, but on 31 August he died there of encephalitis and was buried the next day. As mentioned above, there was a profound sadness at the loss of a champion of Gujarat and Gujarati. Dalpatram continued the work of promoting and modernising Gujarati and its literature until his death in 1898.

CONCLUSIONS

In the introduction to his book on colonialism, Cohn (1996: 4–5) writes, 'The knowledge of languages was necessary to issue commands, collect taxes, maintain law and order – and to create other forms of knowledge about the people they were ruling. This knowledge was to enable the British to classify, categorize, and bound the vast social world that was India so it could be controlled'. He goes on to argue, referring to the forming of texts (dictionaries, grammars, etc.) by Europeans in the late eighteenth century, that these texts 'had the effect of converting Indian forms of knowledge into European objects' and that informants or 'elites had to be found within Indian society who could be made to see that they had an interest in the maintenance of British rule' (ibid.: 21). This could be true of the Orientalists of the eighteenth century and their followers, and Forbes was, initially, in that category. But, as this chapter has shown, the collaboration and friendship between Forbes and Dalpatram went beyond the 'command of language and language of command' (ibid.: 16). In fact, these pioneers facilitated, what we might call modernity, into the language and literature of Gujarat and helped bring about transformations of knowledge and culture to Gujarat, while at the same time, bringing peace and stability to a region that was devastated by wars and rapacity of its rulers for nearly 150 years previously. Forbes' *Ras Mala* inspired Gujarati writers and defined the idea of Gujarat as a historical, cultural and linguistic entity. This could perhaps have been the foundation of what would, in 1960, be the separation of Gujarat as a state from the Bombay province on a linguistic basis. As Kapadia (2010: 63–64) rightly wonders:

> If the 'Ras Mala' was much more a product of exchanges, interactions, and of its author's genuine interest in and love of Gujarat, than simply a manual furthering the aims of the colonial government. At another level, the process of the creation of a united and internally related idea of Gujarat in the Ras Mala also reflects Dalpatram's 'modern' relationship with Forbes as well as the change in his relationship with the Bhats and the Charans [the bards] ... . from the inception of his interaction with Forbes, he became an interlocutor between them and the colonial officer as well as an integral part of the latter's endeavours to promote the 'Gujarati' language.

This is a different view of colonial interactions from the postcolonial discourse presented by Cohn (1996) and Dirks (1993). It is true that Forbes and his mentors and his co-officers, such as T.B. Curtis and T.C. Hope, saw the promotion of Gujarati as a 'civilising' mission, in opposition to Macaulay's (2006: 158) mission to 'form a class who may be interpreters between us and the millions whom we govern; a class of persons Indian in blood and colour, but English in taste, in opinions, in morals, and in intellect'. Perhaps it is ironic that economic globalisation today has brought Gujarat nearer to Macaulay's vision than he perhaps dared! (see Mukadam's chapter in this volume).

This chapter has highlighted how 'native' informants were not passive agents of British rule and that they constructed their own ideas and identities as Gujaratis; that globalisation and language can go hand-in-hand to create new, 'modern' genres of literature and enrich the language. Commenting on the effects of industrialism as one aspect of globalisation, Giddens (1993: 188) points to 'cultural globalisation' as lying behind each of the four dimensions of globalisation.[2] An example of this cultural transformation, as we have seen, was the development of Gujarati as a modern language and the flowering of its literary genres in the mid-nineteenth century. This, in turn, provides some indication of the changing identities of the Gujaratis and of the evolution of the regional identity of Gujarat.

Debates about the role and status of Gujarati, both in Gujarat today and among Gujaratis abroad should, in my opinion, take into account such histories as outlined in this chapter. English is a world language and one of science and technology, but that should not marginalise the vernacular, whose importance administrators like Forbes and his collaborator Dalpatram so presciently recognised: 'They who, in estimating the means available for the mental improvement of the people of India, neglect everything which is not either immediately or derivatively Anglican, narrow their sphere of endeavour very unnecessarily' (Forbes 1849: vii). Some 160 years ago, Forbes had the foresight to recognise the significance of the vernacular, and especially Gujarati and its literature for the peoples of Gujarat.

NOTES

1. The term 'Company' will be used throughout the chapter to refer to the East India Company.
2. The four dimensions of globalisation are: the nation-state system, the world military order, the international division of labour and the world capitalist economy (Giddens 1993).

REFERENCES

Cohn, Bernard S. *Colonialism and its Forms of Knowledge*, New Jersey: Princeton University Press, 1996.

Dalpatram, Daya. *Bhut Nibandh: An Essay*, Ahmedabad: Gujarat Vernacular Society, 1849.

Dave, Mahendra. 'Nandshanker', in *Gujarati Sahityano Itihas*, Vol. 3, edited by Umashankar Joshi, Anantrai Raval and Yashvant Shukla, Ahmedabad: Gujarati Sahitya Parishad, 1978, pp. 90–91.

Desai, Neera A. *Gujaratma Ognismi Sadima Samajik Parivartan*, Ahmedabad: University Granth Nirman Board, Gujarat Rajya, 1978.

Dirks, Nicholas B. 'Colonial Histories and Native Informants: Biography of an Archive', in *Orientalism and Postcolonial Predicament*, edited by Carol A. Breckenridge and Peter van der Veer, Philadelphia: University of Pennsylvania Press, 1993, pp. 279–313.

East India Register, National Archives, Kew, London.

Forbes, Alexander K. *Ras Mala: Hindoo Annals of the Province of Goozerat in Western India*, Delhi: Low Price Publications, 1924.

——. 'Sir John Malcolm', *Bombay Quarterly Review*, Vol. VI (July-Oct. 1857): 139.

——. 'Preface by the Translator', in Daya Dalpatram, *Bhut Nibandh: An Essay*, Ahmedabad: Gujarat Vernacular Society, 1849.

Giddens, Anthony. 'The Consequences of Modernity', in *Colonial Discourse and Post-Colonial Theory*, edited by Patrick Williams and Laura Chrisman, New York: Columbia University Press, 1993, pp. 181–90.

Haileybury College. *The Haileybury Observer*, Haileybury, Hertford: Haileybury College, 1843.

Kapadia, Aparna. 'Alexander Forbes and Making of a Regional History', in *The Idea of Gujarat: History, Ethnography and Text*, edited by Edward Simpson and Aparna Kapadia, Hyderabad: Orient BlackSwan, 2010, pp. 63–64.

Kavi, Nanalal. *Kavishvar Dalpatram*, Vol. 2, Ahmedabad: Gujarat Vidyasabha, 2000.

Macaulay, Thomas B. 'Lord Macaulay's Minute, 2 February 1835', in *Britain in India, 1765–1905*, edited by John Marriott and Bhasker Mukhopadhyay, London: Pickering and Chatto, 2006, pp. 148–49.

Mancherji Kavasji *Share ane Sattabaji*, Bombay: Mancherji Kavasji, Ijukeshan Sosaitina Paresa, 1967.

Mosley, Charles. *Burkes Peerage and Baronetage*, 107th Edition, USA: Genealogical Books, 2003.

Nayak, Ratilal, Somabhai Patel and Prasad Brahmbhatt. *Arvachin Gujarati Sahityano Itihas*, Ahmedabad: Ananda Book Depot, 1989.

Pandya, Natvarlal. 'Dayaram', in *Gujarati Sahityano Itihas*, Vol. 2, edited by Umashankar Joshi, Anantrai Raval and Yashvant Shukla, Ahmedabad: Gujarati Sahitya Parishad, 1976, pp. 635–55.

Parekh, Hiralal T. *Gujarat Vernacular Societyno Itihas*, Vol. 1, Ahmedabad: Gujarat Vidyasabha, 2010.

Pathak, Jayant. 'Navalram', in *Gujarati Sahityano Itihas*, Vol. 3, edited by Umashankar Joshi, Anantrai Raval and Yashvant Shukla, Ahmedabad: Gujarati Sahitya Parishad, 1978, p. 120.

Rawlinson, Henry G. 'A Memoir', in *Ras Mala*, edited by Alexander K. Forbes, Delhi: Low Price Publications, 1924.

Simpson, Edward and Aparna Kapadia. *The Idea of Gujarat: History, Ethnography, Text*, Hyderabad: Orient Blackswan, 2010.

Thaker, Dhirubhai. *Gujarati Vishwakosh*, Vol. 6, Ahmedabad: Gujarati Vishwakosh Trust, 1994.

Yashashchandra, Sitanshu. 'From Hemchandra to Hind Swaraj', in *Literary Cultures in History: Reconstructions from South Asia*, edited by Sheldon Pollock, Berkeley: University of California Press, 2003, pp. 567–611.

Woodruff, Phillip. *The Men Who Ruled India: The Guardians*, London: Jonathan Cape, 1954.

CHAPTER 6

Indobrits

Cultural Hybridity as a Constantly Negotiated Lived Reality

Anjoom A. Mukadam

> 'Either we assimilate or we are ghettoised or we persuade the society that there is a third option.'
>
> —Bhikhu Parekh (Mukadam 2003: 6)

This chapter is primarily concerned with the manner in which young second-generation Indians of Gujarati ancestry in Britain are using hybridity as a constantly negotiated lived reality to overcome imposed boundaries and social inequities. As Kasinitz et al. (2004: 9) outline, the second generation are actively engaged in 'the reshuffling of boundaries and the making of connections across boundaries in new and complex ways'. A lot has been written about second-generation ethnic minorities in the past three decades, ranging from the way in which they were assumed to be 'between two cultures' (Watson 1977), 'neither one thing nor another' (Gidoomal 1997b: 172) or of possessing 'double loyalties' (Ghuman 2003). As with many other first-generation Indians, Lord Noon, a British businessman of Gujarati ancestry, agrees with this scholarship: 'The main problem I see is that they [the second generation] are torn between two cultures. Clearly ... when they go to school or colleges, they see a different culture. They come home and the father and mother say "Sunday you have to come to the temple, you have to go to the mosque" ... so there is a conflict of culture there' (Mukadam 2003: 8). On the one hand, the second generation faced the wrath of the first generation for not strictly adhering to the cultural norms of their community, and on the other, the majority culture continued to view them as immigrants (clearly not possible if they were born in the country to which their parents migrated), referring to them as second-generation immigrants, foreigners and members of the diaspora (another term used incorrectly to describe the second generation) (Mukadam and Mawani 2007a). 'If the word "diaspora" refers to those whose cultural origins are in a different land, then how far do these communities have to go before they are recognised as belonging to the new homeland or will academics and others always refer to them in relation to a past with which many, at best, have symbolic links?' (Mukadam 2003: 195).

As a means of moving forward I refer to the second generation as the 'post-diasporic generation' so as to make a distinction between the generations (ibid.: iii). This is not an ideal term and is problematic in itself, but is a move away from the all-inclusive term 'diaspora' which lacks integrity when applied to the second generation and beyond. What was missing from earlier research conducted either by first-generation Indians or outsiders was the ability to recognise the complexity with which the second generation dealt with what were assumed to be conflicting identities. Perhaps what was needed was the second generation to speak out for themselves and their peers and that is exactly the journey that several of us have taken (Mukadam and Mawani 2007a). At that time, purists in academia, particularly social anthropologists, viewed research on one's own community as an 'insider' as lacking objectivity and therefore flawed. There were no centres for Diaspora Studies or Migration Studies in 1999 when I began my PhD, and even those departments of South Asian Studies at major universities in the United Kingdom that did study the Gujaratis focused on those in India. Despite the barriers, many of us pursued our interests through departments of Linguistics, History or Religious Studies and were fortunate to have the encouragement of academics who were in favour of a more interdisciplinary approach, a method that was generally not looked upon favourably. Over the last decade, times have changed and it is now commonplace for individuals to conduct research within their own communities and for this work to be seen as valid, legitimate and adding to the corpus of academic knowledge on these groups. In fact, there are times when it is only by virtue of being an 'insider' or member of the community that one can gain access to 'closed' sites, community members, their oral histories and, in many cases, documents treasured and preserved within the family. While much progress has been made, there is now a need for a more nuanced approach, so that researchers are more mindful of not mixing respondents into one group without considering differences that may arise based on religious affiliation, age, location of residence, etc. 'Words are never mere words. They embody concepts, are charged with historical memories and associations, and shape our understanding of, and approach to the world' (Parekh 1990: 58). Therefore, care must be taken to avoid using terms, such as diaspora and immigrant, which are more applicable to the first generation, but unsuitable when discussing how the second and subsequent generations negotiate their multiple identities.

DESH PARDES (HOME AWAY FROM HOME – THE EARLY YEARS)

The presence of 'others' in the United Kingdom can be traced back over generations and this history has created the diversity that forms the mosaic of today's multi-ethnic Britain. The Celts, Anglo-Saxons and Normans arrived early in this history, followed by the Irish, Jewish and Eastern Europeans. Jackson (1963) states that in 1851 there were 727,326 Irish immigrants in Britain and that they constituted 2.9 per cent of the population in England and Wales, as well as 7.2 per cent of the population of Scotland. Following them, there was an influx of approximately 120,000 Jews, particularly from Russia, who had fled to avoid persecution. Post World War II a further 460,000 foreigners entered Britain, among them were 115,000 Poles who were invited under the Polish Resettlement Scheme, as well as former prisoners of war and 90,000 European Voluntary Workers (EVWs) from refugee camps in Germany (Anwar 1998). Acute labour shortages continued despite the absorption of white immigrant workers. This resulted in the hiring of migrant workers in the late 1940s and 1950s from the Indian subcontinent and Caribbean to engage in the post-war reconstruction of health services, welfare and transportation. This inflow of visible minority groups was to change the face of Britain and result in racism as well as unrest. Tension increased as the indigenous communities perceived that their own livelihoods were being threatened by this wave of cheap labour (Coward et al. 2000). In reality, the newly arrived workers were engaged in occupations that many of the local population considered undesirable (Desai 1963; Ballard 1994; Brah 1996). Despite the unfavourable conditions, the members of this minority community were industrious in that they invited their family members and friends from the subcontinent to join them in Britain and assisted them with securing jobs. This resulted in chain migration, which is 'the movement in which prospective migrants learn of opportunities, are provided with transportation and have initial accommodation and employment arranged by means of primary social relationships with previous migrants' (Anwar 1998: 2).

In the late 1960s Africanisation was taking place, a process in which Africans and the politicians that represented them began fighting for their rights in an attempt to redress the balance and take control of what they considered to be rightfully theirs. It was a time of discord and many British Asians in Kenya, Tanzania and Uganda fled their homes in search of safety and security by entering the United Kingdom with British passports. The Nationality Act of 1940 had bestowed British citizenship on all colonial and commonwealth citizens thus allowing legal entry into the United Kingdom. This led to further anti-immigration speeches and on 1 July 1962 the government rushed a Bill through parliament imposing strict quotas to curb the inflow of immigrants. No longer could an individual holding a British passport freely enter the United Kingdom unless they were born in the country or descended from a British parent or grandparent. 'Let no one suppose that the flow of dependents will automatically tail off. On the contrary, even at the present admission rate of only 5,000 a year by voucher, there is sufficient for a further 25,000 dependents per annum ad infinitum' (Powell 1968). With his blatant hatred for other 'races' that had entered the United Kingdom and his vitriolic words against them, Enoch Powell had created a name for himself. His following was vast and the country was set into a state of turmoil with skin colour being used as the reason for increasingly vociferous outbursts. Powell had made the 'race' debate public, no longer the whispering conversations of ordinary citizens in the privacy of their homes or among their compatriots. In addition, he advocated the idea of repatriation and undermined the rights of ethnic communities to reside in Britain as rightful citizens (Bourne 1998). Racial exclusionism and intense hostility were to haunt the lives of many, leaving skin colour as an inescapable social marker that continues to be used to this day. The 1971 Immigration Act was introduced and it replaced employment vouchers with work permits, but offered neither permanent residence nor entry rights for dependents. The British public were gradually being lured back into a feeling of safety; the country was being protected from mass invasion and would remain as it had done in the past, predominantly white.

The Ugandan crisis was to bring about an end to the notion that immigration was under control. In August 1972, Idi Amin forced approximately 50,000 East African Asians out of the country, many of whom were from the Gujarati community. The United Nations (1973) office in Geneva estimates that the vast majority affected held British passports and that over 28,000 entered the United Kingdom. The 'twice migrants' (Bhachu 1985) had entered the second phase in their journey from India to East Africa and now to the United Kingdom. The diversity within the ethnic communities of South Asian origin was now clearly visible, they had come from seven countries of the Indian subcontinent: India, Pakistan, Bangladesh, Nepal, Bhutan, Sri Lanka and the Maldives. The largest of those seven countries being India, governed under British colonial rule for over a century and a half until its independence in 1947. These were a people who belonged to many different communities divided along religious, cultural and linguistic lines. The South Asian community in Britain is part of a global diaspora of over 20 million people. Leicester is the second largest city in the world outside India inhabited by post-independence Indians; Durban in South Africa being the largest (Gidoomal 1997a). Figures from the 2011 census show that the number of Indians in England and Wales has risen in the past decade to just over 1.4 million. In total, the South Asian population now makes up 7.5 per cent of the total population (see Table 6.1). The majority of Asians in the United Kingdom live in what Gidoomal (ibid.) refers to as the £5 billion corridor that extends diagonally from Lancashire in the Northwest down to Kent in the southeast. It incorporates the West Midlands and Greater London, areas with a large South Asian presence, and is sometimes also referred to as the 'M1/M6 Corridor' as these are the two main motorways from London to the North. This 'corridor' was in place long before the influx of immigrants in the 1960s, who then simply followed the existing distribution pattern. London still has the greatest concentration of Indians; almost 42 per cent of the Indian population live in and around the capital (Parekh 2001).

Table 6.1 *Growth of Britain's South Asian Population*

Ethnic Group	*1971*	*1981*	*1991*	*2001*	*2011*
Indian	240,730	673,704	823,821	1,053,411	1,412,958
Pakistani	127,565	295,461	449,646	747,285	1,124,511
Bangladeshi	—	64,562	157,881	283,063	447,201
East African	44,860	181,321	*—	—	—
Total South Asian Population	413,155	1,215,048	1,431,348	2,083,759	4,213,531
% of South Asians in England and Wales	0.85%	2.52%	3.04%	4.4%	7.5%

* by 1991 most East Africans identified themselves as Indian.

Source: Ballard 1994: 7; Census UK 2001, 2011.

Migration is an entrepreneurial activity and long-distance migrants are rarely drawn from poor families. The majority of South Asian settlers in Britain primarily came from three regions, the Punjab, Gujarat and Sylhet. They were mainly from peasant farming families, although some were craftsmen and even fewer were professionals. The commonly held assumption that migration was a means of avoiding destitution is ruled out by Ballard (1994) in favour of a view that it was a means of supplementing the family's capital resources and raising their standing in the local social hierarchy or indeed a path to career advancement. Brah

(1996) supports the views of Ballard (1994) with regard to his categorisation of the majority of migrants as being from rural areas of India and belonging to the peasant proprietor class. Desai (1963: 2), however, holds a different view, stating that the reasons for migration by Gujarati and Punjabi migrants was purely economic, based on avoiding poverty: 'there is great pressure on land in Gujarat (and the Punjab) and consequently widespread unemployment and underemployment.'

These once-migrants had come in search of temporary employment with no long-term plans to stay in the country once their objectives had been met. In both the Punjab and Gujarat, emigration was highly valued and did not involve severance of ties with the community. As the years passed the immigrant numbers of South Asian origin increased and they began forming their own communities, retaining unity through their regional culture, language and kinship ties (ibid.). Their image of the homeland was one of nostalgia and idealism and as the years progressed and communication with their past diminished, so did the 'myth of return' (Anwar 1979). No longer sojourners, they began to form roots in Britain. The South Asian diaspora had arrived and was to make its mark in Britain. Brah (1996: 184) defines diasporic journeys as composite in that they are: 'embarked upon, lived and re-lived through multiple modalities: modalities, for example, of gender, "race", class, religion, language and generation.' Immigrants were, more often than not, classified in relation to the majority, as the minority or ethnic minority, and to distinguish them further they were often referred to as 'coloured'. It would seem that this terminology was considered, at that time, appropriate by the majority community, an example of which is evident in an academic paper on racial awareness among adolescents in London comprehensive schools, 'Children from minority groups, particularly coloured' (Dove 1974: 255).

Outsiders can be conceptualised in a variety of ways; they can be described as foreigners, aliens, immigrants, by their national or ethnic origins, religious affiliation and many others. The terminology used is largely dependent on the political and cultural traditions of the country in which they are living, and later on whether the outsiders accept or reject such labelling. In Germany, they are termed *Ausländer*, *immigrés* in France, and ethnic minorities or *etnische minderheden* in Britain and the Netherlands respectively (Parekh 2001). The long associated stereotype of the Indian corner shop was attributed mainly to the Gujaratis, who worked long hours and included their families in all aspects of the business. This commitment to their families and ambition for them has led to this group's success. An article in *The Daily Mail* on 7 February 2002 highlighted how corner shops were in danger of disappearing as the children of the owners are now highly educated professionals: 'They're the daughters of Asian corner shop owners who came to this country with nothing. But now they're all at the top of their professions' (Adam 2002). The Gujaratis are heralded as being among the most affluent and successful of Britain's South Asian settlers. This community boasts a wide range of highly educated professionals, as well as entrepreneurs, many of whom find themselves on Rich Lists published annually. One of them, Manubhai Madhvani, who was among those forced out of East Africa communicates his appreciation to Britain for opening its doors:

> There is gratitude. Especially gratitude to Sir Edward Heath, whose government authorised our entry when we had nowhere to go. What I should like to say to him now is: 'Thank you. We are grateful we were permitted to live in your country. And I would want to say to you that we have not been a burden on you. We have prospered – and our prosperity has benefited Britain'. (Gidoomal 1997b: 15)

This feeling of immense gratitude was to continue among the first generation who had placed themselves as second-class citizens in this country, they had been given another chance and were subservient to the needs of the majority. The winds of change lay ahead and the second generation were to make their mark and stake their place in British society. No longer 'outsiders' as their parents were, they are undergoing a process of change and adaptation, culturally, linguistically and in terms of their identity.

APNA DESH (OUR COUNTRY – OUR HOME)

Sue et al. (1982) outline three historical trends in ethnic minority research: the inferiority model, the deficit model and the bi-cultural or multicultural model. The second generation in Britain have witnessed all three phases and this section will focus on the way in which they have managed to find mechanisms to create a new ethnicity. Where South Asians in the United Kingdom are concerned, Gidoomal (1993) offered four possible mechanisms for coping with identity issues: (1) Wholesale Assimilation, which he warns may create problems at a later stage if the individual feels the need to discover their Asian roots; (2) Asian Ghettos, which he views as being as futile 'as lighting a solitary candle to ward off the night' (ibid.: 149); (3) 'Western Asian,' which he defines as 'not necessarily born in the West, but he/she has lived here so long that Western ways have become part of him/her', thereby creating an individual with 'a combination of the best qualities of the two' (ibid.: 149–50); and (4) 'See-sawing between two cultures', he warns those who see this as their option: 'You can run yourself ragged to no good purpose' (ibid.: 150).

While many individuals may fall into one of these four categories, there is one category that he omitted, a strategy used by many and for which I coined the term Indobrit® at the start of my doctoral studies in 1999. I put forward the idea that these individuals of Indian background and British nationality actually fall along a continuum in which they position themselves so that they can have the best of both worlds – Indian and British. This is different from his category 'Western Asian' which Gidoomal (ibid.: 149) used in reference to the first generation who had adopted 'Western' ways – Indobrits have not adopted Western ways, they have learned how to contextually adapt to a situation utilising the cultures with which they have been brought up. 'Hybrid terms like Indobrit® offer the second and subsequent generation a holistic identity that is inclusive and does not result in an "either/or" misrepresentation of the very complex multiple identities that they possess, yet situates them as belonging to the nation state while maintaining aspects of their ancestral culture' (Mukadam and Mawani 2007b: 203). There is no doubt that the issue of identity is an important one to the majority of South Asians and there appears to be a reconstruction and evolution of self-identification among young second-generation individuals. Do they see themselves as British, East African, Indian, British Asian, or maybe even Indobrit®?

The history of minority individuals and groups has been rife with conflict and accommodations as a result of 'coercive pressures that politically dominant groups exert on their subordinates to gain and to maintain loyalty' (De Vos 1995: 28). It is this pressure for change on the minority groups, which often results in instability in stratified societies. In the past the majority has maintained its position by suppressive measures, which aimed to assimilate the group and thereby resolve the situation by way of disposing of the autonomy and cultural distinctiveness of minority groups. In some cases individuals break away from their ethnic group in order to achieve upward mobility, or in the words of De Vos (ibid.) 'individual evaporation'. He takes this one step further and suggests that upward mobility actually 'weakens ethnic priorities in loyalty and behaviour' (ibid.: 33), which then places the maintenance of ethnicity as an attribute of non-socially mobile and lower-status individuals. Although this may be true in some cases or some communities, the generalisation cannot, in my opinion, be used for all ethnic groups. In fact, there may actually be a case of losing or 'concealing' one's ethnic identity to conform to the pressures of society so as to gain upward mobility and then returning to reclaim or reinstate one's ethnicity at a later stage once success has been attained. At a time of major social unrest in the 1970s and 1980s, it appears that many second-generation individuals responded by hiding or suppressing their ethnicity and developed a Western persona in order to avoid racism and discrimination. Barth's (1969) theory that ethnic groups may become behaviourally assimilated while maintaining a strong sense of ethnic identity is a highly probable outcome in the case of many second-generation Gujaratis. My own experience indicates that this is the way in which many professional second-generation Gujaratis have dealt with the pressure to achieve success and maintain their ethnic identity: a chameleon-like adaptive behaviour that allows for the best of both worlds – economic as well as cultural/religious.

The classic perspective on culture was brought about by anthropological research in the 1950s and 1960s in which culture was perceived as being 'something the members of society have and bear as something shared. They are socialized into a given culture that is handed down from generation to generation as collective meaning homogeneously distributed in society' (Søderberg 1999: 137). While culture was formerly seen as largely homogeneous, bounded and tightly connected to clearly delineated social groups, it is now increasingly conceptualised as an unbounded flow of signification with an uncertain and contestable foundation in social groups. Terms like 'hybridisation' have thus been proposed in order to see culture in a more processual, dynamic light. There are some very good reasons for this reconceptualisation, notably the fact that ethnographic evidence shows much less clear-cut boundaries and less internal homogeneity in social groups than was formerly believed to be the case. More specifically, it could be pointed out that the intensified globalisation processes of recent decades – encompassing the flow of ideas as well as people and commodities – entails an accelerated pace of cultural change as well as an unprecedented degree of cultural complexity in many places (see Mawani's chapter in this volume). On the one hand, cultural universes are increasingly unbounded, mixed and changing. On the other hand, boundaries are being strengthened and recreated through identity politics – be it ethnic, national or religious. Although cultural differences between groups sharing the same space diminish, the social boundaries may indeed be strengthened. Looking at the strategic history of culture in anthropology, there appear to have been two general approaches which, according to Ingerson (2013), emphasise either coherence or creativity, interdependence or independence, holism or differentiation, and continuity or change.

Weller (1999) has likened culture to an Etch A Sketch® – something that can be formed and erased in an instant, constantly changeable and at once fluid in nature. The very fact that we define the term is essentialist in nature and Street (1993: 25) takes an innovative approach to the issue at hand and explains that rather than looking at what culture is, we should look at what it does: 'culture is an active process of meaning making and contest over definition, including its own definition. This, then, is what I mean by arguing that Culture is a verb'. Parents of many second-generation Gujaratis endeavoured to follow the path of assimilation in the hope that their children would benefit from the process and would be accepted as equals. Discrimination continued from the first generation to the second and this lack of acceptance on the part of the majority led to a very strong revival of ethnic identity (Stopes-Roe and Cochrane 1990; Ballard 1994; Mukadam 1994; Dahya 1996; Brah 1996; Anwar 1998; Nielsen 2000). Beverley McLachlin (2003), the Chief Justice of Canada, in the fourth annual LaFontaine-Baldwin lecture, discussing minority ethnic groups in Canada stated:

> the simultaneous pursuit of exclusion and assimilation produced cultural displacement, marginalization, and tragic loss of identity and self-esteem ... the policy of assimilation undermined their identity as members of a group – their shared history, language and culture. The good aspects of their group dynamic – a solid identity rooted in one's history and culture – were weakened with negative aspects – isolation, alienation and lack of opportunity – enhanced.

With regard to the commonly held notion, mentioned earlier, that South Asian youth face a culture clash or are perceived as being between two cultures, Brah (1996: 41) views this argument as being problematic for several reasons: 'to posit a notion of two cultures is to suggest that there is only one "British" and one "Asian" culture'. She goes on to explain how there are significant differences in the upper-, middle- and working-class cultures of Britain and that these are further differentiated in terms of region and gender. Likewise, she makes a strong case for 'Asian culture' being differentiated according to class, caste, region, religion, and gender. Her main objection to the simplistic view of a bi-polar cleavage among South Asian youth is that 'the emphasis on "culture clash" disavows the possibility of cultural interaction and fusion. There is no a priori reason to suppose that cultural encounters will invariably entail conflict' (ibid.).

Hybridity

The term 'hybrid' is commonly used in the biological sciences as an alternative to heterozygous that is the mating of two genetically different forms to create a new species. It is this very nature of creating something different or new by mixing that led to the term being appropriated by academics in the social sciences and subsequently a range of associated terminology emerged, including terms such as diaspora, transcultural, intercultural and syncretism. Ashcroft et al. (1998: 118) state that hybridity is 'one of the most widely employed and disputed terms in postcolonial theory'. In its early form, hybridity was employed to promote white superiority such that miscegenation was deemed to be unnatural and repulsive (Brah and Coombes 2000). Since then the term has been used by several academics, notably Paul Gilroy (1987), Stuart Hall (1989) and Homi Bhabha (1990, 1994), in relation to diaspora and cultural exchange. But it is the very nature of the term that is problematic, as it can mean different things to different people: 'precisely because of its elasticity and open nature, the hybrid model can be appropriated by anyone to mean practically anything. Since the essence of its borders is oscillation, these boundaries can be conveniently repositioned to include and exclude different peoples and communities' (Gómez-Peña 1996: 12–13). In this section I will look at the various ways in which second-generation Gujaratis in Britain use hybridity, including its use as a form of resistance against the prevailing dominant or majority culture.

Post-structuralism is marked by a rejection of totalising and essentialist concepts. It reasserts the importance of process, change and circumstance, and sees human beings as active creators of culture. Within a post-structuralist framework, the discussion of ethnicities and identities has shifted beyond the notion that these concepts are fixed and constructed in isolation. Post-structuralism has made gains in recent years because its allowance of cultural pluralism challenges the fixed status of established categories like sex, class, 'race' and ethnicity. Liberalism, tolerance and pluralism lead us to embrace the idea of multiplicity. One of the central tenets of contemporary Euro-American thought is that the pursuit of personal freedom and, by association, individual autonomy, which is seen as a fundamental human right, should not be affected by the demands of others, including one's immediate family (Ballard 2007). Naturally to those from differing cultural traditions these expectations are unrealistic and undermine the reciprocities and obligations set about by kinship ties. These two faces of liberalism are, therefore, incommensurable. Gray (2000: 1–3, 6) argues that there is no single ideal cultural system on which all humanity can be agreed:

> If liberalism has a future, it is in giving up a search for a rational consensus on the best way of life ... the good life comes in many varieties ... the span of good lives of which humans are capable cannot be contained in any one community or tradition. The good for humans is too beset by conflict for that to be possible. For the same reason, the good life cannot be contained in any one regime.

Gray (ibid.: 6) supports the view that the object of toleration is not about laying down the foundations for consensus, rather to promote mutual coexistence in arenas of diversity:

> A theory of *modus vivendi* is not the search for an ideal regime, liberal or otherwise. It has no truck with the notion of an ideal regime. It aims to find terms on which different ways of life can live well together. *Modus vivendi* is liberal toleration adapted to the historical fact of pluralism. The ethical theory underpinning *modus vivendi* is value-pluralism. The most fundamental value-pluralist claim is that there are many kinds of human flourishing, some of which cannot be compared in value. Among the many kinds of good lives that humans can live there are some that are neither better nor worse than one another, nor the same in worth, but incommensurably – that is to say, differently – valuable.

Parekh (2001: 22) echoes the views of Gray (2000) and states that if Britain is to be at ease with its cultural diversity and foster a common sense of belonging, then

> Britain needs a broadly agreed body of shared values. These include such procedural values as respect for civil authority, tolerance, mutual respect, freedom of expression and commitment to the democratic resolution of differences as well as such basic ethical norms as respect for human dignity, belief in the equal worth of all human beings and the equality of races and sexes and respect for privacy. Although these and related values do not eliminate deep differences about the content of the good life and are not by themselves enough to foster a sense of common belonging, they provide a basic framework for social co-operation, for resolving such differences as remain and for developing common bonds of citizenship.

Ballard (2007) stresses that most human societies are culturally plural and that cultural pluralism is a regular feature of human social organisation and that exposure to and familiarity with a range of cultural codes is a normal human experience. The Parekh Report (Runnymede Trust 2000: 27) questions fixed boundaries that are implied when referring to members of so-called communities:

> Post-migration communities are distinct cultural formations, but they are not cut off from the rest of British society. It is true that maintaining tradition is critical to their self-identities, but their sense of community owes as much to how they are treated as to where they came from. These communities are not, and have never aspired to be, separate enclaves. They are not permanently locked into unchanging traditions, but interact at every level with mainstream social life, constantly adapting and diversifying their inherited beliefs and values in the light of the migration experience.

Brah (1996: 137–38) holds similar sentiments and clearly shows how the lives of South Asians in Britain are lived through multiple modalities:

> Asian-British cultures are not simply a carry-over from the sub-continent but are now 'native' to different regions and localities of Britain. Asian cultures of London, for example, may be distinguished from those of Birmingham. Similarly, East London cultural life has its own distinctive features compared with the local cultures of West London. There are some commonalities, of course, dependent on which particular modality – religion, region, language, class, etc. – is singled out. For example, Panjabi cultures have their own specificities compared with Gujerati or Bengali cultures. On the other hand, all Muslim groups, be they Panjabi, Gujerati or Bengali, share certain cultural specificities. But each case is simultaneously a dimension of region and locality – of 'Englishness', 'Scottishness', 'Welshness', 'Irishness', and so on … . They can not be disaggregated into 'Asian' and 'British' components. They are fusions such that 'Asian-British' is a new ensemble created and played out in the everyday life world.

It is this changing view of culture, as fluid and multiple, that is the essence of the second generation's trajectory.

The Second Generation

The South Asian presence in Britain has added a new dimension to the discourse on culture and identity. Both culture and identity are inextricably linked and debates on these issues are increasingly taking centre stage in the post-modern world alongside globalisation and Europeanisation. South Asian communities have often been portrayed as encapsulated (Khan 1974; Anwar 1979; Shaw 1988; Werbner 1990), that is, they follow their own value systems and live within closely defined ethnic boundaries (Bhatti 1999). However true this was for the first generation, it now appears that second-generation Indians born and/or brought up in Britain are challenging the stereotypes attributed to the older generation. Culture is far from being a static reality and while differing groups in society will have particular characteristics, they will also share aspects of each other's culture as a result of socio-political and economic forces (Brah 1996). It is this amalgamation or fusion of cultures that will be examined in detail regarding second-generation Indians in London and its environs. Chambers (1993: 74) summarises the position of those living in a multicultural society and the myth of achieving an authentic culture: 'Post-colonialism is perhaps the sign of an increasing awareness that it is not feasible to subtract a culture, a history, a language, an identity from the wider transforming currents of the increasing metropolitan world. It is impossible to "go home" again'. In the case of second-generation Indians, this challenges the older generations' definition of 'home' and of their ideal authentic culture, putting these second-generation individuals in the position of cultural negotiation and interaction with wider society. Their culture is no longer solely the culture of their parents and their home is not the land of their forefathers, rather, the land in which they were raised and in which they are integrated. Theirs is uncharted territory that is evolving with each day and each turn of events, from the riots in Oldham in May 2001 to the tragedies of 11 September 2001 and 7 July 2005.

These individuals were born and brought up in Britain; they are not outsiders and have a sense of loyalty to the country. This is a generation that has struggled to gain acceptance and which now celebrates its multiple identities, its plurality, and its difference in a Britain that is more accepting of its global status as a multi-ethnic nation. Hybrid identities are celebrated as progressive, as shown in the work of Hall (1990) and Gilroy (1987). Bhabha (1990: 211) defines hybridity as the 'third space': 'This third space displaces the histories that constitute it, and sets up new structures of authority, new political initiatives, which are inadequately understood through received wisdom. The process of cultural hybridity gives rise to something different, something new and unrecognisable, a new arena of meaning and representation'.

The term 'hybridity' is complex and encompasses a range of possibilities. In order to lead to a more nuanced understanding of how the second generation have utilised hybridity in their everyday lives I propose that there are, in fact, three types of hybridity: (1) distinct hybridity, where cultural aspects remain separate but together; (2) integrated hybridity, where two cultural aspects are fused; and (3) contextual hybridity, where cultural aspects alternate depending on context. These three types of hybridity can be illustrated through the example of language use among the second generation, where code-switching, moving back and forth between two or more languages, demonstrates distinct hybridity; code-mixing, using two or more languages in conversation, exhibits integrated hybridity; and alternating between Gujarati and English, depending on the context, shows contextual hybridity. Table 6.2 provides further examples, which are indicative of the cultural adaptation strategies of second-generation Gujaratis in Britain.

In the same way as a second-generation individual's identity is fluid, so is the way in which they manoeuvre between these three types of hybridity. They have developed the skill, probably as a result of all the environmental factors they faced being brought up with two cultures, and created strategies that would enable them to access the 'best of both'. Further research will need to be conducted to ascertain if there are specific conscious decision-making strategies employed or if the choices evolve instinctively, as a type of

Table 6.2 *Three Types of Hybridity as Employed by Second-Generation Gujaratis*

Cultural Element	*Distinct Hybridity*	*Integrated Hybridity*	*Contextual Hybridity*	
			Indian Context	*Western Context*
Language Use	• code-switching	• code-mixing	• Gujarati	• English
Food and Drink	• *gulab jambu* (deep fried doughballs soaked in syrup) with ice cream • masala omelette with baked beans • roast chicken with masala *bateta*	• chicken tikka pasty • chocolate samosas • naanwich • *kesar* (saffron) and *elchi* (cardamom) fudge • chai tea latte	• daal and rotis (dinner at home)	• cheese sandwich (school lunch)
Clothes	• Indian *kurti* on jeans • *pachhedi* used as a scarf with woollen coat	• denim *kurti* • silk blouse with Indian design	• Punjabi suit or sari (evening wear)	• Western suit (work)
Music Interest	• Zakhir Hussain's use of the *tabla* with other styles, e.g., Irish folk	• Karmacy • Raghav	• Indian classical music	• Western classical music
Film Interest	• The Best Exotic Marigold Hotel • Run Fat Boy Run	• East is East • West is West • The Namesake • Bend it Like Beckham • Anita and Me	• popular Hindi cinema	• popular Hollywood movies
Celebrations	• wedding celebration with Indian religious ceremony followed by a dinner/dance with bride and bridegroom in Western attire	• registry wedding in Indian attire	• Indian wedding celebration	• Western wedding celebration

second nature. One thing is certain, these adaptive strategies employed by the second generation were a direct result of assimilationist policies and an environment of distrust and hatred towards these 'outsiders', even though the majority had been born and brought up in Britain. Perhaps the second generation should be grateful that the political climate at that time 'allowed' them the opportunity to experiment and be defiant – theirs was a generation that held bhangra parties at the night club, 'The Empire', in Leicester Square during school hours, who were not going to allow the majority to treat them in the way their parents had been treated and this anger and resentment at being labelled 'paki' or being told to 'go home' would be their strength rather than their weakness. This arena of hybridity would open up new opportunities and allow them to create a 'new ethnicity' and give them the confidence to feel that they, too, belonged on this small island. Little did they know that the culture that they had created in their homes would transform the British cultural landscape and leave a mark for generations to come.

Masala to Mainstream

Commodification is defined as the process of developing things, concepts and even people into saleable products. Hassan (1999) states that today's shrinking material world has led corporations to take commodification into 'identity spaces' of culture and society. Research conducted on Indian-American college students by Maira (1999) indicated that Indian parties were an important context in which these second-generation youth were creating and contesting their identity. Their music is one of Indian remixes blended with techno, rap and reggae. When asked to explain the importance of this youth culture, Maira (ibid.: 179) states: 'This popular culture is significant because it provides a public space in which second-generation Indian-Americans can socialize with one another, a space not created by their parents or by community institutions but by the youth themselves – with a little help from popular culture entrepreneurs'. Similarly, the needs of Indian youth in Britain were not met by mainstream society resulting in the creation of their own temporary autonomous zones, arenas where they were free to express themselves as they chose. An identity evolved from this removal, an identity built on tradition, creativity, and freedom of expression. At some point, entrepreneurs noticed the marketability of this subculture and began exploiting this niche market as well as creating a new trend for things exotically Indian ranging from clothing, accessories and henna to music, theatrical productions and restaurants (Mawani and Mukadam 2010).

British society has recognised this subculture and it has been accepted as a part of mainstream culture such that it is hard to believe that in the early 1960s the early migrants had difficulty finding the basic ingredients for their cuisine, in fact, fresh vegetables, such as okra and aubergines, lentils, yogurt, spices, pickles and other such items were seen as luxuries. Over time, these items became more accessible, first in Indian corner shops, then in specialised Indian grocery stores, and today they can also be found on the shelves of large British supermarkets. It appears that the once-maligned Indian culture reached its pinnacle in Britain in 2002, under the slogan 'Indian Summer,' during which London was engulfed in a Bollywood extravaganza where the media capitalised on the British public's fascination of the exotica of South Asia. The popular culture and fashion magazine, *Vanity Fair*, had a special Bollywood issue in May with the Hindi cinema actress Aishwarya Rai on the cover; a photo essay on the leading figures of Hindi Cinema, including Amitabh Bachchan, Aamir Khan and Rekha; a feature piece celebrating the haute couture of Indian designers, including Rohit Bal and Rina Dhaka; as well as contributions by British-Asians, including comedian Meera Syal and musician Nitin Sawhney. During the same month, the high-end department store Selfridges on Oxford Street chose the theme of '23½ Days of Bollywood' for its annual one month in-store extravaganza. Selfridges called on the talents of Nitin Desai, Hindi cinema's production designer, famed for his work on Hindi cinema blockbusters like *Jodhaa Akbar* and *Devdas*, to provide the building with an Indian makeover. Its façade garlanded with marigolds and the interior shimmering in silks and sequins. Selfridges also hosted fashion shows showcasing the latest Indian designs, as well as interviews with Indian authors. A section of the store was dedicated to the recreation of the opulent home of Dimple Kapadia, a leading Hindi Film actress of the 1980s. In the following month the Victoria and Albert Museum hosted a special exhibition entitled 'Cinema India', which featured over 70 Hindi cinema posters, free film screenings and workshops on Bollywood dance and Indian jewellery making. The British composer, Andrew Lloyd Webber's theatrical production 'Bombay Dreams', featuring music from Indian composer A.R. Rahman, ran at the Apollo Victoria Theatre for two years from June 2002. This recognition was exciting and there was a sense within the Indian community of well-deserved validation. Finally, the community and its traditions appeared to be valued.

Basically, this was commercialism at its height and the only language used in association with such hype was the global language, English. An opportunity to promote linguistic diversity, mutual understanding and tolerance was completely sidetracked in favour of the hard sell. This celebration of Indian culture inevitably moved into the religious domain, an arena not unfamiliar in the subcontinent. While images of deities are common in Indian advertising, there is an unquestionable reverence for the divine. When these images are transported to the West and placed on lunchboxes and t-shirts, consumers who do not attach religious significance to these icons are drawn to them due to their exotic nature, and often, sometimes unintentionally, respect is replaced by impudence.

What has subsequently evolved is a multi-billion pound industry, especially in the food sector, where leading British and American companies have taken centre stage with products which are a form of integrated hybridity, a fusion of Indian and traditional British cuisine. Birds Eye offers a range of Indian frozen meals including Chicken Tikka Masala, Chicken Balti Pie and Rice Fusions Aromatic Vegetable Pilau Rice. Heinz has a variety of products which recently included Tomato Ketchup Blended with Indian Spices and Mean Beanz Tikka and Curry Beanz. Ginsters produce a Spicy Chicken Slice, flavoured with Madras curry paste, Chicken Tikka Stuffed Sub and Chicken and Mango Flatbread Sandwich. Subway's sandwiches include Chicken Tikka and the recently introduced Sag Paneer. The British snack food manufacturer, Walkers, caters to the Indian palette in its Sensations Range with Bengali Spice Coated Peanuts and Lime and Coriander Chutney Poppodoms.

The success of these products has also led second-generation individuals to create their own varieties of hybrid foods. Devnaa Chocolates, a London-based company specialising in Indian inspired confectionaries, which are suitable for vegetarians and are alcohol-free, combine the finest Belgian chocolate with Indian spices. Their products include White Chocolate Saffron Caramels, Coconut and Cardamom Dark Chocolate and Chai Masala Blend Drinking Chocolate. According to MasterChef presenter, Greg Wallace, 'With flavours like Coconut Karma and Cinnamon Chai, they're [as] exotic as a trip to the Taj Mahal' (Devnaa 2013). The television chef, Anjum Anand launched her own range of spice kits, The Spice Tailor, in mid-2011. The kits consist of a marinade, sauce and Guntur chilli, with flavours including Rustic Rogan Josh and Spiced Spinach Curry. The family run company, Holy Cow!, produces sauces and dips, including Spicy Bombay Ketchup and Mango and Chilli BBQ Sauce. They claim that their sauces are 'really versatile' and can be used 'as accompaniments to dishes like fish and chips, pizza, tapas or nachos' (*Daily Mail* 2009), thereby demonstrating the hybrid nature of these products. Mamajaan's Curry Sauces, established in late 2010 uses this form of integrated hybridity in an exemplary manner. Their product range includes Belsize Bhuna, made with green chilli and coriander and Hampstead Harooni, which is infused with lemongrass and mustard seeds.

There appear to be two sides to the argument when it comes to commodification of Indian cultures and religions. For some it is blatant consumerism, an easy way to gain financially from this trend; for others, it is an opportunity to educate the majority about Indian culture and tradition. Looked at cynically this is blatant exploitation of South Asian culture, but in many ways there may be some truth in the idea that the commodification of Indian culture has actually helped to educate many and enabled society to understand the rich heritage of the Indian subcontinent (Mukadam and Mawani 2007b; Mawani and Mukadam 2010). The integrated hybrid culture of young second-generation Gujaratis has entered mainstream culture in a manner that could never have been predicted.

From a personal perspective, I am envious of all those Indian youngsters at school who no longer shun their own culture in favour of the dominant culture. They are the fortunate ones who are not forced to live two separate lives in order to maintain the culture and traditions of their parents. This is their home and their inherited Indian culture has found its way onto the High Streets for all to enjoy and celebrate. If popular culture is a measure of the situation of the masses, then it appears that second-generation Gujaratis are paving a new route for themselves and entering arenas that their parents never considered possible. Their culture has become part of the mainstream, and in so doing, their art forms and way of life, which were once seen as alien, exotic and in many cases, undesirable, have risen in status and become an acceptable, almost naturally occurring fabric of British society. The key to their success appears to lie in this complex process of hybridity, a blend of East and West that allows for mutual understanding and respect in a multi-ethnic society that now thrives on the notion of diversity and pluralism. The image of South Asians in London has changed from that of an immigrant culture to that of an upwardly mobile professional and business culture, whose two worlds co-exist to create a space, which is inspired by the best of both. Whether or not individuals are pleased by the so-called 'arrival' of their culture needs further investigation, but my own discussions with friends and family have led to very mixed feelings regarding this emotive topic. Some are resentful of the way in which majority acceptance gives the culture status, yet for others it is all part and parcel of the Western material society in which we live. Ambiguity and fluidity best describe the position faced by many second-generation Gujaratis as they negotiate between the contrasting terrains of Indianness and Britishness. One can perhaps suggest that it was fate, destiny or maybe even chance (Mattausch, 2007) that brought the Gujaratis to Britain, but it was racism and rejection that forced their children to position themselves as game changers, innovators and survivors – cultural hybridity would be the key to their success and would give them back their dignity and self-respect, as well as allow them to maintain aspects of their ancestral culture in a manner that has created a kaleidoscope of possibilities and added a bit of spice to British life.

> To study a banyan tree, you must not only know its main stem in its own soil, but also must trace the growth of its greatness in the further soil. Only then you can know the true nature of its vitality.
>
> — Nobel laureate Rabindranath Tagore

REFERENCES

Adam, Robina. 'From Corner Shop to High Flyers', *The Daily Mail*, 7 February 2002.

Anwar, Muhammad. *Between Cultures: Continuity and Change in the Lives of Young Asians*, London: Routledge, 1998.

——. *The Myth of Return*, London: Heinemann, 1979.

Ashcroft, Bill, Gareth Griffiths and Helen Tiffin. *Key Concepts in Post-Colonial Studies*, New York: Routledge, 1998.

Ballard, Roger. 'Living with Difference: A Forgotten Art in Urgent Need of Revival?', in *Religious Reconstruction in the South Asian Diasporas: From One Generation to Another*, edited by John R. Hinnells, London: Palgrave Macmillan, 2007, pp. 265–301.

Ballard, Roger (ed.). *Desh Pardesh: The South Asian Presence in Britain*, London: Hurst & Co., 1994.

Barth, Fredrik. 'Introduction', in *Ethnic Groups and Boundaries: The Social Organization of Culture Difference*, edited by Fredrik Barth, London: George Allen and Unwin, 1969.

Bhabha, Homi. *The Location of Culture*, London: Routledge, 1994.

——. 'The Third Space', in *Identity: Community, Culture, Difference*, edited by Jonathan Rutherford, London: Lawrence and Wishart, 1990, pp. 207–21.

Bhachu, Parminder. *Twice Migrants: East African Sikh Settlers in Britain*, London: Tavistock, 1985.

Bhatti, Ghazala. *Asian Children at Home and at School*, London: Routledge, 1999.

Bourne, Jenny. 'UK: The Powell Effect', *Race and Class*, Vol. 39, No. 4 (1998): 59–62.

Brah, Avtar. *Cartographies of Diaspora*, London: Routledge, 1996.

Brah, Avtar and Annie Coombes. *Hybridity and its Discontents*, London: Routledge, 2000.

Census UK. *Ethnicity*. 2001 and 2011. <www.ons.gov.uk> (19 September 2013).

Chambers, Iain. *Migrancy, Culture, Identity*, London: Routledge, 1993.

Coward, Harold G., John. R. Hinnells and Raymond Brady Williams (eds). *The South Asian Religious Diaspora in Britain, Canada, and the United States*, New York: State University of New York Press, 2000.

Dahya, Badr. 'Ethnicity and Modernity: The Case of Ismailis in Britain', in *The Racism Problematic*, edited by Rohit Barot, New York: The Edwin Mellen Press, 1996, pp. 106–38.

Daily Mail. 'Holy Cow! Mother of Five Hits Jackpot as Asda Pays £300,000 to Stock Her Homemade Curry Sauce', 7 May 2009, <http://www.dailymail.co.uk/femail/food/article-1178286/Holy-Cow-Mother-hits-jackpot-Asda-pays-300-000-stock-homemade-curry-sauce.html> (5 September 2013).

De Vos, George A. 'Concepts of Ethnic Identity', in *Ethnic Identity: Creation, Conflict and Accommodation*, edited by Lola Romanucci-Ross and George A. De Vos, Walnut Creek: Alta Mira, 1995, pp. 15–47.

Desai, Rashmi. *Indian Immigrants in Britain*, London: Oxford University Press, 1963.

Devnaa. *Indian Inspired Chocolate*, <www.devnaa.com> (16 September 2013).

Dove, L.A. 'Racial Awareness among Adolescents in London Comprehensive Schools', *New Community*, Vol. 3, No. 3 (1974): 255–61.

Ghuman, Paul A.S. *Double Loyalties*, Cardiff: University of Wales Press, 2003.

Gidoomal, Ram. *Building on Success: The South Asian Contribution to UK Competitiveness*, London: Business Link, 1997a.

——. *The UK Maharajahs*, London: Nicholas Brealey, 1997b.

——. *Sari 'n' Chips*, London: Monarch, 1993.

Gilroy, Paul. *There Ain't No Black in the Union Jack*, London: Hutchinson, 1987.

Gómez-Peña, Guillermo. *The New World Border: Prophecies, Poems and Loqueras for the End of the Century*, San Francisco: City Lights, 1996.

Gray, John. *Two Faces of Liberalism*, Cambridge: Polity Press, 2000.

Hassan, Robert. 'Globalization: Information Technology and Culture within the Space Economy of Late Capitalism', *Information, Communication and Society*, Vol. 2, No. 3 (1999): 300–17.

Hall, Stuart. 'Cultural Identity and Diaspora', in *Identity: Community, Culture, Difference*, edited by John Rutherford, London: Lawrence and Wishart, 1990, pp. 222–37.

——. 'New Ethnicities', in *Stuart Hall: Critical Dialogues in Cultural Studies*, edited by David Morley and Kuan-Hsing Chen, London: Routledge, 1989, pp. 441–49.

Ingerson, Alice. 'A Critical User's Guide to 'Culture' in Anthropology', <www.icls.harvard.edu/ecology/culture.html> (14 September 2013).

Jackson, John A. *The Irish in Britain*, London: Routledge & Kegan Paul, 1963.

Kasinitz, Philip, John Mollenkopf and Mary C. Waters. 'Worlds of the Second Generation', in *Becoming New Yorkers: Ethnographies of the New Second Generation*, edited by Philip Kasinitz, John Mollenkopf and Mary C. Waters, New York: Russell Sage Foundation, 2004, pp. 1–19.

Khan, Verity S. 'Pakistani Villagers in a British City: The World of the Mirpuri Villager in Bradford and in His Village of Origin', Unpublished PhD Thesis, University of Bradford, 1974.

Maira, Sunaina. 'The Politics of 'Cool': Indian American Youth Culture in New York City', in *Encounters: People of the Asian Descent in the Americas*, edited by Roshni Rustomji-Kerns, Rajini Srikanth and Leny Mendoza Strobel, New York: Rowman & Littlefield, 1999, pp. 177–93.

Mattausch, John. 'We are Family: The Changing British Gujarati Hindu Community', in *Gujaratis in the West: Evolving Identities in Contemporary Society*, edited by Anjoom A. Mukadam and Sharmina Mawani, Newcastle: Cambridge Scholars Publishing, 2007, pp. 127–43.

Mawani, Sharmina and Anjoom A. Mukadam. 'Living in a Material World: Religious Commodification and Resistance', in *Religion, Consumerism and Sustainability: Paradise Lost?*, edited by Lyn Thomas, Basingstoke: Palgrave Macmillan, 2010, pp. 55–71.

McLachlin, Beverley. 'The Civilization of Difference', Institute for Canadian Citizenship, 10 March 2003, <http://www.icc-icc.ca/en/lbs/docs/BeverleyMcLachlinEN.pdf> (25 September 2013).

Mukadam, Anjoom A. 'Gujarati Speakers in London: Age, Gender and Religion in the Construction of Identity', Unpublished PhD Thesis, University of Reading, 2003.

——. '"Until Death Do Us Part", Language as a Factor of Group Identity: Gujaratis', Unpublished MA Thesis, University of Reading, 1994.

Mukadam, Anjoom A. and Sharmina Mawani (eds). *Gujaratis in the West: Evolving Identities in Contemporary Society*, Newcastle: Cambridge Scholars Press, 2007a.

——. 'Diaspora Revisited: Second-Generation Nizari Ismaili Muslims of Gujarati Ancestry', in *Global Indian Diasporas: Exploring Trajectories of Migration and Theory*, edited by Gijsbert Oonk, Amsterdam: Amsterdam University Press, 2007b, pp. 195–209.

Nielsen, Jørgen S. 'Muslims in Britain: Ethnic Minorities, Community, or Ummah?', in *The South Asian Religious Diaspora in Britain, Canada, and the United States*, edited by John R. Hinnells, New York: State University of New York Press, 2000, pp. 109–25.

Parekh, Bhikhu. *Integrating Minorities*, London: Institute of Contemporary Arts, 2001.

——. 'Britain and the Social Logic', in *Britain: A Plural Society*, London: Commission for Racial Equality and the Runnymede Trust, 1990, pp. 58–76.

Powell, Enoch. 'Rivers of Blood Speech', *The Sterling Times*, 1968, <http://www.sterlingtimes.org/text_rivers_of_blood.htm> (20 September 2013).

Runnymede Trust. *The Future of Multi-Ethnic Britain: The Parekh Report*, London: Profile Books, 2000.

Shaw, Alison. *A Pakistani Community in Britain*, Oxford: Blackwell, 1988.

Søderberg, Anne-Marie. 'Do National Cultures Make a Difference', in *Language, Culture and Identity*, edited by Torben Vestergaard, Aalborg: Aalborg University Press, 1999, pp. 137–71.

Stopes-Roe, Mary and Raymond Cochrane. *Citizens of this Country: The Asian-British*, Clevedon: Multilingual Matters, 1990.

Street, Brian. 'Culture is a Verb: Anthropological Aspects of Language and Cultural Process', in *Language and Culture*, edited by David Graddol, Linda Thompson and Mike Bryam, Clevedon: Multilingual Matters, 1993, pp. 23–43.

Sue, S., J. Ito and C. Bradshaw. 'Ethnic Minority Research: Trends and Directions', in *Minority Mental Health*, edited by Enrico E. Jones and Sheldon J. Korchin, New York: Praeger, 1982, pp. 37–58.

United Nations. 'Asians from Uganda in European Transit Camps', *New Community*, Vol. 2, No. 3 (1973): 276–77.

Watson, James L. (ed.). *Between Two Cultures*, Oxford: Basil Blackwell, 1977.

Weller, Robert. *Alternate Civilities: Democracy and Culture in China and Taiwan*, Boulder: Westview Press, 1999.

Werbner, Pnina. *The Migration Process: Capital, Gifts and Offerings among British Pakistanis*, Oxford: Berg, 1990.1

CHAPTER 7

Identity and Belonging

The Case of the Gujarati Diaspora Community in the United Kingdom, Singapore and South Africa

Sheena Shah

Defining identity is important for a person's sense of self. This chapter examines how second and subsequent generations of Gujarati young adults living in the UK, Singapore and South Africa perceive their Indian identity. I apply a mixed methods analysis and my conclusions are drawn from sixty in-depth interviews. It appears that for the participants in this study being Indian is associated with factors such as a strong sense of community and participation in Indian cultural activities. I discuss the role of heritage language schools in passing on aspects of Indian identity, in particular, ethnic culture, religion and language. In addition, the chapter illustrates difficulties with being a member of the Gujarati community which arise when ethnic cultural ideas contrast with the local mainstream mindset. Using these young adults' own words and insights, I will highlight how their identity is multiple, fluid and at times hybrid (see Mukadam's chapter in this volume), and demonstrate how they negotiate these identities. By undertaking a multi-site analysis in similar educational but different local settings, this chapter also serves to illustrate similarities and differences in acculturation processes into the host society and highlights how this impacts the formation of identity.

THE CONSTRUCTION OF IDENTITY

Identity is often defined through various 'identity markers'. In order to assess the way in which Gujarati young adults identify themselves, I looked out for several identity markers during the interviews to determine which variables are considered important in the construction of their Indian identity. Despite 'widely discrepant definitions and measures of ethnic identity' (Phinney 2003: 500), certain common elements are found in most definitions and descriptions of ethnic identity. These include a common language, culture, religion, 'race' and place of origin. One of the most powerful markers of ethnic identity is a shared language (Edwards 1985; Fishman 1989; Woolard 1991; De Vos 1995). But if language is no longer present, then ethnic minority communities in diaspora contexts may resort predominantly or solely to cultural markers, like traditional arts, dance, festivals and food to express their ethnic identity (Khemlani-David 1998; Canagarajah 2008). While ethnic identity is closely related to cultural identity, definitions of cultural identity seem to place more importance on behaviours, practices and traditions (Jackson and Garner 1998; Lustig and Koester 1999). Ethnicity is 'a dynamic, multidimensional construct that refers to one's identity, or sense of self as a member of an ethnic group' (Phinney 2003: 63). Subjective identification, that is, self-identifying as a member of an ethnic group, is just as important in ethnic identity as is being accepted and acknowledged by 'ingroup' and 'outgroup' members (Collier and Thomas 1988; Saharso 1989). According to Phinney (2003: 23), 'ethnic identity is not a fixed categorization, but it is rather a fluid and dynamic understanding of self and ethnic background. Ethnic identity is constructed and modified as individuals become aware of their ethnicity, within the large (sociocultural) setting'. The view that ethnic identity is more of an ongoing process than a static product is shared by many scholars working in a social constructionist vein (Hall 1992; Bucholtz 1995; Blackledge and Pavlenko 2001; De Fina, Schiffrin and Bamberg 2006), and can be applied to all groups, not just particular ethnic groups in the diaspora.

GUJARATIS IN THE UK, SINGAPORE AND SOUTH AFRICA

Gujaratis, renowned as traders and businessmen, have a long-standing tradition of migration to various destinations around the world. This has resulted in the development of large Gujarati diaspora and post-diaspora communities outside of India (Mukadam and Mawani 2007; Mawani and Mukadam 2012). This chapter will look at those communities who have settled in the UK (via East Africa), Singapore and South Africa.

The Gujarati community in the UK is composed of immigrants who arrived directly from Gujarat, as well as those who arrived via East Africa and have been classified as 'twice migrants' (Bhachu 1985). As a result of labour shortages in the 1950s and 1960s in certain industries, (e.g., health, transport, service and manufacturing) at a time when Britain's industry was expanding, the UK actively pursued labour migration. Indian men, the majority of whom were Gujaratis and Punjabis, came directly from India between 1955 and 1970 as unskilled migrant workers and provided cheap labour (Poros 2011). However, the majority of the Gujaratis in the UK (approximately 70 per cent) came via East Africa (Price 2000). The construction of the railway lines resulted in the development of towns, thereby attracting Gujarati merchants from the 1880s onwards, who came to East Africa to set up businesses in these newly developed towns. However, after several African states gained their independence and due to Africanisation policies, life became increasingly difficult for Indians. Many East African Gujaratis had received the right to possess a British passport and many Gujaratis thus migrated to the UK. Gujarati immigration to the UK was boosted further by the decision of Idi Amin, former president of Uganda (1971–1979), to expel South Asians, including Gujaratis, from Uganda (Twaddle 1975).

Gujaratis began migrating to Singapore in the late nineteenth century. They originated primarily from areas in and around the urban centres of Gujarat, such as Ahmedabad and Surat, and transferred to Singapore either directly from their home provinces or via Bombay (Sandhu 1969). They arrived as traders, with the intention of returning to India after they had made their fortune in Singapore.

In addition to the migration of Gujarati entrepreneurs to East Africa, another group ventured to South Africa from the early 1870s. A major destination was Natal and its sugar plantations; many Gujarati immigrants subsequently migrated to the Transvaal. A large majority of the early Gujarati immigrants were Muslims. These Gujaratis earned their living by trading in Indian goods, such as spices and clothing, mostly to their fellow Indians who worked as indentured labourers.

Some notable differences in the socio-political setting of these three countries exist which are relevant for the purposes of this study. First, as a result of the early arrival of Gujaratis to Singapore and South Africa, up to five generations of Gujaratis are currently present in these two countries. By contrast, Gujaratis are more recent immigrants in the UK, with three generations of British Gujaratis currently residing in the UK (Frübing 2008). Second, the size of the Gujarati and Indian communities in these countries varies. Indians are the largest non-white ethnic group in the UK. Approximately 1.5 million Indians currently live in England and Wales, of which a third are based in London (Office for National Statistics 2009). More than 700,000 Gujaratis are estimated to reside in the UK (Mawani and Mukadam 2007), making them one of the larger Indian subgroups (Poros 2011). By contrast, in Singapore and South Africa, both the Gujarati and Indian communities are considerably smaller in size. Indians constitute about 8.4 per cent of the Singaporean population, according to a 2004 estimate (Rai 2006), with the majority being of Tamil origin (64 per cent). Gujaratis form a very small minority community. According to the 2000 Singapore census, there are 3,260 Gujaratis in Singapore (Leow 2001, cited in Mehta 2009: 303). In South Africa, the Indian population is approximately 1.2 million (Lal, Reeves and Rai 2006) and constitutes about three per cent of the total South African population. The majority are of Tamil origin; the Gujarati population constituted about three per cent of the minority Indian population (Desai 1997) and thus totals about 36,000 members.

Third, the public discourse about ethnicity is also markedly different in each of these countries. In Singapore, in an attempt to build and foster national identity and unity after the post-colonial nation-state was established in 1965, and to ensure that ethnic ties were not destroyed, the hyphenated identity, national-ethnic, was adopted, for example, Singaporean-Indian (Rai 2006). In the UK, the term British Asian is frequently used to refer to individuals of Indian, Pakistani or Bangladeshi descent. These individuals may employ the term 'British South Asian' to describe themselves, though they tend to prefer using specific ethnic categories, such as Indian, Pakistani or Bangladeshi (Runnymede Trust 2006; Jaspal 2011). In South Africa, during apartheid and as a result of the Population Registration Act of 1950, South Africans were classified based on one of four racial classifications, Black, White, Coloured or Indian. However, in the post-apartheid period, there seems to be a shift among certain South African groups, including the South African Indians, from employing an ethnic identity label to using a more national and inclusive South African identity label (Goldschmidt 2003).

THE STUDY

The participants in this study are in their twenties and were born and grew up in a predominantly Indian neighbourhood in their respective countries: Croydon (UK), Eastern and Central Singapore and Lenasia (South Africa). They all had abundant opportunities to hear and use the Gujarati language and take part in Indian cultural and religious events during their childhood. In addition, they all attended a Gujarati School, where they received intensive language and ethnic culture exposure. Semi-structured interviews were conducted individually with twenty participants in each country to determine the ways in which identity is perceived, defined, experienced and expressed by these communities.

Several identity markers were frequently cited by participants as being part of their definition of Indian ethnic identity. These included language, a sense of community, family values and morals, Indian cultural activities, religion and food, which is in line with previous studies (Mukadam 2003; Mawani 2006). I discuss two of these, a sense of community and Indian cultural activities, in detail below.

Sense of Community

The strong sense of community that exists among Gujaratis was unanimously cited by participants in all three sites as one of the most defining characteristics of Indian identity. In Indian culture, family includes not only immediate family, but also extended family. Participants compared this to the mainstream culture in which they were living. Participants from the UK described the typical white British family as being composed solely of the immediate family members, which was in stark contrast to their situation, where three generational households were common and close contact was maintained with extended family members and the community:

> I know of ... British white families who ... have their own immediate family and then they are quite disjoint[ed], ... maybe not from their grandparents, but from other brothers or sisters of their parents and their children kind of thing and they're very distant. Whereas ... . I think we have a strong sense of family and that reaches out to a sense of community even between families ... . Just treating everyone like brothers and sisters ... even, say, friends of parents. (Anand, UK)

The idea of closeness within the community is also portrayed through kinship terms, such as *bhai* (brother) to refer to male cousins, *ben* (sister) to refer to female cousins and aunty to refer to any older female figure, for example, a Gujarati teacher. While the idea of a close-knit community was viewed in a positive light by most participants, some also highlighted the problematic aspects of this: 'People are in your space all the time. In other cultures, if you're family, it's your immediate family and that's it. Whereas here, you have to worry about a hundred thousand people other than just yourself' (Hiral, SA). Other negative aspects included gossip, competitiveness and concern about personal reputation in the community.

Indian Cultural Activities

Taking part in Indian cultural activities was mentioned as an aspect of being Indian which distinguished participants from their non-Indian friends. Many reported that they spent a good amount of their free time in their childhood engaging in Indian cultural activities, such as Indian classical dancing, (e.g., *kathak*), playing Indian instruments, (e.g., the harmonium) or learning to sing Hindu devotional songs (*bhajans*). In the UK and South Africa, many of the cultural activities were incorporated as part of the Gujarati School day or were organised through the school. In

Singapore, this was not the case due to state policy which dictates that language education should be of a secular nature. Nevertheless, there are many opportunities for Singaporean Gujaratis to undertake Indian cultural activities through various organisations. Participants in all three sites were heavily involved in Indian cultural activities during their childhood. As they grew older, they generally participated less in such activities, due to lack of time, lack of interest, etc. So, this marker of ethnic identity, while acknowledged by most to constitute a general Indian identity, was no longer relevant for some participants in definitions of their *own* ethnic identity. However, not all individuals held the opinion that being Indian meant participating in Indian cultural activities: 'Everyone was constantly telling me that I'm Indian and that I should behave more appropriately … . But I didn't know what it meant to be Indian. The only experiences I had were at Gujarati School, and the dance and harmonium classes we did, you know all that Indian stuff we did as kids, but that doesn't really mean you're Indian' (Reena, UK). During a trip to India, Reena found that many young Indians there were not involved in such activities, a trend noted by other participants as well: 'Even though we are British born, I think we embrace a lot of Indian culture, more so because I recently was in Mumbai and I felt like everything is trying to be so westernised' (Minal, UK).

The Role of the Gujarati School

For Gujaratis in the diaspora, their ethnic identity has been successfully maintained through a number of means, including traditional home environments and the setting up of linguistic, cultural and religious organisations (Desai 1997; Creese et al. 2006; Kelly 2007). In this study, the Gujarati School was recognised as being very efficient in fostering feelings of belonging and a shared sense of Indian identity:

> Going to Gujarati classes made me feel proud of my culture and background and my family life. I'm proud to be Indian. (Karishma, UK)

> [Had I not gone to Gujarati School], I would probably be so English. (Anjali, Singapore)

Despite residing in Singapore, Anjali uses the word English and not Singaporean. Her word choice here highlights how 'being English' is being associated with 'being Western', and thus how Gujarati School played a role in helping to maintain her ethnic identity.

In South Africa, where the vast majority of the participants were third, fourth or fifth generation Gujaratis, Gujarati School was an important site from which they could gain knowledge about aspects of their heritage which their locally-born parents might not have been able to pass on to them:

> [At Gujarati School,] we would do the *Ramayan* [ancient Indian religious epic], we would do the *Mahabharat* [ancient Indian epic], we would do the *Bhagvat Gita* [700-verse Hindu scripture that is part of the *Mahabharat*], they used to teach us Hindi, so the *bens* [literally, sisters, here used to refer to their Gujarati teachers] were more like mothers that taught me those small things that my parents, being South African, couldn't. (Kinari, SA)

Gujarati School provided an opportunity to forge friendships with other children of the same age and ethnic background, which some regarded as an important defining characteristic of being Indian: 'If I would never have gone to Gujarati School in the first place, I would never have had any Gujarati friends, so I would feel kind of awkward calling myself Gujarati' (Bhavik, Singapore). Gujarati School also provided regular contact with the Gujarati community and aided in integration into Gujarati society: 'Probably the biggest advantage with Gujarati School is that it helps you integrate into the Gujarati society, whereas people who don't go to Gujarati School have a hard time integrating into the Gujarati society, so they don't come to any of the functions and stuff' (Jyoti, Singapore). Even those who did not particularly enjoy attending Gujarati School highlighted that they would nevertheless send their children there, as 'it's not just about learning the language, it's about mixing with people from the same background as you, taking part in shows and celebrating festivals together' (Karishma, UK).

Challenging Traditional Ideas

In descriptions of their identity, it emerged that clashes were sometimes caused between generations living in the diaspora as a result of changing lifestyle patterns and views (traditional vs. western): 'Basically, I'm very westernised and my parents are still very traditional, so obviously there's going to be a lot of clashes, innit?' (Pritesh, UK). While Pritesh and other participants often equated 'being traditional' with 'being Indian', a change in lifestyle with each new generation in these countries is almost certainly inevitable, but this does not necessarily mean that their ethnic identity is weakened, but rather that it may be of a different form than that of previous generations (Isajiw 1990; Mawani 2006).

Participants described what they considered to be outdated viewpoints held by the older generation. They simultaneously depicted the struggles they faced with some of the demands and expectations associated with belonging to the Gujarati community. These included the search for a life partner and gender role differences. The question arises whether generational differences in viewpoint threaten Indian ethnic identity or rather whether challenging certain rules, expectations and behaviours that are typically associated with being traditionally Indian has little to do with the strength of ethnic identification, but rather portrays an evolution of ethnic identity rather than assimilation – that is, a complete shift towards another (local) identity.

For many of the participants, the majority of whom were in their twenties, marriage was a topic that had begun to emerge in discussions with parents, extended family or with the community: 'She [my unmarried sister] is 28. Not only my parents, but everyone in the family, my mother's sisters and her brother, everyone's telling her, "You must come to weddings so you can meet guys and get proposals" and all that. She gets angry, she doesn't like that' (Keval, SA). Many of the participants' parents and grandparents had been married at an early age. It was generally unthinkable in their time to be female and unmarried at the age of 28. However, there is a shift among the new generation of Gujaratis in these countries, with several articulating their wish to delay marriage or not get married at all for a number of reasons, including their desire to establish a career beforehand or to travel. Despite these preferences, many participants, especially females, felt the pressure from the Indian community to be married by a certain age and portrayed the struggles they faced in adhering to traditional Indian marital norms:

> I'm 26. Pressure's on [to get married], pressure's on … . It's quite grating and draining … . I guess it's instilled in everyone who's Indian that … you must get married quite young, because you know, you don't want to end up alone and you've got to have children. There's kind of this whole path that's set out for you. You go to school, you go to university, you get a good job, then you get married, then you have babies. Well … . I don't want that life. (Reena, UK)

One of the biggest differences between the Indian and the mainstream local culture was the role that others had in the choice of their future spouse. Participants discussed their parents' wish that their future spouse would belong to the same caste, a point raised most frequently by participants in South Africa and the UK. Some participants expressed the difficulty they felt in accepting such restrictions: 'For them [my parents] ideally, they'd want us to find someone from the same caste. That was my mother's hope, and then that obviously didn't happen. Then they said "anybody Gujarati", but I mean you don't just choose these things' (Hiral, SA). In Singapore, where the Gujarati population is much smaller in number than in South Africa and the UK, spouses were often sought overseas, as the number of potentially eligible spouses in Singapore was limited. In some cases, marrying outside the Gujarati community but remaining within the North Indian community, but not the South Indian community, was acceptable (Rai 2004). In Indian culture, parents traditionally have a big influence on the choice of potential marriage candidates for their child, either directly through the traditional Indian method of spousal selection, an arranged marriage, or through an adapted version of the practice, parent-assisted marriage (Raja 2012). Some participants did not object to the continued practice of arranged marriages, believing that 'arranged marriages work out much better than love marriages' (Asha, SA). Such viewpoints were found more among the South African Gujaratis than among the British and Singaporean Gujaratis. For others, remaining within one's culture and community meant more long-lasting marriages: 'My mum has the idea that if I marry a Gujarati, it won't end in a divorce, that the marriage will last for a 100 years until death do us apart. And she assumes that if I marry a Chinese or a Malay, I'll break up in two or three years' (Amit, Singapore); and would result in fewer problems with children: '[When you mix cultures], there's a problem with your children' (Rakesh, SA). On the other hand, there were some who felt that intercultural and interethnic marriages could be successful: 'There are many successful [intercultural and interethnic] marriages, it depends on the two of you and what you make of it' (Payal, SA).

Keval's (SA) and Reena's (UK) narratives highlight the external pressure that women in particular experience in relation to marriage. This pressure continues after marriage where demarcation in gender roles still exists both among Gujaratis in Gujarat (Twamley, Pryce and Kielmann 2012) and outside of Gujarat (Mehrotra 2004). Such gender differences were experienced by the female participants in this study: 'At home, being a girl ... you must cook, you must clean, you must learn to do this, you must learn to do that' (Rupal, SA). Given the gender bias that females encountered, it is not surprising that participants describe the Indian culture as male chauvinistic: 'There's still a slight emphasis on men. It bugs me because a lot of times people ask me it's only you and your sister, you don't have a brother?' (Kajal, Singapore). Female participants indicated the restrictions they encountered as females and the frustrations that they felt:

> She [my mother] is very conservative about what I can wear ... . Even though it's so hot in Singapore, I'm not allowed to wear shorts. I'm not allowed to wear short skirts ... . She's like 'We're Indian, You have to keep your culture, blah, blah, blah blah ... . I think it's quite nonsense actually, because ... when I go back to India, I see all these Indian girls wearing the same kind of clothes that Singaporean girls wear ... . I guess she's still stuck in the Indian mentality when she was there, when she left India. (Nima, Singapore)

Nima's experiences highlight how the physical separation from India has resulted in her mother, who was born and raised in India, developing a static view of Indian culture, one which represents a past Indian culture. Her narrative illustrates the difficulty she faces in conforming to a conservative dress code, which her mother enforces on her, when she is aware that even the culture's place of origin, India, has changed in this regard. Her point echoes the sentiments expressed by Reena (UK) earlier, that Gujaratis outside of Gujarat may in fact be (expected to be) more 'traditionally Indian' than Indians in India themselves.

Another participant, Radhika, highlights how the gender bias has extended to areas which are generally highly valued by Indians, such as education: 'A lot of people think that it's good to be educated, but for girls, it's not good to be educated over a certain amount. Well, it's like, why not? (Radhika, UK). In addition, females encountered restrictions in career choice. Careers which were traditionally deemed inappropriate for females or ones which would put strain on the family and prevent them from carrying out household chores typically performed by Indian women, such as cleaning and cooking, were not viewed favourably:

> Rupal (SA): So they say that being a pilot is strenuous on family, because after you get married, you have a responsibility towards your in-laws and that you should look after your husband and you should be able to be at home and not up in the sky and some other continent.
>
> Sheena: And what are your thoughts about that?
>
> Rupal (SA): Personally I feel that's very selfish … . I believe that if it is meant to be, it will happen, and that if I do get married and have those responsibilities, I believe that my in-laws or my husband should understand and respect me and support me on the decision.

Rupal's narrative is not unique. Several of the female participants described how traditional views on gender roles were still upheld by many. This is not surprising when considering that it was previously customary for males to be the sole breadwinners of the family and for females to play the role as homemakers, with the responsibility of looking after and caring for the children. This pattern is still found in many Gujarati households, more so in South Africa and Singapore than in the UK. Females expressed the struggles and frustrations they felt with accepting this outdated gender bias: 'I've heard that in studying [to become] a doctor, that most … . Indian ladies or girls that study to become a doctor, they don't practice it after university ... I don't think that's fair ... I think that everyone should have the right to work, and not just doing housework, but ... everything' (Anushka, SA).

OTHERS' AND SELF PERCEPTIONS OF IDENTITY

The way others view an individual plays an important role in how the individual's identity is formed and developed. Some participants considered the adoption of an Indian identity compulsory, because of factors, such as their Indian physical appearance: 'You can be the most British person you want, but you'll never be fully British, cos you're brown' (Pratik, UK). Participants also admitted that they were not fully Indian and were not regarded as Indians in India: 'There [in India], you are seen as the Westerner, so you are treated as a guest' (Jayni, UK).

Displaying the expected norms and behaviours of a certain group may lead to identity labelling. Jayni, a participant in this study, discusses how people consider her to be very Indian, but also very Western. She describes how she finds these groupings, based on somewhat superficial qualities, both simplified and problematic:

> The interesting thing is how other people see you. Some people see me as extremely Indian, because I religiously have to have my *rotli, dar, bhat, shak* (a typical Gujarati meal consisting of chapatti, lentils, rice, and curry) every day and I'm quite into Jainism, so I'm very Indian in that sense. Then a lot of people think I'm completely white, a complete coconut, because I reject Bollywood and I reject Hip-Hop and R&B, I'm not really a fan of Jay Sean or any of that sort of stuff. So sometimes I almost feel like being Indian has become a bit simplified, so if you like Bollywood, that equates to you being Indian and that's really problematic. My best friend is actually an Indian, but is a South Indian, and he said that he still feels really Indian, but he isn't into all that Bollywood and stuff. So to compensate for all of that, he is a bit of an intellectual Indian and knows all about Indian history and politics, which your average Indian who considers themself as very Indian probably wouldn't have a clue about. (Jayni, UK)

Other researchers have also mentioned how heritage language learners tend to be more familiar with popular culture, (e.g., music, cinema, fashion) than with the geography, history and politics of their ancestral country (Ilieva 2012). Jayni's quote illustrates how deviations from the expected group norm generate the idea that one does not belong in a certain identity category.

Tempting as it may be for others to infer a person's ethnic identity from concrete traits, such as their physical features, or their adherence to expected group norms, these signs may in fact be quite deceptive. This leads to how the participants self-identified and their claims of having multiple identities. Most participants described their identity as national-ethnic, (e.g. Singaporean Indian), but insisted that identity is not a fixed category, but rather dynamic, fluid and multi-faceted. Participants described having the 'best of both worlds', that is more choices than some of the native locals who did not have another ethnic identity to draw on: 'I'm obviously a citizen of Britain and I respect and follow all the ideals that this country is based on, but I bring to that a heritage which is beyond that, which is an Indian heritage. It's almost a shame that you can't also throw in Kenyan, because there's obviously that factor as well' (Jayni, UK). They also described how they were actively 'picking and choosing' (Seema, UK) which aspects of their Indian side they identified with: 'Even though I'm not interested in it [the Indian entertainment industry], I like the fact that it has got its own film industry, its own music industry, and it's doing well, cos it's something that I can be proud of, even though it's not something I like' (Seema, UK). Seema's comment further portrays a sense of flexibility that participants felt they had in choosing when to express their ethnic or local identities. Different situations determine which aspect of their identity gets accentuated at a given moment (Mukadam 2003; Nesbitt 2004): 'Parts of me feel I'm more British, but then again, when I do stuff like Gujarati class or ... go to [Indian] events, or something like that, that's when I feel more Indian. So I think it depends on ... where I am, what I'm doing' (Bina, UK). Several British and South African participants, having been interviewed just before or soon after the World Cup in South Africa (2010) and the Olympics in Britain (2012), discussed how such events heightened their sense of local identity: '[I felt] totally South African last year at the World Cup. That feeling was amazing. I mean, you didn't even feel different to anybody else, because everyone is in the same excitement. So that's when I really felt totally South African' (Payal, SA). In the South African case, where skin colour marked different races during Apartheid, such sporting events promote displays and feelings of national identity and pride and seem to be important in uniting the different races.

Contrary to dominant stereotyping, many scholars have shown that the second generation does not suffer from an identity crisis (Mukadam 2003; Rayaprol 2005). However, Mukadam (2003) points out that not all researchers agree and second- and later-generation Indians have been categorised as 'neither one thing nor another' (Gidoomal 1993), 'between two cultures' (Anwar 1976; Watson 1977) and as 'the half-way generation' (Taylor 1976) (see Mukadam's chapter in this volume). My data is in agreement with that of Mukadam (2003: 44): 'there in fact appears to be a fusion of East and West' among second and subsequent generation of Gujaratis, who are seen to be achieving 'a balance between the culture of their parents and that of the ethnic majority' (2007: 122):

> We feel different to British white people. We are doing things our way, we have our culture, we are kind of trying to live up to that, we are trying to maintain the language. You feel that way but going there [India], you see ... [those who are] non-Westernised, who have never may be been outside their country's borders ... . You recognise a lot of aspects which are the same ... but I definitely feel different to them. It's kind of like we build our own community of how to adapt to that lifestyle ... in the Western world. (Anand, UK).

Participants who self-reported as suffering from an identity crisis were often those who attempted to reject their ethnic identity, but found that certain aspects could not be excluded, such as skin colour, making the adoption of a partial Indian identity compulsory for all. Some of these participants portrayed the difficulties they faced as they tried to bring their Indian and non-Indian worlds together, which at times they described as being complete opposites of one another: 'At least two different worlds. It's really different. You can't balance them and you can't bring them together' (Meeta, SA).

When participants were asked to describe their identity in their own words, it often emerged that their identity was hybrid. One participant, who identified strongly with her British side, admitted at a later point in the interview that she could not really claim to be fully British: 'I wanted to originally say British, but then I do feel that I want to hold on to my roots and that I want to pass them on and they are important to me, so I wouldn't want to just constitute as British' (Pooja, UK). Another participant, who also identified strongly with her British side, reconstructed her identity with each new question I asked, going from 'I definitely feel British' to 'I would call myself a British citizen, (*long pause*) British Indian' to 'Oh my God, you're making me think now. I feel like I'm not from India, but at the same time I am kind of … . I feel Indian because of this bit and that bit' (Seema, UK).

Ultimately, the participants acknowledged in their narratives that it was difficult to choose just *one* identity label and words like 'confusion', 'uncertainty' and 'indecisiveness' came up frequently in their descriptions of their identity. This may be because these participants, like others in society, had not given too much thought to their identities until they encountered my questions in the interviews.

> I am a Singaporean by blood and I am proud of that. Having relatives in India also makes me an Indian. It seems to be an indecisive decision between choosing from one of them. (Priyanka, Singapore)

> It's a really tough question [about how I identify], because you become patriotic, but you also become … aware of where your roots are from … if you look at a typical India-South Africa match in cricket, I'd support India. But I'd choose not really to watch those games because it puts you in the middle. (Payal, SA)

> I consider myself to be British. I feel I relate more to the culture and way of life here. However, if I was being completely honest, I'd say I don't completely identify with either culture and am torn between the two, which at times can be very difficult and other times quite enriching. But mostly it leads to confusion. (Reena, UK)

Despite the sentiments felt by Priyanka, Payal and Reena, many readily described how they had in fact taken aspects of both cultures to create a flexible and multi-faceted identity, leading to the conclusion that both their local and ethnic identities are fostered and neither is being completely jeopardised.

CONCLUSION

This study has shown that Gujarati young adults in the UK, South Africa and Singapore have held on to their Indian identity, which they express through various identity markers, such as being part of a close-knit Gujarati community and participating in Indian cultural activities. Institutions, such as the Gujarati schools, foster these identity markers and reinforce individuals' ethnic cultural identity. Struggles that these individuals face as they try to understand competing mainstream and ethnic cultural ideas highlight and support the statement that they are 'not completely like their parents, nor completely like their white peers' (Bhatti 1999: 238). While their ethnic identity may not be of the same form as that of the first generation (Isajiw 1990), no evidence emerges from the interview data that their ethnic identity is threatened. Through ethnic self-identification and cultural adaptation, they are far from losing their Gujarati identity, they are in fact actively attempting to make sense of their unique position as they navigate their various and variegated identities and seem to take the best of both worlds by adopting a fluid, multi-faceted and, at times, hybrid identity.

REFERENCES

Anwar, Muhammad. *Between Two Cultures,* London: Community Relations Commission, 1976.

Bhachu, Parminder. *Twice Migrants: East African Sikh Settlers in Britain,* London: Tavistock Publications, 1985.

Bhatti, Ghazala. *Asian Children at Home and at School: An Ethnographic Study,* London: Routledge, 1999.

Blackledge, Adrian and Aneta Pavlenko. 'Negotiation of Identities in Multilingual Contexts', *International Journal of Bilingualism,* Vol. 5, No. 3 (Sept. 2001): 243–57.

Bucholtz, Mary. 'From Mulatta to Mestiza: Passing and the Linguistic Reshaping of Ethnic Identity', in *Gender Articulated: Language and the Socially Constructed Self*, edited by Kira Hall and Mary Bucholtz, London: Routledge, 1995, pp. 351–73.

Canagarajah, Suresh. 'Language Shift and the Family: Questions from the Sri Lankan Tamil Diaspora', *Journal of Sociolinguistics*, Vol. 12, No. 2 (April 2008): 143–76.

Collier, Mary Jane and Milt Thomas. 'Cultural Identity: An Interpretive Perspective', in *Theories in Intercultural Communication*, edited by Young Yun Kim and William B. Gudykunst, Newbury Park, California: Sage Publications, 1988.

Creese, Angela et al. 'Multilingual, Heritage and Learner Identities in Complementary Schools', *Language and Education*, Vol. 20, No. 1 (January 2006): 23–43.

De Fina, Anna, Deborah Schiffrin and Michael Bamberg. 'Introduction', in *Discourse and Identity*, edited by Anna De Fina, Deborah Schiffrin and Michael Bamberg, Cambridge: Cambridge University Press, 2006, pp. 1–23.

Desai, Usha. 'An Investigation of Factors Influencing Maintenance and Shift of the Gujarati Language in South Africa', Unpublished PhD Thesis, University of Durban-Westville, 1997.

De Vos, George A. 'Ethnic Pluralism: Conflict and Accommodation', in *Ethnic Identity: Creation, Conflict, and Accommodation*, edited by Lola Romanucci-Ross and George A. De Vos, Walnut Creek, CA: Alta Mira Press, 1995, pp. 15–47.

Edwards, John. *Language, Society and Identity*, Oxford: Basil Blackwell, 1985.

Fishman, Joshua. *Language and Ethnicity in Minority: Sociolinguistic Perspective*, Clevedon: Multilingual Matters, 1989.

Frübing, Judith. 'The Third Generation of Indians in Britain: Cultural Identity and Cultural Change', Unpublished MA Thesis, Universität Potsdam, 2008.

Gidoomal, Ram. *Sari 'n' Chips*, London: Monarch, 1993.

Goldschmidt, Myra M. 'Identifying Labels among University Students in the New South Africa: A Retrospective Study', *Journal of Black Studies*, Vol. 34, No. 2 (Nov. 2003): 204–21.

Hall, Stuart. 'The Question of Cultural Identity', in *Modernity and its Futures*, edited by Stuart Hall, David Held and Anthony McGrew, Cambridge: Polity Press, 1992, pp. 273–325.

Ilieva, Gabriela Nik. 'Hindi Heritage Language Learners' Performance During OPIs: Characteristics and Pedagogical Implications', *Heritage Language Journal*, Vol. 9, No. 2 (2012): 18–36.

Isajiw, Wsevolod W. 'Ethnic Identity Retention', in *Ethnic Identity and Equality: Varieties of Experience in a Canadian City*, edited by Raymond Breton et al., Toronto: University of Toronto Press, 1990, pp. 34–91.

Jackson, Ronald L. and Thurmon Garner. 'Tracing the Evolution of 'Race', 'Ethnicity', and 'Culture' in Communication Studies', *The Howard Journal of Communication*, Vol. 9, No. 1 (1998): 41–55.

Jaspal, Rusi. 'The Construction and Management of National and Ethnic Identities among British South Asians: An Identity Process Theory Approach', Unpublished PhD Thesis, Royal Holloway, University of London, 2011.

Kelly, Melissa. 'Negotiating a Gujarati Identity in Vancouver', in *Gujaratis in the West: Evolving Identities in Contemporary Society*, edited by Anjoom A. Mukadam and Sharmina Mawani, Newcastle: Cambridge Scholars Publishing, 2007, pp. 42–58.

Khemlani-David, Maya. 'Language Shift, Cultural Maintenance, and Ethnic Identity: A Study of a Minority Community: The Sindhis of Malaysia', *International Journal of the Sociology of Language*, Vol. 130, No. 1 (January 1998): 67–76.

Lal, Brij V., Peter Reeves and Rajesh Rai. *The Encyclopedia of the Indian Diaspora*, Singapore: Editions Didier Millet, 2006.

Leow, Bee Geok. *Census of Population 2000: Education, Language and Religion*, Singapore: Department of Statistics, 2001.

Lustig, Myron and Jolene Koester. *Intercultural Competence: Interpersonal Communication across Cultures*, Menlo Park, CA: Addison-Wesley, 1999.

Mawani, Sharmina. 'The Construction of Identities amongst Young Adult Nizari Ismaili Muslims in Toronto and Mumbai', Unpublished PhD Thesis, SOAS, University of London, 2006.

Mawani, Sharmina and Anjoom A. Mukadam (ed.). *Gujarati Communities across the Globe: Memory, Identity and Continuity*, Stoke-on-Trent: Trentham, 2012.

——. 'Introduction: A Journey Enriched by Tradition', in *Gujaratis in the West: Evolving Identities in Contemporary Society*, edited by Anjoom A. Mukadam and Sharmina Mawani, Newcastle-Upon-Tyne: Cambridge Scholars Publishing, 2007, pp. 1–9.

Mehrotra, Meeta. '"Triple Outsiders": Gender and Ethnic Identity among Asian Indian Immigrants', Unpublished PhD Thesis, Virginia Polytechnic Institute and State University, 2004.

Mehta, Kalyani K. 'The Nexus of Ageing and Migration in Singapore', in *Older Persons in Southeast Asia: An Emerging Asset*, edited by Evi

Nurvidya Arifin and Aris Ananta, Singapore: Institute of Southeast Asian Studies, 2009, pp. 301–13.

Mukadam, Anjoom A. 'Shattering Stereotypes: Post-Diasporic Swaminarayan Gujaratis in London', in *Gujaratis in the West: Evolving Identities in Contemporary Society*, edited by Anjoom A. Mukadam and Sharmina Mawani, Newcastle: Cambridge Scholars Publishing, 2007, pp. 106–26.

——. *Gujarati Speakers in London: Age, Gender and Religion in the Construction of Identity*, PhD Thesis, University of Reading, 2003.

Nesbitt, Eleanor. 'I am a Gujarati Lohana and a Vaishnav as Well: Religious Identity Formation among Young Coventrian Punjabis and Gujaratis', in *Religion, Identity and Change: Perspectives on Global Transformations*, edited by Simon Coleman and Peter Collins, Aldershot: Ashgate, 2004, pp. 174–90.

Office for National Statistics UK. *Resident Population Estimates by Ethnic Group, All Persons*, 2009, <http://neighbourhood.statistics.gov.uk> (24 April 2011).

Phinney, Jean S. 'Ethnic Identity and Acculturation', in *Acculturation: Advances in Theory, Measurement, and Applied Research*, edited by Kevin Chun, Pamela B. Organista and Gerardo Marin, Washington, DC: American Psychological Association, 2003, pp. 63–81.

Poros, Maritsa. *Modern Migrations: Gujarati Indian Networks in New York and London*, Palo Alto, CA: Stanford University Press, 2011.

Price, Glanville. *Encyclopedia of the Languages of Europe*, Oxford: Wiley-Blackwell, 2000.

Rai, Rajesh. 'Indians in Singapore', in *The Encyclopedia of the Indian Diaspora*, edited by Brij V. Lal, Peter Reeves and Rajesh Rai, Singapore: Editions Didier Millet, 2006, pp. 176–88.

——. '"Race" and the Construction of the North-South Divide amongst Indians in Colonial Malaya and Singapore', *South Asia: Journal of South Asian Studies*, Vol. 27, No. 2 (Aug. 2004): 245–64.

Raja, Sheena. 'A Match Made in Heaven: A Study of Changing Hindu Marriage Practices amongst Gujarati Eligibles', in *Gujarati Communities across the Globe: Memory, Identity and Continuity*, edited by Sharmina Mawani and Anjoom A. Mukadam, Stoke-on-Trent: Trentham Books, 2012, pp. 123–39.

Rayaprol, Aparna. 'Being American, Learning to be Indian: Gender and Generation in the Context of Transnational Migration', in *Transnational Migration and the Politics of Identity*, edited by Meenakshi Thapan, Thousand Oaks, CA: Sage Publications, 2005, pp. 130–49.

Runnymede Trust. *Connecting British Hindus: An Enquiry into the Identity and Public Policy Engagement of British Hindus*, London: Hindu Forum of Britain, 2006.

Saharso, Sawitri. 'Ethnic Identity and the Paradox of Equality', in *Ethnic Minorities: Social Psychological Perspectives*, edited by Jan Pieter van Oudenhoven and Tineke M. Willemsen, Amsterdam: Swets and Zeitlinger, 1989, pp. 97–114.

Sandhu, Kernial Singh. *Indians in Malaya: Some Aspects of their Immigration and Settlement (1786–1957)*, Cambridge: Cambridge University Press, 1969.

Taylor, J.H. *The Half-Way Generation: A Study of Asian Youths in Newcastle upon Tyne*, Windsor: NFER, 1976.

Twaddle, Michael. *Expulsions of a Minority: Essays on Ugandan Asians*, London: Athlone Press, 1975.

Twamley Katherine, Anthony Pryce and Karina Kielmann. '"I Want Love to be Arranged!" Courtship and Marriage in the Context of Globalisation: Baroda, India', in *Gujarati Communities across the Globe: Memory, Identity and Continuity*, edited by Sharmina Mawani and Anjoom A. Mukadam, Stoke-on-Trent: Trentham Books, 2012, pp. 107–21.

Watson, James L. *Between Two Cultures: Migrants and Minorities in Britain*, Oxford: Basil Blackwell, 1977.

Woolard, Kathryn A. 'Linkages of Language and Ethnic Identity: Changes in Barcelona, 1980–1987', in *Language and Ethnicity: Focusschrift in Honor of Joshua A. Fishman*, edited by James R. Dow, Philadelphia: John Benjamin's Publishing, 1991, pp. 61–81.1

Part III

INCLUSION/EXCLUSION

CHAPTER 8

Contesting 'Purity' and Zones of Inclusion and Exclusion among the Gujaratis in Contemporary Zanzibar

Akbar Keshodkar

In Zanzibar, notions of 'roots' have always been shaped by the 'routes' (cf. Clifford 1997) that have facilitated constructions of specific identities for different groups of people within this diverse, multi-ethnic social milieu. While all inhabitants have and continue to identify themselves as Zanzibaris, their simultaneous efforts in identifying themselves through association to places elsewhere and constructing social boundaries for legitimising these alternative identities remains a primary dimension of the local politics of belonging. Based around perceived places of origin outside of Zanzibar, each ethnic group within this contested landscape aspires to acquire some notion of social centrality through different social practices in specific, private spaces[1] inaccessible to other Zanzibaris (Keshodkar 2010). Through such demarcations, Zanzibaris maintain their strangeness towards each other (cf. Simmel 1971).

For the Gujarati community of Zanzibar, which started emigrating to the islands from the late nineteenth century and continue to represent the majority of the South Asian population in Zanzibar, formulations of *jat* (caste)[2] demarcates additional social boundaries to distinguish themselves not only from other Zanzibaris, but also from other Asians[3] around them. It facilitates their strangeness vis-à-vis other Zanzibaris. Based around notions of purity associated with specific religious traditions (different castes among the Hindus or sectarian differences among the

Muslims) and exercised through the practice of endogamy,[4] the designation of *jat* serves as the primary marker of asserting exclusivity for these Gujaratis, the majority of whom are Muslim (Hindus make up less than 15 per cent of the local Gujarati population today in Zanzibar). It also reinforces their social isolation and provides rigid boundaries to mark their difference from other Asians and the surrounding Swahili[5] majority. With specific types of marriage practices, centred around endogamy serving as the route for preserving certain roots, members of the Gujarati community that have pursued alternative routes, either hypergamy or more importantly, hypogamy[6] (voluntary or involuntarily), have faced the consequence of expulsion from or marginalisation within the zone of inclusion defined around the construction of *jat*.

While endogamy among the Gujarati prevailed during the colonial era, inter-marriages between the Gujarati and non-Asians became more widespread after the 1964 revolution. In the aftermath of the revolution, the majority of Asians fled Zanzibar. The government instituted an era of forced marriages between Swahili men and Asian women as part of official state policy and there was a general lack of availability of suitable partners from within the *jat* on the islands. As a result of these developments, the role of marriage for maintaining one's purity within the Gujarati community became further concretised. The descendants of inter-marriages, particularly from those with Swahili, became regarded as *chotarda*[7] (half-caste), and often faced stigmatisation from the 'pure' members of the *jat* and the broader Asian community. In light of the constant marginalisation that Gujarati descendants of such inter-marriages faced, this chapter, based on several years of ethnographic research in Zanzibar,[8] examines how the orientation of *jat*, now increasingly defined around questions of 'race' rather than religious tradition, forces the Gujarati descendants of these inter-ethnic marriages to cope with their stigmatisation in the community, imposing new notions of impurity on them. Furthermore, by questioning the premise on which ideas of purity now exist among the Gujaratis, the chapter explores how, within this new discourse, Gujaratis imposed with ideas of impure status employ new routes to transform their position vis-à-vis other Gujaratis to construct notions of roots based around the ideology of *jat* membership in contemporary Zanzibar.

THE PROBLEM OF PURITY AND THE ASIAN EXPERIENCE IN ZANZIBAR

Ideas of purity demarcate structural distance through the construction and maintenance of symbolic boundaries between individuals and groups. An individual or group maintains such purity by avoiding social practices that are considered polluting in nature. Consequently, taboos provide the social framework to restrict engagement with impure activities (Douglas 1966). In the ancient Hindu tradition of *varna,* boundaries associated with ideas of purity demarcated different people on the premise of their occupations, which defined their ritual roles in society. The pollution associated with the occupations of individuals from the lower *varna* was instrumental in enabling those higher than them to fulfil their ritual obligations. Though ideas of purity separated the population, maintenance of purity necessitated interaction and interdependence between members of the different *varna.* However, under the hegemony of British colonial rule, these relationships were transformed and gave rise to new ideas of purity, concretised around *jat,* caste-based communities, which now physically separated the population (Dirks 2001). Previous notions of social separation based on ritual roles gave way to constructing specific ideas of purity and impurity for distinguishing new primordial identities for different members in society.

As the Gujaratis left their Indian homeland in pursuit of economic prosperity under the auspices of colonial rule, they renegotiated their understanding of purity, often transforming practices through which they maintained their social distinctions. In the case of the Hindus moving to East Africa, many of them, particularly those that categorised themselves as members of higher castes, abandoned important pillars of Hindu purity, based around maintaining vegetarianism, consumption of alcohol and leaving the purity of their home environment as a consequence of their overseas travel (Oonk 2004; Mukadam 2007). In pursuit of *dharm ane dhando* (religion and business), virtues of the Gujarati community (Dwivedi 2010), many relinquished *dharm*, the premise of their purity, for the economic and social benefits they received in the new lands[9] (Oonk 2004).

In East Africa, their favourable socio-economic position in comparison to Africans around them (ibid.: 2006) enabled the Gujaratis to construct new premises for constituting ideas of purity, primarily around marriage within the *jat*. Facilitated by British policies which developed a social structure based on skin colour, with Europeans at the top, Asians in the middle and Africans at the bottom (Gregory 1993b; Twaddle 2001; Mukadam and Mawani 2009), Asians organised themselves into independent and socially exclusive communities in which association with *jat* often served as the primary means of socialisation within colonial society (Walji-Moloo 1996). Having forsaken traditional models of purity, social discourses of purity and honour also demarcated new boundaries along the lines of 'race' (Nager 1998) within this multi-cultural milieu.[10] Furthermore, by associating with and perceiving themselves primarily as British (Chauhan 1994), rather than African, the majority around whom they lived, the codification of *jat* as the institution for preserving purity enhanced sectarian fragmentation and greater separation from the African population (van den Berghe 1970). Though the Gujaratis relaxed norms of ritual purity to accommodate their emerging westward orientation in East Africa, discourses of sexual purity became a crucial feature for constructing new zones of inclusion and exclusion within the *jat* (Nager 1998; Oonk 2004).

During the colonial era, the Gujaratis in Zanzibar predominately married within their *jat*. By the late 1940s, approximately 20,000 Asians lived in Zanzibar and accounted for about six per cent of the islands' population, the majority of whom were Shia Muslim Gujarati (Lofchie 1965; Bharati 1970).[11] The minority Hindu Gujarati community consisted of the Bhatia, Lohana and Vania castes. In pursuit of their commercial interests, they were accompanied by the majority Gujarati Shia Muslim communities of Khoja Nizari Ismailis,[12] Bohras and Ithna'asharies, along with other Sunni groups such as the Kumbara, Memon, Kokni, among others.[13] Though Hindus made up the majority of South Asians in

East Africa, the prevalence of Islam on the islands encouraged Hindus to immigrate to mainland East Africa (Mangat 1969). Furthermore, despite the small presence of the Hindus on the islands, the terminology of *jat* became an important marker for differentiation among all Gujaratis, irrespective of their religion, and other Asians in Zanzibar (Keshodkar 2010). This affiliation with *jat* also ensured that marriage practices remained controlled within the boundaries of the caste.

While earlier immigrants brought their wives from India, the subsequent generations of Gujaratis living in Zanzibar predominately acquired their marriage partners from within their *jat* in East Africa. By the 1950s, contact with India had waned and East African Asians considered themselves more urban and western-oriented than their counterparts in India (Mangat 1969). However, inter-caste marriage among Asians remained a rare phenomenon (Bharati 1970). Additionally, with the wealth and status enjoyed by some of these Asian communities, ideas of purity associated with marriage also became delineated along lines of class. The Gujaratis from the lower socio-economic classes often had no alternatives but to either marry women from different castes or local Swahili or African women (Nager 1998).[14] Though Gujarati men married Swahili women, prospects of marriage between Gujarati women and Swahili men, who were perceived as not only threatening the honour of the women, but also of the *jat*, were outright rejected (ibid.: 2000). In instances where Asian women married outside their *jat*, even to other Asians, they were shunned by their communities (ibid.: 1998). Moreover, women who married outside their caste lost their caste identity and no longer enjoyed access to religious places of worship or ceremonies (Oonk 2004). One premise for endogamy asserted by Asians was that for them, marriage was a one-time event, in contrast to the Swahili and Africans who married numerous times (Walji-Moloo 1996). With ideas of 'race' now influencing their perceptions of purity, marriage with Swahili, who they perceived as socially and structurally inferior, was categorised as disgraceful (Larsen 2004). Consequently, by virtue of their socio-economic positions under British rule and with the incorporation of new models of purity based on 'race', the Gujaratis were able to demarcate these boundaries to maintain zones of inclusion and exclusion of membership within the *jat*.

It was only after the 1964 Revolution, when the ruling Arabs were deposed and a new government oriented towards mainland Africa sought to seek revenge on those categorised as foreigners (Clayton 1981), that Asians lost much of the socio-economic prestige they previously enjoyed in Zanzibar. The majority of Asians were forced off the islands (Martin 1978). Those remaining behind, predominately the poor, were subject to new, harsh policies that punished and marginalised Asians. Subsequently, forced inter-racial marriages between the leaders of the state and Asian women were implemented under the policy of promoting racial harmony and eradicating tribalism (Amory 1994). According to respondents, these forced marriages were carried out predominately with Muslim Asian women.[15] Through this sexual subjugation of Asian women, the taboo of sexual purity for demarcating boundaries of the *jat* was violated, in turn symbolising a defeat of a community (Jones 2011). Furthermore, with limited access to networks outside Zanzibar to acquire marriage partners and constant harassment from the government, many Gujarati and other Asian men and women remained bachelors and spinsters in order to save their family's reputation and maintain their position within their *jat* (Keshodkar 2010).

Ideas of purity, as they were transformed with the migration of the Gujaratis to East Africa, and then the colonial experience, were once again redefined as a consequence of post-colonial developments in Zanzibar. The pollution of ritual purity exercised by the Gujaratis affected individual lifestyles but did not significantly impact the structural framework of the *jat* or membership in it. However, with the pollution of sexual purity, the system of patriarchy which has given form to specific ideas and functions of *jat* in East Africa and the role they occupied in a multi-racial society, were considered violated. While the infraction of ritual purity only impacted the individual, the violation of sexual purity forced the Gujarati community to re-evaluate its identity and the routes through which it defined its roots in Zanzibar. Consequently, with these forms of impurities impacting the orientation of the *jat*, the Gujaratis have now redefined their ideas of purity and imposed new boundaries for including and excluding members into their communities.

NEW MARKERS OF INCLUSION AND EXCLUSION

For the Asian community in Zanzibar, the revolution and its aftermath represented a new era of psychological trauma. Closed from the outside world and unable to practice their faith or openly interact with other members of the *jat*, religion often became secondary in their efforts to survive and overcome the marginalisation they faced in their own society. Stigmatised as non-Africans, their experiences under the emerging politics of 'race' directed by the state concretised new forms of antagonisms towards the Swahili and Africans around them. Though this animosity has not erupted in any form of violence or direct opposition against the authority of the state, it is clearly visible in the attitudes developed by the Gujaratis and other Asians in redefining the framework of the *jat* in contemporary Zanzibar. The role of marriage and the values associated with it now occupy central significance among Asians for constructing their sectarian identities as well as maintaining Asian roots in Zanzibar (ibid.).

The liberalisation of Zanzibar's political economy in the mid-1980s enabled the local Asians to overcome the economic marginalisation and other forms of stigmatisation they endured for over 20 years. The freedom of access enjoyed as a consequence of the transformation of the state empowered the Gujaratis and other Asians to reconnect with their *jat* not only throughout East Africa, but once again in India and other parts of the world. With very few members of the *jat* remaining on the islands, interaction with relatives abroad and the transnational orientation of *jat* in the era of globalisation became important markers for reviving the centrality of *jat* in distinguishing their social identity in Zanzibar (ibid.: 2005). Through this interaction with their *jat* counterparts elsewhere, they are able to pursue new routes for constructing their roots in Zanzibar.

Revival of *jat* networks provides the Gujaratis of Zanzibar with one of the most crucial elements required for reconstituting ideas of purity, namely Asian marriage partners. Those Gujaratis in

Zanzibar that have substantially improved their socio-economic status in the current era of liberalisation with the support from transnational networks often acquire their marriage partners from wealthy counterparts within their *jat* from abroad, ranging from parts of East Africa to India. In such instances, brides are 'imported' to Zanzibar from these places, while daughters of wealthy Gujaratis are additionally 'exported' to Europe and North America. For financially impoverished Gujaratis, they continue to primarily marry members of the *jat* with similar socio-economic status in Zanzibar, and in instances where this is not possible, then members of other *jat*. However, Asians are still seen to be the most suitable marriage partners (ibid.: 2010). By virtue of these marriage strategies, ideas of sexual and racial purity, defined on the premise of ethnicity, regulate the basis of inclusion into the *jat*. Through their membership in the *jat*, irrespective of their socio-economic position within it, they maintain ideas of purity and enjoy access to various religious networks, as well as financial and social resources, which are inaccessible to the rest of the population. *Jat* membership not only offers a means to redefine one's identity in this multi-ethnic social landscape, but also facilitates access to resources for impoverished members of the community through prevailing patron-client relationships within which one can alleviate one's financial situation at a time when the majority of Zanzibaris continue to struggle to survive in the prevailing neo-liberal economic environment.

The Gujaratis that remain excluded from accessing the newly communally sanctioned routes within the revised boundaries of the *jat* are predominately those that have inter-married with either other Asians outside the *jat*, or more importantly, non-Asians. Inter-racial marriages between Asians of different *jat* or between Gujaratis and non-Asians is not a new phenomenon in Zanzibar, but in light of the new political and racial discourse introduced under colonial rule and cemented during the revolutionary era, those engaged in such marriage practices are now subject to search for new routes for determining their roots in this multi-ethnic landscape. No longer accepted as Gujaratis and Asians, these individuals and increasingly, their children, who are labelled as *chotardas*, by those that consider themselves 'pure', face a continuous social struggle and marginalisation in the process of accessing these zones of inclusion defined around the *jat*. With marriage to the local Swahili considered disgraceful, those categorised as *chotardas* are left with no alternatives but to affiliate with their non-Asian, Swahili or African origins and in the process of doing so, their position is further compromised within the *jat* (ibid.: 2010). In addition, given the religious orientation of *jat*, it being based around a belief system, these individuals, if they are able to retain their membership in the *jat*, are now forced to move through the same spaces as those claiming a higher degree of purity within the *jat*. However, in attempting to establish their roots, they are denied access to the routes which facilitate the construction of religious identity for the other Gujarati members of the *jat*. Even in instances where the descendents of these inter-marriages learn to speak Gujarati, a defining feature for constructing notions of a Gujarati identity, they are not recognised as Gujaratis by other members of the *jat*.

Within the Hindu and the Shia Muslim sectarian communities, inter-marriage is highly discouraged. Among the local Hindus, according to respondents, there is no inter-marriage with the Swahili. If locally unavailable, marriage partners are often acquired from the different Hindu castes on mainland Tanzania and Kenya. There have only been a few cases in which Hindu men have married non-Hindu Asian women. In all such instances, the women were often integrated into the community. However, the purity of the family was often put into question by other members of the community in light of the marriage from outside the *jat*. The majority of Hindu men that have married women from outside their *jat* in recent years have left Zanzibar, though it is not clear if the social position of the family was the motive for their departure. Irrespectively, there remains minimal inter-marriage among the Hindu community.[16]

The Shia Bohra community, who have historically been more conservative than other *jat* (Gregory 1993b), also consider any form of inter-marriage outside the *jat* as unacceptable. Bohra men who have married Asian women from other *jat* have often found themselves marginalised in the community. In instances where Bohra men married Swahili women, they were excommunicated from the *jat*, losing all privileges of membership and more importantly, an integral aspect of their identity in Zanzibar. The movement of Bohra women in Zanzibar is also strictly controlled to ensure that they have limited social interaction with 'strange' men, thus facilitating their marriage only to Bohra men. In instances when I inquired about the marriage of Bohra women to Swahili men, respondents readily indicated that they would kill their sisters or daughters for bringing shame associated with such marriages to the family (Keshodkar 2010).

Inter-marriage, though discouraged, has nonetheless become a prominent feature within the Shia Ismaili community since the revolution. The Ismaili community was the most prominent Gujarati community in Zanzibar during the colonial era. However, today, its membership is roughly a little over 100 people. With the majority of Ismailis fleeing Zanzibar after the revolution, impoverished Ismaili men remaining behind had difficulty marrying Ismaili Asian women. Consequently, they married Swahili women and now have children who have part Swahili ancestry. Since religion forms the premise of the community, children from these marriages have access to the communal ceremonies and gatherings. However, they often face marginalisation at the hands of those that identify themselves as 'pure'. While the language of pollution is used to draw ideas of strangeness between the different members of the community on the premise of 'race', the religious orientation of the community prevents the excommunication of these 'polluted' members (ibid.). These individuals, forced into a marginal position in this private space as a result of the designation placed upon them, are now forced to establish new roots for defining their Ismaili identity by virtue of their position in the *jat*, which facilitates their movement as Ismailis, but not as Asians in the local landscape. On the basis of patriarchy, these children remain of Indian origin. However, due to their skin colour, they are primarily categorised as Swahili and marginalised accordingly.

As the size of these castes have decreased substantially in the aftermath of the 1964 Revolution,[17] the notion of racial purity now dictates how members of these communities construct their *jat* identities. This approach however, becomes problematic for the Gujarati-speaking Kumbara community, who are predominately

Sunni Muslims, and who have historically inter-married with Swahili women. In light of the lower socio-economic status they historically occupied, marriage with Swahili women was often the only option accessible to many Kumbara men. Additionally, such marriages were facilitated by the fact that these Asian Sunnis and Swahili Zanzibaris practiced the Shafii tradition of Islam, sharing similar religious beliefs and ideologies. However, today, particularly as the Kumbara have abandoned their traditional occupation as potters and moved to urban areas of Zanzibar where they are engaged in trade, there is a conscientious effort among wealthy Kumbara traders to pursue different marriage strategies. Given the emerging prominence of 'race' as a marker of distinction, some Kumbara men have tried to marry Asian women from other *jat*, who they perceive as 'pure' Indian. One respondent indicated that it was important to preserve Indian culture, and by marrying a woman of Indian origin, they can achieve that goal.[18]

Even among the Sunni Memons, marriage is preferred within the *jat*. Memons have historically married primarily within the caste (cf. Gregory 1993b). Memons only consider it acceptable for their men to marry Swahili women and women from other *jat*. In order to maintain their association with Indian traditions and culture, many Memon men often married women from other *jat*. However, the prospects of a Memon woman marrying a local Swahili Muslim man is considered unacceptable. Memons, like all the other *jat*, rely upon their networks in East Africa to ensure that endogamy prevails. Consequently, many Memon women end up marrying Memon men from outside Zanzibar. However, for those women who are unable to find partners from within the Memon community, often the case for women from poor families, then, according to respondents, the only other option available to them is to marry some Asian from another *jat* or for the women to live out their life in Zanzibar as spinsters (Keshodkar 2010).

In defining their roots, the Gujaratis of Zanzibar have created different mechanisms at different times to preserve the patriarchal system associated with the *jat* and their ideas of Indian heritage. From the preservation of ritual purity to sexual purity and now racial purity, these mechanisms are directed to expunge different forms of pollution that affect their ability to maintain their roots in this foreign land.[19] Respondents argue that *chotardas* have lost their purity (of skin) which can never be regained. By utilising 'race' to mark such differences, the Gujaratis now risk challenging the very system of patriarchy that defines the framework of *jat*. Asian Zanzibaris characterised as *chotardas* are predominately children of Asian men and non-Asian women. On the premise of patriarchy, on which the *jat* system is defined, these children, irrespective of their skin colour, are of Asian descent and not Swahili or African. However, in light of being rejected as Asian and marginalised due to their skin colour, they often have no alternative but to associate with their maternal cultures.

One route accessible to some Asians of mixed descent in order to acquire a degree of acceptance and gain a marginal space within the *jat* is for them to enter into various forms of patron-client relationship with other Gujarati members of the *jat*. Historically, such patron-client relationships served as the basis of social interaction between the Gujarati and members of the Swahili community. Many Gujaratis in Zanzibar have improved their financial conditions in the liberalisation era with the assistance of family and *jat* networks abroad. However, Gujarati men who married Swahili women have often been unable to benefit from such networks. Their socio-economic conditions and marginalisation within the *jat* has limited their ability to improve their conditions. However, they and their children, by virtue of still remaining members of the *jat*, can improve their status in the community by entering into patron-client relationships with those who occupy more central positions within the caste. These patron-client relationships enable Asians of mixed descent to engage in various forms of economic activities so as to overcome their impoverished state. However, the level of assistance offered to those of mixed descent is often lower in comparison to that offered to poor members of the *jat* that are categorised as 'pure'. One Gujarati respondent of mixed descent indicated that, 'the light skin Asians, while helping us, want us to realise that we are better off only because of them. They do not want the dark skin Asians to do well ... they always want you to beg from them' (interview January 2011). The unwillingness to accept these Gujaratis as equals on the premise of their 'race' ensures that those that consider themselves 'pure' remain at the centre of the *jat*, while those of mixed descent always occupy marginal positions within the community.

Given the significance of endogamy for constructing the orientation of the *jat*, these Asians of mixed descent also find themselves in situations where they are unable to acquire marriage partners from within the caste. Asians that consider themselves 'pure' adamantly refuse to marry their daughters to Gujaratis of mixed descent within their *jat*. Some go as far as restricting any social interaction between their daughters and these men. At the same time, Gujarati men often treat Gujarati women of mixed descent as sexualised objects, claiming that these women offer sexual enjoyment that an Indian woman is incapable of providing (Nager 2000). Gujarati men often violate their own ideologies of sexual purity by engaging in affairs with Swahili, African, Arab and Gujarati women of mixed descent while at the same time punishing their women for such infractions (ibid. 1998). There have been a few instances where Gujarati men have married Gujarati women of mixed descent within their *jat* but in the majority of cases, these women end up marrying outside the *jat*, as a result of which, they lose their position within the community. One respondent who ended up marrying outside the *jat* indicated that her marriage offered her a new sense of freedom that she could not previously experience. She was never accepted as an equal within the *jat* and was always marginalised. Through her marriage, she no longer has to worry about how people will evaluate her on the basis of her skin colour.

For Gujarati men of mixed descent, marriage within the *jat* also remains problematic. These men face challenges not only in acquiring marriage partners from families that consider themselves 'pure', but also from families within the *jat* that have daughters of mixed descent. In one instance, when a wealthy Gujarati man of mixed Asian and Swahili descent approached a poor family from within the *jat* with a marriage proposal for their daughter, who was of mixed Asian and Arab descent, the latter outright rejected the proposal. Lacking the specific social capital (cf. Bourdieu 1984) of a 'pure' Asian identity, these men are unable to enhance their social position within the community. Consequently, they often end up marrying non-Asian women (Keshodkar 2010). However, by virtue of their marriages, they are then further marginalised for bringing in a greater degree of impurity within the *jat*.

While the patriarchal nature of *jat* remains relatively intact for the Gujaratis in Zanzibar, the growing emphasis on 'race' for demarcating ideas of purity highlights how only specific routes are recognised for establishing their roots in Zanzibar. The antagonism towards the Swahili and Africans emerging from the experience of the revolution and its aftermath seems to have become the primary mechanism which moulds the construction of boundaries to articulate new identities of the Gujaratis in Zanzibar. Those advocating racial purity argue that the *chotardas* have lost their purity and can never regain it. In light of the recent history of rape and forced marriages of Indian women to Swahili men following the revolution, some respondents have even gone as far as to argue that it is better for an Asian woman to be raped by an Indian man than an African because at least, if the woman is impregnated, the child will be of Indian origin and not African. Such formulations of purity disregard the fact that definitions of religion, caste, 'race' or class have been constructed by Asians in East Africa in relational terms (Nager 1998). If ideas of purity were absolute, their own violations of various pillars of purity as a consequence of their own migratory experience in East Africa, such as eating meat, drinking alcohol (Oonk 2004) and sexual liaisons with non-Asian women among others, would result in them also now becoming polluted, and thus no longer being able to enjoy membership within their *jat*.

By categorising some violations as aspects of individual choice and others as detrimental to communal and religious identity, the Gujaratis in Zanzibar are engaged in transforming the framework on which ideas of purity and impurity are defined. In the process of this exercise, they are manipulating modes of inclusion and exclusion to ensure that they retain their membership within the community. Furthermore, through this process, only specific routes facilitate the development of Gujarati roots in Zanzibar, which despite their premise on loyalty to some idea of tradition and homeland based in India (cf. Sahoo 2006; Dwivedi 2010), the majority are either unaware of or consciously reject these Gujarati traditions due to their immigrant experience in East Africa. Consequently, the routes highlighting the efforts to define their roots, on the basis of which different ideas of purity mandate zones of inclusion and exclusion could be considered flawed. Through the exclusion of Gujaratis of mixed descent from the *jat* on the premise of 'race', the Gujaratis are upholding a fallacy that only one route defines their roots as Gujaratis and as Asians in Zanzibar. They fail to recognise that as a consequence of their movement through different social spaces, they have acquired multiple identities which subsequently facilitate their ability to constantly develop new routes to define their roots in Zanzibar (Keshodkar 2005). Accordingly, the Gujaratis that have inter-married, and their descendants, have developed new routes to define their identities as Gujaratis, as Asians, as Swahili, as Zanzibaris, and as Africans, each as relevant and meaningful as those who have taken different routes to construct different identities within the same social landscape.

CONCLUSION

Questions of purity have been instrumental for dictating zones of inclusion and exclusion among the Gujaratis in Zanzibar. Through the practice of endogamy, the different Gujarati *jat* have sought to maintain their distinctiveness vis-à-vis other Zanzibaris around them. Their ability to maintain specific levels of distinctiveness, however, was compromised in the aftermath of developments following the 1964 Revolution. In an era of liberalisation, the Gujarati are now emphasising notions of racial purity through endogamy to distinguish themselves and construct their roots and identities in Zanzibar. These marriage practices mandate very specific routes to facilitate the development and maintenance of roots in Zanzibar. The primacy attributed to *jat* through such practices, which frames notions of purity and ideas of inclusion in a rigid form, fails to recognise that no one identity is self-sustaining across time and space (Castells 2001). Through their own migratory experience, they have constantly negotiated and redefined ideas of purity. It is for these reasons that the orientation of *jat* in Zanzibar and other parts of East Africa remain different from their counterparts in India and elsewhere. Yet, in light of memories of the revolution and the subsequent psychological trauma through which they continue to live, questions of racial purity now lie at the centre of governing modes of inclusion and exclusion for membership within the *jat*.

The Gujaratis that find themselves excluded or marginalised within the *jat* as a consequence of these developments are those of mixed Asian and Swahili descent. Stigmatised through the label, *chotardas*, these individuals continue to lack access to routes to construct their identities as Gujaratis in Zanzibar. By virtue of their marginality, defined on the premise of their perceived racial impurity, these Gujaratis of mixed descent remain unable to engage in endogamy to strengthen their position within the *jat*. Unable to define their roots as Gujarati, they subsequently associate with their Swahili or African roots. The construct of purity among the Gujarati in Zanzibar today, defined through absolute rather than relational terms, and the zones of inclusion and exclusion they have constructed, limits the routes through which individuals can identify themselves as Gujarati and Asian in Zanzibar. For the Gujaratis of mixed descent, unless the contexts in which prevailing ideas of purity change, they will remain marginalised and outside the zone of inclusion within the *jat*.

NOTES

1. The ability to move into and out of different spaces, I propose, determines the identities that prevail within the given spaces. As such, every social space exists in the form of a public and private space and the degree of accessibility into these spaces, at a given time, shapes what meanings self and other can construct within them to develop a particular identity. A space in which 'self' is able to restrict the movement of the 'other' becomes a private space and the identity that emerges in this space is different from when both self and other are able to access the same space. For example, a house can serve as both a private as well as a public space. As a place for family activities, the house acts as a private space, restricting non-family members from accessing this space. However, at a time of death in the family, members of the broader community acquire access into this space and interact with the family, thus making it more public. Viewed from this perspective, the public and private dimensions of

space are not in opposition, but rather different perspectives of the appropriated and re-appropriated social space. The forces of production that construct the different meanings for the same space determine the public or private value of the appropriated spaces (Keshodkar 2005, 2010).

2. The term '*jat*' refers to both South Asian Hindus and Muslims. Refer to Ahmed (1973) for a broader discussion on the existence of the caste system among South Asian Muslims.
3. The term 'Asian' will be used throughout the chapter in reference to South Asians.
4. Endogamy is the practice of marriage within one class, ethnic or social group.
5. The Swahili make up the majority indigenous population in Zanzibar, many of whom are descendants of inter-marriage between Arab men and African women over centuries. Meanwhile, ideas of being African in Zanzibar are more specifically associated with tracing one's heritage to mainland Africa. Refer to Caplan and Topan (2004) for a broader discussion of how ideas of Swahili identity vary along the East African coast.
6. Hypergamy is the marriage practice where an individual marries a person of higher social status, while hypogamy represents marriage practices in which one marries someone of lower social status.
7. The term has a derogatory connotation, and is rarely used in public spaces or in front of someone considered half-caste, but was often heard in private discussions in which Asians referred to such individuals.
8. The ethnographic research examining marriage practices and the state of affairs of the Asian community in Zanzibar commenced in 1998 and continues today (Keshodkar 2005, 2010).
9. Mukadam (2007: 113) indicates that for some Hindu communities, for example, in the case of the Swaminarayans, Lord Swaminarayan provided his followers with 'scriptural sanction to migrate beyond the sacred land of India ... and even recommend[ed] it be used as a method of fleeing destitution or harm'.
10. While this notion of 'purity' is based around concepts of ethnic origin, being Asian and African, elements of race are integrated within it. Originating from perceived Aryan and Dravidian differences in India and facilitated by British racial policies in East Africa, many Asians in East Africa have carried with them the concept that fair skin denotes superiority (cf. Gregory 1993a). Since ideas of race are intertwined with complexities of ethnicity in developing this

form of classification in the Zanzibar context, no single determinant can be used as a primordial marker of identity (Keshodkar 2010).

11. Discussion of Asians in the context of Zanzibar implies reference to the Gujarati speaking community, since they continue to constitute the majority of the Asian community in Zanzibar.
12. The term 'Ismaili' will be used throughout this chapter to refer to the Khoja Nizari Ismailis.
13. Other Asian groups that lived in Zanzibar included the Parsis, Goans Christians and Sikhs. Many of these groups continue to live in Zanzibar in small numbers.
14. Such practices were more prominent among the poor members of the Sunni, who in sharing the Shafii tradition of Islam with the indigenous population, were not bound by any religious restrictions from marrying African women. However, among the Sunni Memons, marriage predominately took place within the caste (Keshodkar 2010). Furthermore, the Sunni Memons exhibit a closed Sunni conservatism, building their own schools and mosques and rarely marry beyond the extended family. They, unlike other Sunnis who married non-Asian Sunnis, have largely remained a 'closed' community (Gregory 1993a: 31).
15. Arab women were also subject to these forced marriages. According to respondents, Hindu women were apparently spared from such marriages because of the role that the Hindu community played in supporting the efforts of the African government to come into power at the end of the colonial era.
16. One reason why there is limited inter-marriage between Hindus and other sectors of the Asian and non-Asian population is because over 95 per cent of the population of Zanzibar is Muslim. Thus, marriage does not take place on the basis of religion.
17. There were approximately 120 Ismailis, 400 Bohras, and less than 300 Hindus living in Zanzibar. Of the 4,000 or so Asians still living in Zanzibar, now composing less than 0.2 per cent of the entire population, approximately 3,000 are Sunni (Keshodkar 2010).
18. Given that these Asians have lived in Zanzibar for generations and have inter-married with the Swahili, questions emerge over how they perceive and understand ideas of Indian culture. This warrants further research.
19. Though the majority of Asians in Zanzibar have no association with India, having lost all contact for over two generations, they continue to utilise affiliation with India as a premise to maintain their strangeness in Zanzibar (Keshodkar 2010).

REFERENCES

Ahmed, Imtiaz. *Caste and Social Stratification among Muslims in India*, New Delhi: Manohar, 1973.

Amory, Deborah. 'The Politics of Identity of Zanzibar', unpublished PhD Thesis, Stanford University, 1994.

Bharati, Agehananda. 'A Social Survey', in *Portrait of a Minority: Asians in East Africa*, edited by Dharam P. Ghai and Yash P. Ghai, Oxford: Clarendon Press, 1970, pp. 15–67.

Bourdieu, Pierre. *Distinction: A Social Critique of the Judgement of Taste*, translated by Richard Nice, Cambridge, Massachusetts: Harvard University Press, 1984.

Caplan, Pat and Farouk Topan. *Swahili Modernities: Culture, Politics and Identity on the East Coast of Africa*, Trenton, New Jersey: Africa World Press, 2004.

Castells, Manuel. *The Power of Identity*, Oxford: Blackwell, 2001.

Chauhan, Jaya. 'Bridging Different Worlds: Accounts of South Asian Woman Born in Kenya Who Moves to England', *Canadian Woman Studies*, Vol. 14, No. 2 (1994): 34–37.

Clayton, Anthony. *The Zanzibar Revolution and its Aftermath*, London: C. Hurst and Co., 1981.

Clifford, James. *Routes: Travel and Translation in the Late Twentieth Century*, Cambridge, Mass.: Harvard University Press, 1997.

Dirks, Nicholas. *Castes of Mind: Colonialism and the Making of Modern India*, Princeton: Princeton University Press, 2001.

Douglas, Mary. *Purity and Danger: An Analysis of Concepts of Pollution and Taboo*, London: Routledge, 1966.

Dwivedi, Manan. 'Gujarati Diaspora on a Global Platform: Perceptions, Contributions and Experiences', *Diaspora Studies*, Vol. 3, No. 2 (2010): 161–85.

Gregory, Robert G. *South Asians in East Africa: An Economic and Social History, 1890–1980*, Oxford: Westview Press, 1993a.

——. *Quest for Equality: Asian Politics in East Africa, 1900–1967*, London: Sangam Books, 1993b.

Jones, Stephanie. 'The Politics of Love and History: Asian Women and African Men in East African Literature', *Research in African Literature*, Vol. 42, No. 3 (2011): 166–86.

Keshodkar, Akbar. 'Marriage as a Means to Preserve 'Asian-ness': The Post-Revolutionary Experience of the Asians in Zanzibar', *Journal of Asian and African Studies*, Vol. 45, No. 2 (April 2010): 226–40.

——. 'Movement of Asian and Swahili Identities: Impact of Tourism on Constructions of Community, Ethnicity, and Gender Relations in Zanzibar Town', Unpublished PhD Thesis, University of Oxford, 2005.

Larsen, Kjersti. 'Change, Continuity and Contestation: The Politics of Modern Identities in Zanzibar', in *Swahili Modernities: Culture, Politics, and Identity on the East Coast of Africa*, edited by Pat Caplan and Farouk Topan, Trenton: New Jersey: Africa World Press, 2004, pp. 121–43.

Lofchie, Michael. *Zanzibar: Background to Revolution*, Oxford: Oxford University Press, 1965.

Mangat, Jagjit S. *A History of the Asians in East Africa, 1886–1945*, Oxford: Clarendon Press, 1969.

Martin, Esmond B. *Zanzibar: Tradition and Revolution*, London: Hamilton, 1978.

Mukadam, Anjoom A. 'Shattering Stereotypes: Post-Diasporic Swaminarayan Gujaratis in London', in *Gujaratis in the West: Evolving Identities in Contemporary Society*, edited by Anjoom A. Mukadam and Sharmina Mawani, Newcastle: Cambridge Scholars Press, 2007, pp. 106–26.

Mukadam, Anjoom A. and Sharmina Mawani. 'Excess Baggage or Precious Gems? The Migration of Cultural Commodities', in *Muslim in Britain: Race, Place and Identities*, edited by Peter Hopkins and Richard Gale, Edinburgh: Edinburgh University Press, 2009, pp. 150–68.

Nager, Richa. 'Communal Discourses, Marriage, and the Politics of Gendered Social Boundaries among South Asian Immigrants in Tanzania', *Gender, Place, Culture*, Vol. 5, No. 2 (1998): 117–39.

——. 'Religion, Race and the Debate over Mut'a in Dar es Salaam', *Feminist Studies*, Vol. 26, No. 3 (2000): 661–90.

Oonk, Gijsbert. 'South Asians in East Africa (1880–1920) with a Particular Focus on Zanzibar: Toward a Historical Explanation of Economic Success of a Middlemen Minority', *African and Asian Studies*, Vol. 5, No. 1 (2006): 57–89.

Oonk, Gijsbert. 'The Changing Culture of the Hindu Lohana Community in East Africa', *Contemporary South Asia*, Vol. 13, No. 1 (2004): 7–23.

Sahoo, Ajaya. 'Issues of Identity in the Indian Diaspora: A Transnational Perspective', *Perspectives on Global Development and Technology*, Vol. 5, Nos 1–2 (2006): 81–98.

Simmel, Georg. 'The Stranger', in *On Individuality and Social Forms*, edited by Donald Levine, Chicago: University of Chicago Press, 1971, pp. 143–50.

Twaddle, Michael. 'The Development of Communalism among East African Asians', in *Community, Empire and Migration: South Asians in Diaspora*, edited by Crispin Bates, New York: Palgrave, 2001, pp. 109–22.

van den Berghe, Pierre L. 'Asians in East and South Africa: A Comparison', in *Portrait of a Minority: Asians in East Africa*, edited by Dharam P. Ghai and Yash P. Ghai, Oxford: Clarendon Press, 1970, pp. 151–71.

Walji-Moloo, Parveen. 'Women's Position and Fertility: The Case of the Asians in Kenya', in *Shifting Circles of Support: Contextualising Gender and Kinship in South Asia and Sub-Saharan Africa*, edited by Rajni Palriwala and Carla Risseeuw, London: Alta Mira Press, 1996, pp. 221–48.

CHAPTER 9

'Wherever there is one Gujarati, there is Gujarat'

The Integration of Hindus in the United Kingdom

John Mattausch

In the preface to his study of *Indian Immigrants in Britain* published in 1963 Desai recounts what may well be an apocryphal story about the arrival and integration of Parsis (Zoroastrians) in tenth century Gujarat:

> The Parsees, persecuted in their own land because of their religious beliefs, came one day to the port of Sanjan in Gujarat. Their leader sent a petition to the local Raja seeking permission to stay. The Raja sent him a glass of water filled to the brim. The Parsee added sugar to the water and sent it back. The Raja was pleased when he tasted the water and found it sweet. He knew then that the Parsees would mix with his subjects as sugar does with water. They would become 'one with the people'.

Desai (1963) tells us that the Raja's judgement proved prescient, that Parsis did indeed become as one with Gujaratis, not by abandoning their ancient religious culture but instead by preserving it: 'By paradox they have become integrated through voluntary segregation' (ibid.: np). Turning to the subject of his own study, chiefly Gujaratis who had settled in Birmingham, Britain's second largest city, Desai (ibid.) claims that 'this is the form of integration which Indian immigrants in the United Kingdom desire'. Now, over fifty years since Desai published his study we may take stock of how far Gujaratis have been successful in sweetening the waters of British society, whether or not they have achieved integration through voluntary segregation, and also whether this apparently paradoxical strategy of integration demands that we reconsider what belonging to a nation-state might entail.

The Gujaratis, mainly Hindus, whom Desai (ibid.) studied, had arrived in Britain and had settled in Birmingham before the crises arose in East Africa. Although a small number of Asians[1] had begun to travel from East Africa to live, usually temporarily, in Britain in the early 1960s (Desai 1963; Michaelson 1979), Desai's (1963) study was of the first phase of British Gujaratis, of settled immigrants who, rather than assimilating with the host society, chose instead to 'accommodate' to their new British homeland. In the way of expats the world over, they sought to build what Desai (ibid.) termed an 'internal' social space where they could live and mix with fellow immigrants, preserving their religious culture in a foreign milieu.

'The immigrant takes up membership of his village-kin group immediately upon arrival and obtains a number of benefits out of such membership' (Desai 1963: 122). Most often already married before emigrating (Desai 1963), it was this village-kin group membership and identity which defined these settlers' relationships with fellow immigrants and with the wider society in Birmingham. Though Hindu caste placements remained salient, and informed the immigrants' dealings with Indians back in India, in the UK the 'wider caste system' along with the caste hierarchy were absent and the immigrants' social compass was given by their village-group membership which united them 'into a linguistic-regional community' (ibid.: 17) that connected those living in Birmingham to other members of their village group living in other towns and cities throughout Britain. Who the immigrants lived with and ate alongside, who they socialised with and where they shopped, all this and much more was steered by this group membership as was the kind of work they undertook. Returning home from work, these early Gujarati settlers entered houses they either owned, possibly housing other Gujarati or Indian tenants, or similar houses where they themselves rented a room, entering a private space where English was not spoken even by the children (ibid.: 9), closing the front door upon a world they had accommodated to but had not joined any more than was functionally necessary. Desai's (ibid.) study paints a picture of a self-contained, self-referential community preserving as far as possible its native culture and shunning any real contact with other Brummies (residents of Birmingham), even from their closest non-Indian neighbours about whose neighbourhood patterns of behaviour they 'were totally ignorant' (ibid.: 30). The 'immigrant's house is,' Desai (ibid.: 55) remarks, 'so to speak an immigrant's castle' which the non-Indian did not enter any more than these early Indian immigrants visited their neighbours' homes: rows of houses sited side by side but wholly culturally discrete.

Perhaps this style of expat living is what we should expect to find practised by early immigrants of small number, too small for example to bear the costs of building and maintaining public *mandirs* (Hindu temples) (ibid.), an expat world of mutual support and familiarity preferable to the chilly offerings from the native hosts. Desai (ibid.) concluded his study with his thoughts upon how the community might develop in future. Noting that a satisfactory definition of 'integration' could not be reached, Desai (ibid.: 149) wisely opted instead to question whether the settlers' current form of integration by minimal accommodation was sustainable or whether the immigrant community would dissolve as future generations opted instead for integration through assimilation, a question to which he concluded 'there can be no answer' because the possible influences upon the community's development were too unpredictable. Such influences included the level of education achieved by future generations, the level of hostility expressed by other Britons, whether greater geographical dispersal would weaken the community, and also the affects of recent restrictions on migration to Britain (Desai 1963). In many ways, it would be the last of these influences that would come most to affect the British Gujarati Hindu community along with British Hinduism.

British migration policy and legislation, along with its political sibling citizenship, have, since the end of the Second World War, been reactive in character and the restrictions on immigration Desai foresaw as affecting the frontier community are a prime example of this national governance trait (Mattausch 2012b). Classified under the terms of the 1948 *British Nationality Act* as

Citizens of the UK and Colonies, Gujaratis living in the colonial East African countries of Malawi, Tanzania, Uganda and Kenya held the unrestricted right to enter and reside in the United Kingdom. Many presumed this right to be unaffected by the 1962 *Commonwealth Immigrants Act* which, with the introduction of vouchers based upon employment criteria, ended this automatic right of free entry for other Commonwealth peoples and ended too the old imperial ethic of equity between all Commonwealth citizens. After the 1962 restrictions were enacted, few new non-dependent immigrants from India joined the British frontier community. However, following the two East African Asian Crises, first in Kenya in 1967/68 then in Uganda in 1972, the British Gujarati frontier community was greatly swollen by the arrivals of those departing or fleeing the consequences of post-independence Africanisation. The details of this unhappy chapter in British Gujarati history have been well documented, as too have been the machinations of prominent Labour and Conservative politicians in the face of the African Asians' plight (Hansen 1999). Equally, the history and sociology of Asians in the British colonies, is now reasonably familiar; in fact more studies have been published about Gujaratis in East Africa than have been published on the early frontiersmen community in Britain (Desai [1963] being a rare exception). For the purposes of this discussion, I want to focus upon the form of integration that had been constructed by Asians in the sixty or so years since settling in Africa, rather than as had previously been their custom of seasonally visiting the coastal ports as traders.

Both Desai's British Gujarati immigrants and the Gujaratis who moved to East Africa were voluntary migrants which, as Gupta (1998) noted, distinguishes them from involuntary Indian migration to other countries. Both East African and Birmingham Gujaratis were pioneers and in the case of Gujarati Hindus, moving to East Africa meant not only crossing the Indian Ocean but also for the first time defying the religious prohibition on crossing the *kalipani* (the black sea), the crossing of which defiled the transgressor and was met by caste ostracism of the kind visited upon Gujarat's most famous son, Gandhi, when he left Bombay aboard a ship bound for London's Inns of Court.[2] How Gujaratis lived alongside Africans and Europeans in the colonies mirrors the patterns of integration through accommodation and voluntary segregation which Desai traced in his study of frontiersmen Gujaratis in Birmingham. There were of course some sharp differences in the character of the two diasporic communities, unsurprisingly, not least in the economic sphere: whereas Desai's Gujaratis in Birmingham owned a small number of shops serving the needs of their community, or earned their living as hawkers or as factory workers, in Africa by the time of the crises, markedly in Uganda, the Asians owned and ran the majority of the colonies' commerce which for some firms extended internationally.[3] Whereas the small British Gujarati community could not financially support public *mandirs*, in Africa, *mandirs* along with mosques and *gurudwaras* (Sikh temples) had long been established along with community associations, schools, colleges and hospitals. Unlike their already married migrant counterparts in Birmingham, Asians in Africa, many of whom by the time of the crises had been born on African soil, were caught up in the business of contracting marriages. However, common to the two communities whether living under cold dreary grey, or warm clear blue skies was that pattern of integration through limited accommodation and voluntary segregation, a pattern which in both continents preserved the family-based religious cultures of the Asians in their private social world.

For the majority Hindu Gujarati population in the East African countries, the migratory passage along with the types of employment the migrants undertook, were novel (Twaddle 1975): there was no tradition of Gujarati Hindus seasonally trading, let alone permanently settling, in East Africa; no tradition of working as *dukanwallas* (shop-keepers), civil servants, teachers, factory owners, etc. Africa was in many, many ways a new departure, comparable in novelty to the transition made by Desai's frontiersmen when they arrived in Birmingham. Just as in Britain, as Desai noted, the Hindu caste system had not been imported intact, so too in Africa the migratory patterning of Gujarati Hindus had led two Vaniya castes – Lohanas and Lewa Kanbi Patidars – who share the surname Patel, to be numerically overrepresented with other caste strata there in short measure. The form of Hinduism that was lived and practised in Africa, in common with all cultures and religions exported from their native soil, was not a replica of that found in Gujarat or the Punjab, nor were the expressions of the other Indian religious cultures found in the African countries such as, Nizari Ismailism and other Muslim persuasions, Jainism, Sikhism and Christianity. Expatriate Hindus, argued Bharati (1976), were adapting their religious practices by permitting ritualistic tolerance while at the same time trying to maintain what they regarded to be ideological rigour. Sixty years of adaptation to the African context had fostered innovations both subtle and gross (Oonk 2008), much as one would expect given the length of time the Asians were settled in Africa and the disparities between the Saurashtrian peninsula and the African lands. But underlying these innovations and changes at the cultural level, the integral sociological underpinning of Gujarati, and indeed of all Asian societies, was maintained and perpetuated under African skies as too it was under Birmingham's grey clouds. As Desai (1963: 16) noted the 'joint family' was the basic social unit for the frontiersmen he studied, the sociological lode for the 'village-kin and relatives' community and the immigrants' identity, and this was equally true in Kenya and Uganda. Though the composition of the Asian families adapted to meet the demands of African life, it was this social feature of African and Birmingham Gujarati cultures which was preserved and perpetuated and which in its turn knitted the common pattern of what Desai (ibid.: 145) had called 'integration through voluntary segregation'.

In Africa, as in Birmingham, Gujaratis lived together. As in Birmingham, when they returned from the public world of work the African Gujarati men entered a house where only other Gujaratis lived, changed out of their work clothes into Gujarati garb, ate their regional diet, albeit adapted to locally available produce, spoke in Gujarati, performed *puja* (worship) to the *murtis* (idols) housed in the family *mandir*, and continued to eat food only with their right hands. As in Gujarat, and in Birmingham, Asians functioned as families, both at home and then at the weekends when for example Lohana families met each other for their regular picnics where large aluminium cooking pots full of *undhyu* (a Gujarati regional vegetarian stew) bubbled away as the women rolled out *rotlee* (chapattis), while the men played at tug-of-war. Just as Desai's frontiersmen kept their

Brummie neighbours at arms length, so too in Kenya and Uganda Gujaratis enjoyed circumscribed social relations with native Africans and with expat Europeans, the former kept as servants or employees, the white-skinned latter met at work, maybe later for a sundowner. There were, of course, differences between inter-racial contacts made by Gujarati men and women, between countries, and also by individuals, some of whom counted individual Africans and Europeans among their close friends but, crucially, not as relatives, for in Africa Gujaratis very rarely crossed the racial divide. Both Muslims and Hindus inter-married ethnic coreligionists, but crossing the racial divide threatened family dishonour and social ostracism. Initially, in the early days of the Indian-African chapter, it had been men who had migrated in the classic pattern of chain migration, and these single men would sometimes form liaisons with African women. The offspring of these mixed relationships numbered some 3,000 and lived chiefly in coastal towns or on Zanzibar (Bharati 1970), reflecting the earlier settlement of Indian migrants before the African hinterland was opened up by the Railway (see Keshodkar's chapter in this volume). As the Asian communities matured and women migrants joined their menfolk these earlier cross-racial affairs declined. Even innocuous inter-mixing could be scandalous, as the Ugandan-born journalist Yasmin Alibhai-Brown (1995) recalled when she was cast as Juliet to play alongside an African Romeo, a taboo also in force among Desai's frontiersmen; as Desai (1963: 27) observes, 'Indians regard any relationship with unrelated women as potentially sexual'. Gujarati businessmen might share a drink with an English colleague or a cigarette with an African employee (both drugs formerly culturally illicit, now presented as tokens of progressive Westernisation), but they did not share their daughters despite having lived, and quite possibly having been born, in the same African towns. Marriage marked the boundaries of integration and perpetuated the sociological lode that bound together the Gujarati families, binding families to their in-laws in related families, to their religious community and back to communities and kin in India.

The Gujaratis' chosen pattern of integration in Africa allowed many of them to lead comparatively secure and profitable lives, with the wealthy funding the building of community resources from the profits of their businesses. These concrete expressions of cultural achievement marked religious distinctions in the small community, as too did the religious divides in spouse selection, leading the African Asians to be divided among themselves, a division which grew as the community became wealthier. As long as British colonial rule continued, the Asians' strategy of integration through limited accommodation remained viable but with the rise of *uhuru*, the African version of *swaraj* (self-rule), this mode of living led to accusations that this highly visible though numerically small and divided community, which was comparatively wealthy, and included conspicuously rich families, had failed to integrate sufficiently. This accusation had several dimensions: Asians were perceived as unwilling to support the African political struggle, maybe becoming willing collaborators in the Europeans' colonial exploitation of Africans (Tangri 1966; Gregory 1981); in the economic sphere Asians were accused of sharp business practices, of remitting profits back to India rather than investing in Africa, and of excluding Africans from higher positions in their businesses; and, damningly, of not assimilating, of remaining socially aloof and discrete, a social distancing epitomised by the absence of mixed marriages, of mixed children, with no African and Asian families related one to another by love and law. It was to be this latter dimension of social distancing that Idi Amin, then the President of Uganda, exploited in his campaign to expel the Asians from Uganda, when for illustration in December 1971 speaking to the crowds gathered for an independence rally he said that the Asians: 'must come out and identify with Ugandan Africans. You must go with them and stop isolating yourselves .... I want to see Africans marrying Asians and vice versa. I will attend those weddings myself' (Okaya-Lakidi 1975: 96).

The actual truth of these social, economic and political accusations became irrelevant as independence soured and Kenya's new political leaders, though supportive of capitalism (Gupta 1998), began to squeeze Asians from the economy by restricting their work permits and commercial licenses, discouraging Asians from relinquishing their British citizenship in favour of Kenyan, and encouraging them to think instead of migration as preferable, migration in keeping with their assumed British citizenship. With the sudden arrival of the African Asians, the British Gujarati community grew significantly and at the same time was defined by the arrival of their fellow countrymen from East Africa where they had been living as a successful expat community until the winds of change swept away their prosperity and safety.

The first tranche of East African Asians arrived from Kenya at a time when immigration and 'race' relations had risen to prominence on the British political agenda, with persistent worries over 'race' relations and the politicisation of 'race' having prompted the Labour Party a couple of years earlier to introduce a Bill to enact anti-discrimination legislation, the 1965 *Race Relations Act*. Anti-discrimination legislation had long been in the minds of leading Labour politicians, manifest from at least 1958 when Lord Pakenham moved the Labour motion to debate 'Colour Prejudice and Violence'. Prejudice and violence were all too evident earlier that year in Nottingham and Notting Hill. These riots introduced 'race' relations to mainstream political discourse in Britain and eventually led the Conservative Party to introduce the first restrictions upon Commonwealth immigration, reactive restrictions that bedevilled the Kenyan Asian Crisis. In a 1958 House of Lord's debate the Labour peer Lord Pakenham had called for a Bill to outlaw what was then known as colour discrimination (HL Deb 1958: cc642–44). Seven years later, and a year after they returned to power, albeit with a perilously slender majority, Labour kept its manifesto promise and moved Britain's first anti-discrimination bill. In the second reading of this bill in parliament the debate raised issues that would come to be added to the existing political agenda on 'race' relations, the agenda which also included the topic of integration.

In the second reading of the *Race Relations Bill*, some of those present were puzzled by the use of the category 'ethnic', the members of which, along with those classifiable by 'colour' and 'race', were intended to be protected from discrimination in the provision of public services by the new legislation. The Conservative MP Anthony Buck interrupted the introduction of the debate to question the meaning of this novel category, soon to be joined by his fellow Conservative Bernard Braine inquiring whether the proposed Act would protect British Jews whom, up to that point, had not been classified as an 'ethnic group' (HC Deb 1965: cc932–33). In addition to questioning the exact meaning and membership criteria for this novel category, the opposition also questioned the wisdom of extending criminal, public law to cover what previously had been considered private civil matters and they argued strongly that the proposed legislation threatened the cherished, long-standing right of Britons to free speech (ibid.: c948 and passim). By the time the bill was passed into law, Labour, then in power with a bare majority of just four seats, had been forced to concede to the opposition's demand that violation of the Act would be a civil rather than criminal legal offence but the positioning of the divide between the public and the private areas of British life, anxieties over threats to private freedoms, and the wisdom of classifying some sections of British citizenship in ethnic terms became standing items on the political agenda on immigration, and also informed the debate over the issue of integration.

By 1976, four years after the refugees from Uganda had arrived, the final group of East African Asians from Malawi joined those already settled in Britain. 1976 was also marked by the passing of the *Community Relations Act*, a further Labour measure intended to widen the scope of anti-discrimination legislation, and by a significant research study (Anwar 1976) concerning issues affecting the upcoming generation of young Asians raised in Britain. This study was initiated by the concerns of elders in the Asian community and the study's central theme, that Asian youngsters were finding 'living between two cultures' problematic, was taken up by James Watson in an edited collection of essays under the title *Between Two Cultures* (1977) and although this research focus would soon become contested (Brah 1996; Mukadam 2003) the theme entered into the public discourse over the integration of minority ethnic communities. A new agenda of research and political measures was being written as the topics of immigration and racialist discrimination were joined by issues arising from the growth of settled British Asian communities, communities now coming routinely to be classified under the rubric of ethnicity, a categorical triumph secured in 1991 when for the first time all Britons were legally obliged to classify themselves in ethnic terms on their census returns. The 'new agenda' grew and developed as unexpected events such as the riots in Brixton and Liverpool in the early 1980s, or in the Northern cities twenty years later, demanded a public political response, as too did the equally unexpected ebbs and flows of migration with net migration starting, from 1983, to become positive in first faltering but then widening annual steps as new national immigrant groups and asylum seekers joined or numerically superseded the old black and Asian Commonwealth inflows. However, none of the new agenda items – for instance, the episodic riots, the generational issues, anti-asylum sentiment and rhetoric, opposition to new EU migrants, vacillations over multi-culturalism, British-born terrorists, political moves against immigration, etc. – were referenced to either British Hindus nor to British Gujaratis. In fact, as I have noted in another publication (Mattausch 2012), there has been only one occasion when British Hindus have taken to the streets of Britain to speak up for what they perceived to be their rights, when the International Society for Krishna Consciousness was defending their British headquarters at Bhaktivedanta Manor (a present from George Harrison in 1973) against the local council's plans. Indeed British Hinduism, and British Hindus, the majority of whom are Gujarati, are seldom mentioned in British newspapers or political discourse, as the Runnymede Trust noted when publishing in 2006 the findings of research commissioned by the Hindu Forum of Britain and the Government's Department for Communities and Local Government, although Hindus formed the third largest religious community in Britain 'we know remarkably little about them, their needs, or experiences' (Runnymede Trust 2006: 3).

When British Hindus do come to wider attention then it is invariably favourable; they are routinely presented as a welcome, prosperous, culturally enriching British minority community, their religion seen as non-threatening, their religious festivals supported by the local councils in towns and cities where they live in significant number. It would seem that British Gujarati Hindus have, like Desai's (1963) Parsi refugees, sweetened the national water, and like the Parsis have done so not by assimilating but by becoming 'integrated through voluntary segregation' (Desai 1963: 145). The findings from the Runnymede Trust's report, *Connecting British*

Hindus, gives a picture of British Hindus which in many ways echoes the communities formed by Desai's (1963) frontiersmen in 1960s' Birmingham, and also by the East African Asian communities; whereas 89 per cent of this study's research sample reported feeling either 'mostly' or 'completely' integrated in English society (Runnymede Trust 2006: 24), there had been by 2001 negligible inter-marriage with 97 per cent of Britain's 558,342 Hindus declaring they were Asian/British Asian in the 2001 census, with 93 per cent, of those who were married, having a co-religionist spouse (at the time of writing, comparable data had not yet been released from the 2011 census). This low level of mixed marriages may be accounted for by the high proportion of foreign-born Hindus (63 per cent of the report's sample) (ibid.: 14) and by the nature of Hindu religious identity, for given that Hinduism is an ascribed religion and that by custom women take on the caste of their husband's family, 'marrying out' may involve considerable personal, as well as familial costs but nonetheless the fact that British Gujarati Hindus have not in any number moved outside the Hindu fold is symptomatic of their accommodation to British society being restricted to the public sphere. In this capitalistic public sphere Gujarati Hindus have, as I have already observed (Mattausch 1998), been strikingly successful within a very short period. In the forty years since the arrival of Ugandan Asians, building upon the earlier arrival of Kenyan Asians, they had laid the foundations for the British Gujarati ascent from among the poorest to one of the wealthiest British minority ethnic communities. Research carried out by the Policy Studies Institute (Brown 1984) showed that merely within a decade, between 1974 and 1984, East African Asians, many of whom had arrived traumatised and penniless, were now among the best economically performing British 'black' groups. Twenty years later, the Runnymede Trust's (2006) research findings showed British Hindus were outperforming the majority of Britons in terms of educational qualifications; in their occupations (More than one in three Hindus in employment is in professional or senior management positions [Runnymede Trust 2006: 19]); and in terms of home ownership. This remarkably rapid rise to prosperity was made possible, I have argued (Mattausch 2012), by chance opportunities becoming available when East African Asians arrived in Britain, in particular opportunities to buy small businesses, in the early days often small Confectioner-Tobacconist-Newsagent cornershops, opportunities eagerly exploited by Asians who had already known success in the trying context of East Africa, who could draw upon family labour from within families who had often arrived intact from East Africa, and who placed great store upon self-employment, for the Gujarati Vaniya castes a mark of identity achievement. Desai's pioneer frontiersmen, if they were self-employed were small shopowners or hawkers catering exclusively for their own immigrant community. But, as I have noted elsewhere (ibid. 2007), East African Asians quickly moved their businesses out from ethnic niches toward a diverse customer base, and younger generations of British Gujaratis, capitalising on those impressive educational qualifications, moved out from behind their parents' cornershop counters and into a wide range of occupations, with British Gujaratis now found in all professions, in many, many kinds of businesses, and in a wide range of public and professional positions. Just as in East Africa, their wealth has funded the building of religious and community resources, resources they have built for themselves drawing upon their ethic of community self-sufficiency as the Runnymede report noted (2006: 20): 'Participants were also proud to report the successes of their communities in organising support for themselves. This self-sufficiency was a source of pride and frustration at the lack of support from outside their own immediate community. The levels of contributions, both financial and otherwise, to set up temples and community centres have been impressive in a relatively short space of time'.

In the round and on many fronts, British Gujarati Hindus are a successful British minority ethnic community and they feel well integrated in British society; in fact, British South Asians reportedly feel more integrated than white Britons in their neighbourhood:

> There were differences in sense of belonging by ethnicity. Asian groups were more likely than other ethnic groups to feel a strong sense of belonging to their neighbourhood. Bangladeshi (88%), Pakistani (83%) and Indian (81%) people felt a stronger sense of belonging to their neighbourhood than White (77%), Black Caribbean (76%), Black African (74%),

> Other ethnicity (72%), Chinese (70%) and Mixed Race (69%) people. There was little variation in terms of strength of belonging to Britain among these groups. (HM Department of Communities and Local Government 2012: 35)

Furthermore, if integration is measured, like ethnicity, in terms of values, then African Asians hold to values largely indistinguishable from the majority of white Britons, as my re-analysis of the data presented in chapter nine of the 4th PSI report (Modood et al. 1997) indicates (Mattausch 2000). In the case of modern Britain, the issue of values has special eminence because it has been shared values that has come to be presented as the hallmark of integration, with those minority ethnic groups, especially some British South Asian Muslims, who are subject to political and media identification as not sufficiently integrated being thought of as not sharing 'core' national British values. Indeed, British citizenship too has come to be defined in terms of values. British citizenship was not defined legally until 1981 with the passing of the *British Nationality Act*. However, this legal definition, as politicians soon realised, lacked substance and meaning and this lacuna came to be filled, by politicians of all persuasions, with talk of national values, as this excerpt from a speech given by Tony Blair in 2006 signalling his retreat from multiculturalism in the wake of the 7 July 2005 London bombings, illustrates: 'Integration, in this context, is not about culture or lifestyle. It is about values. It is about integrating at the point of shared, common unifying British values. It isn't about what defines us as people, but as citizens, the rights and duties that go with being a member of our society' (Blair 2006). Blair's emphasis upon 'common unifying British values,' along with his disavowal of multiculturalism, has been echoed by the current Coalition Prime Minister David Cameron (see, for example, his Munich speech given in February 2012), and it is values which now take strategic centre stage in Coalition integrationist policies:

> Our history and our shared values mean we are better placed than many other countries to meet the challenges of integration. We believe that core values and experience must be held in common. We should be robustly promoting British values such as democracy, rule of law, equality of opportunity

> and treatment, freedom of speech and the rights of all men and women to live free from persecution of any kind. It is these values which make it possible for people to live and work together, to bridge boundaries between communities and to play a full role in society. (HM Department for Communities and Local Government 2012a)

Nowadays, both integration and citizenship are measured and defined by value adherence and once again British Gujarati Hindus do well, they are both well integrated and are seen to be good citizens. And yet, they have sweetened the waters of British national life, not by assimilating in the conventional sense of adopting British customs and sharing values at the expense of their Gujarati identity, but rather by their fortuitous placement in the British public/private polity, which permits their religious culture to be sustained, without being troublesome to the wider British community.

As I noted earlier, when discussing the second reading of the *Race Relations Bill* in 1965, a concern to demarcate strictly the boundaries between public and private sectors, joined to an often fierce defence of private freedoms, has long been a feature of the discourse over migration and citizenship in Britain: *plus ça change*. Modood (2003) has argued that a key reason British Muslims are perceived as insufficiently integrated, and as a problematic community, lies in their wish to have equality with other citizens understood not in the traditional British sense of equality in the public sphere with differences permitted in the private, but rather 'the right to have one's "difference" (minority ethnicity, etc.) recognised and supported in both the public and private spheres' (ibid.: 105). By transgressing the orthodox distinction between the public and the private Muslims are set on a hazardous political path paved with potential conflicts over religious and secular values, for by demanding public equality they are demanding that other non-Muslim Britons accept their values (for obvious example, over the limits to free speech).[4] Whereas, in contrast, British Gujarati Hindus, by following their strategy of successful integration in the public sphere while practising what Desai (1963: 145) termed 'voluntary segregation' in the private sphere have managed to avoid the stigmatisation landed upon some British Muslim communities while retaining their cultural legacy.

In conclusion, it may be worth pausing to consider the reasons for the persistence of this profitable form of Gujarati Hindu integration through voluntary segregation. One simple explanation for the persistence of this strategy is to be found in the history of Gujarat. It was only in 1960, that Gujarat emerged in its current form as a state, thirteen years after India had declared itself a republic, freeing the Gujarat region from six and a half centuries of foreign paramountcies. Gujaratis had not developed a public polity comparable to that which had emerged in European nation states by the time the British, in the early eighteenth century, first began their move from merchant capitalists to paramountcy in the region as the East India Company men started to sign treaties with local rulers and then, in 1759, accepted an invitation to provide security for merchants trading at Surat (Copland 1982; Torri 1998). In neither the geographically small area under direct governance from the Bombay Presidency, one-seventh of the region[5] comprising the prosperous bangle of Ahmedabad, Kaira, Bharuch and Surat that were designated British Districts, nor in the 300 or so native kingdoms and fiefdoms covering sixth-sevenths of the region, which the British demoted to the status of 'Princely/Native States', was there a secular regional identity or ambition which could have overridden the parochial feelings of belonging to a particular religious community and a specific locality. Yagnik and Sheth (2005) have claimed that Gujaratis had long enjoyed a commonality owing to their common language, but this linguistic fellowship did not find public, political expression until Gujaratis and Gujarat fell under British suzerainty. Only toward the end of the nineteenth century, when literate westernised Gujarati elites, many clustered on Bombay (Mallison 2007), began to write their own history (Isaka 2006; Shukla 2007), and the introduction of British technologies such as the railways, the telegraph and the postal service overran the borders of districts and kingdoms, might we say that a regional Gujarati political identity began to emerge. This is not to imply that the development of modern public life always lagged behind the British Gujarati Districts to the same degree, in fact the Gujarati Native States were in every way diverse and the most advanced, for example Baroda, could boast a public polity rivalling, or bettering that found in the British Districts wherein foreign rule excluded Indians from complete political participation. In fact, it was to be the oppositional 'Indian' identity championed by the nationalist movement which became precious, not least for Gandhi, but by the time that the British left India Gujaratis had been established in East Africa for half a century and had not exported the nationalist cause alongside their religious, village-kin sentiments. In East Africa, Gujaratis did not figure as anti-British freedom fighters.

In a sense, Gujarati migrants are living in ways familiar to all expats the world over, hanging on to their native customs, their old religion, their diet and dress – much the same as do many of the 4.7 million or so British citizens living abroad (Osborne 2012); for example the 808,000 Britons living in Spain, eating fish and chips, drinking beer, going to church on high days and holy days, housed in sun-bleached expat settlements dotted along the coast. Unlike the millions of expat Britons however, Gujaratis in the UK are preserving, not just native dress, diet, etc., but also the family basis to their culture, the sociological lode, and in this sense their voluntary segregation differs from that of Britons in Marbella, for the orthodox distinction between the public and the private conceived the latter in terms of private individuals, individuals protecting their right to live their lives as they saw fit with the state sovereign only in the public sphere. This western, individualised dual polity had not developed in Gujarat and in the Gujarati migrant version the private became home to their family-based culture, not to a family of individuals. It has been this unorthodox, fortuitous version of the public/private distinction that has supported the many achievements of British Gujarati Hindus, allowing them to sweeten the waters of British life while simultaneously maintaining their native identity. In contradistinction to current political thinking, British Gujarati Hindus have successfully integrated precisely by not assimilating, by not sharing 'core' national values.

NOTES

1. The term 'Asian' will be used throughout this chapter to refer to South Asians.
2. This prohibition on crossing the *kalipani*, which Gandhi as a young man chose to disregard so that he could pursue his legal career, may have rather prosaic functional origins and, like all Hindu practices

form part of a Behavioural Immune System that has evolved to protect the health of Hindus (Mattausch 2012, 2012a).

3. For a detailed history of the rise of an African Asian family firm from small beginnings to an international business, see Oonk (2009).
4. It should be noted that this perception should not be taken to be a general statement pertinent to all Muslim communities in Britain.
5. In 1861 British Gujarat was expanded when the Panch Mahal, previously ruled by the Scindia Maratha clan, was taken over by the Bombay Presidency. In geographical terms this expanded British Gujarat from 1/7th to 1/6th of the region.

REFERENCES

Alibhai-Brown, Yasmin. *No Place Like Home: An Autobiography*, London: Virago, 1995.

Anwar, Michael. *Between Two Cultures: A Study of Relationships between Generations in the Asian Community in Britain*, London: Community Relations Council, 1976.

Bharati, Agehananda. 'A Social Survey', in *Portrait of a Minority: The Asians of East Africa*, edited by Dharam Ghai and Yash Ghai, Chicago: Nelson Hall, 1970, pp. 15–67.

——. 'Ritualistic Tolerance and Ideological Rigour: The Paradigm of the Expatriate Hindus in East Africa', *Contributions to Indian Sociology*, Vol. 10, No. 2 (1976): 317–39.

Blair, Tony. Lecture given on the 18th of December 2006 in Downing Street, <http://*news.bbc.co.uk/2/hi/uk_news/politics/6219626.stm*> (18 January 2012).

Brah, Avtar. *Cartographies of Diaspora: Contesting Identities*, London: Routledge, 1996.

Brown, Colin. *Black and White Britain: The Third PSI Survey*, London: Heinemann, 1984.

Copland, Ian. *The British Raj and the Indian Princes*, Bombay: Orient Longman, 1982.

Desai, Rashmi. *Indian Immigrants in Britain*, Oxford: Oxford University Press, 1963.

Gregory, Robert. 'Co-operation and Collaboration in Colonial East Africa: The Asians' Political Role, 1890–1964', *African Affairs*, Vol. 80, No. 319 (1981): 259–73.

Gupta, Desh. 'South Asians in East Africa: Achievement and Discrimination', *South Asia* (Special Issue), Vol. XXI (1998): 103–36.

Hansen, Randall. 'The Kenyan Asians, British Politics, and the Commonwealth Immigrants Act, 1968', *The Historical Journal*, Vol. 42, No. 3 (1999): 809–34.

HC Deb. 3 May 1965. Vol. 711: cc 932–33.

HL Deb. 19 November 1958. Vol. 212: cc 642–44.

HM Department for Communities and Local Government. *Creating the Conditions for Integration*, February 2012.

——. *Community Spirit in England: A Report on the 2009–10 Citizenship Survey*, 2012a.

Isaka, Riho. 'Gujarati Elites and the Construction of a Regional Identity in the Late Nineteenth Century', in *Beyond Representation: Colonial and Postcolonial Constructions of Indian Identity*, edited by Crispin Bates, Oxford: Oxford University Press, 2006, pp. 151–76.

Mallison, Françoise. 'Bombay as the Intellectual Capital of the Gujaratis', in *Bombay: Mosaic of Modern Culture*, edited by Sujata Patel and Alice Thorner, New Delhi: Oxford University Press, 2007, pp. 76–87.

Mattausch, John. 'With Whom May British Gujaratis Identify, to Whom May they be Compared?', in *Gujarati Communities across the Globe: Memory, Identity and Continuity*, edited by Sharmina Mawani and Anjoom A. Mukadam, London: Trentham Books, 2012, pp. 27–42.

——. 'Gandhi's Prescription: Health and Hygiene in the Struggle for *Swaraj*', Paper presented at the 4th meeting of the Gujarat Studies Association, Dubai, February 2012a.

——. 'Unsettled Citizens? British South Asians', Paper presented at the 22nd meeting European Conference on South Asian Studies, ISCTE-Lisbon University Institute, July 2012b.

——. 'A Chance Diaspora: British Gujarati Hindus', in *Global Indian Diasporas: Exploring Trajectories of Migration and Theory*, edited by Gijsbert Oonk, Amsterdam: Amsterdam University Press, 2007, pp. 149–66.

——. 'A Case of Mistaken Identity: Why British 'African Asians' are Not an 'Ethnic' Community', *South Asia Research*, Vol. 20, No. 2 (2000): 171–81.

——. 'From Subjects to Citizens: British East African Asians', *Journal of Ethnic and Migration Studies*, Vol. 24 (1998): 121–42.

Michaelson, Maureen. 'The Relevance of Caste among East African Gujaratis in Britain', *New Community*, Vol. 11, No. 3 (1979): 350–60.

Modood, Tariq et al. (eds). *Ethnic Minorities in Britain: Diversity and Disadvantage*, London: PSI, 1997.

Modood, Tariq. 'Muslims and the Politics of Difference', *The Political Quarterly*, Vol. 74 (2003): 100–15.

Mukadam, Anjoom A. 'Gujarati Speakers in London: Age, Gender and Religion in the Construction of Identity', Unpublished PhD Thesis, University of Reading, 2003.

Osborne, Hilary. 'Where do UK Expats Live?', *The Guardian*, 26 November 2012.

Okaya-Lakidi, Dent. 'Black Attitudes to the Brown and White Colonisers of East Africa', in *Expulsion of a Minority: Essays on Ugandan Asians*, edited by Mike Twaddle, London: Athlone Press, 1975, pp. 81–97.

Oonk, Gijsbert. *The Karimjee Jivanjee Family: Merchant Princes of East Africa, 1800–2000*, Amsterdam: Pallas Publications, 2009.

——. 'Negotiating Hinduism in East Africa, 1860–1960', *Transforming Cultures eJournal*, Vol. 3, No. 2 (2008), <http://epress.lib.uts.edu.au/journals/TfC> (10 January 2012).

Runnymede Trust. *Connecting British Hindus: An Enquiry into the Identity and Public Policy Engagement of British Hindus*, London: Hindu Forum of Britain, 2006.

Shukla, Sonal. 'Gujarati Cultural Revivalism', in *Bombay: Mosaic of Modern Culture*, edited by Sujata Patel and Alice Thorner, New Delhi: Oxford University Press, 2007, pp. 88–98.

Tangri, Roger. 'Asians in Kenya: A Political History', *Africa Quarterly*, Vol. 6, No. 2 (1966): 107–27.

Torri, Michelguglielmo. 'Mughal Nobles, Indian Merchants and the Beginnings of British Conquest in Western India: The Case of Surat 1756–1759', *Modern Asian Studies*, Vol. 32, No. 2 (1998): 257–315.

Twaddle, Michael (ed.). *Expulsion of a Minority: Essays on Ugandan Asians*, London: Athlone Press, 1975.

Watson, James (ed.). *Between Two Cultures: Migrants and Minorities in Britain*, Oxford: Basil Blackwell, 1977.

Yagnik, Achyut and Suchitra Sheth. *The Shaping of Modern Gujarat: Plurality, Hindutva and Beyond*, New Delhi: Penguin, 2005.

CHAPTER 10

A Religious Education Curriculum

Addressing the Challenges Faced by Canadian Adolescents of Gujarati Ancestry

Shezeleen Kanji

Why is it that I don't seem to be able to feel a part of the fabric of the Canadian landscape that boasts inclusivity and multiculturalism? As an Ismaili Muslim religious education teacher, questions like this are often posed to me by the high school students that I teach, who wonder why they continue to be victims of discrimination based on phenotype, as did their parents and grandparents when they initially migrated to Canada. This chapter explores the potential of a religious education (RE) curriculum, *Ethical Pathways to Human Development,*[1] in helping to address social challenges such as discrimination[2] faced by Canadian Nizari Ismaili Muslim students,[3] of whom a significant percentage are of Gujarati ancestry.[4] This chapter will provide a context in which the new RE curriculum for the teaching of Ismaili secondary students has been introduced. Additionally, it will outline different components of a curriculum generally, as well as the role of the teacher in contextualising the curriculum and providing examples of cultural links to students' Gujarati ancestry, guided by intended aims and outcomes. This chapter will illustrate how the curriculum employs a universal perspective of achieving peaceful co-existence by including content about the ethics and values underpinning Islam, including aspects of citizenship education, understanding of human rights and cosmopolitanism. The curriculum aims to complement the values of mainstream society with those seen as essential to Islam and Ismailism. Following exposure to the curriculum, students have begun to openly express elements of their Gujarati identity while also learning to respond to discrimination through the use of an ethical framework.

OVERVIEW OF THE CANADIAN CONTEXT

Canada and Multiculturalism

Canada is a country that is viewed as exemplary in terms of its multi-ethnic and multicultural composition. Toronto is the largest city in Canada and comprises a large South Asian community. As a country that is made up of diverse cultures and ethnicities, Canada has a Multiculturalism Act that seeks to 'assist ethno-cultural minority communities to conduct activities with a view to overcoming any discriminatory barrier and, in particular, discrimination based on race or national or ethnic origin' (Government of Canada 1988). In spite of the initiation of this Act since 1988, Ismaili[5] secondary students in grades seven to ten in Toronto have expressed in class how they continue to experience or witness issues emanating from discrimination which surround their social and educational environment. In Canada, Ismailis are seen to be 'visible minorities'. According to the 2001 census (Statistics Canada 2008), visible minority is a term used in Canada to refer to ethnic minorities, which would include the students that are part of this study. For these students, this label can be traced back to the time when their parents and grandparents initially arrived in Canada and where their immigrant status deemed them a minority 'race' in relation to the white majority.

Migration of Ismailis to Canada from East Africa

In the early 1970s a large number of Gujarati families found themselves suddenly displaced almost overnight by then Ugandan President Idi Amin, who ordered the expulsion of all Asians from Uganda (Twaddle 1975). These once prominent and thriving Gujarati families lost most of their belongings and almost immediately found themselves migrating as refugees headed to unknown lands with the hope of a safe future. Canada was one of the countries that received these refugees (Pereira et al. 1978). Forty years later, the children and grandchildren of these Gujarati immigrants continue to experience forms of discrimination which has led to issues of low self-esteem, isolation and identity crisis (Raby 2004; Mawani 2006; Richardson 2009). Even though they are born and raised in Canada, they are still classified as part of the visible minorities of Canada and are viewed as immigrants (Mawani 2006). If in the secular school environment these individuals have not found a sense of belonging, then this raises the question of the role that RE can play in helping to address these issues.

Religious Education Classes

The Religious Education (RE) system for Ismailis in Canada was formally established to facilitate the teaching of RE to students from kindergarten to the secondary level after the early Ismaili settlers migrated to Canada in the 1970s. Currently the RE system is implemented by the Ismaili Tariqah and Religious Education Board (ITREB), which is run by both voluntary and full-time paid management and academic personnel. This RE system is deemed as supplementary education (Osler and Vincent 2002) as it falls outside the scheduled secular school times and students participate on a voluntary basis.

Since the early 1990s the primary RE system has been taught using curriculum materials developed by the Institute of Ismaili Studies (IIS) in London, United Kingdom. Operating across six regions in Canada, Ismaili students attend these classes once a week, usually at the weekend, for approximately two and a half to three hours and have the opportunity to learn about, and express their identity in various ways while feeling a sense of belonging within the Ismaili community. In Canada, the RE system is termed Bait-ul Ilm (BUI) meaning 'house of knowledge.' The entire primary and secondary system is overseen by the full-time national Academic Director who works with an educational team as well as the ITREB Canada governance board to guide the implementation of the RE programme from kindergarten to Grade 12. Each city has part-time or full-time Professional Teacher Educators (PTE) who train voluntary RE teachers at the primary school level to implement the content and appropriate pedagogical strategies in the classroom. Each primary classroom across the country is staffed by volunteers who provide their personal time to teach young students once a week. The primary RE classes are taught using the *Ta'lim* curriculum developed by the Department of Curriculum Studies at the IIS. The aim of the programme 'is to educate students in the faith, history and cultures of Muslim societies, and of the Ismaili Muslim community in particular' (IIS 2010b: 6). The *Ta'lim* curriculum draws on modern principles in education presented through various teaching materials and has been translated into eight languages including Gujarati.[6] The primary *Ta'lim* curriculum is divided into three teaching levels: pre-school, lower primary and upper primary and is taught using a thematic approach seeking to provide a foundation of RE through the introduction of basic principles and content around Islamic beliefs, ethics, history and culture (ibid.).

Prior to 2009, the secondary system was also overseen by the national board and senior personnel mentioned above. The instructional content for the secondary curriculum was developed by academic personnel, including curriculum writers at the national ITREB level, as the IIS had not yet produced secondary level materials. Like the PTE role for the primary sector, the secondary system had Secondary Teacher Educators (STE), who, by profession, were secular teachers and whose role was to equip volunteer secondary teachers with teaching strategies to implement the content in the classrooms.

In 2007, Aga Khan IV introduced the Secondary Teacher Education Programme (STEP), a joint endeavour between the IIS and the Institute of Education, University of London. The programme was originally piloted in five countries (Mukadam 2012) and has now expanded to include students from thirteen countries. The aim of STEP is to cultivate an international cadre of professionally qualified RE teachers to facilitate the teaching of the IIS' secondary curriculum (SC) for secondary level Ismaili students worldwide. Individuals accepted onto this two-year double Masters scholarship programme obtain a Master of Teaching (MTeach) and a Master of Arts in Education (Muslim Societies and Civilisations), gaining knowledge in subject matter pertaining to the SC, as well as insights and understanding of pedagogic practices. In 2009, the first group of professional teachers returned to Canada having graduated from the double Masters programme. With the continuing aid of support staff at the management and board level, these teachers are in the process of transforming a system once run by voluntary teachers into a system with full-time professionally trained secondary RE teachers.

The SC's philosophical principles employ a humanistic, civilisational and normative perspective to the study of Islam, providing a tapestry with which the richness and diversity of the Muslim world, both past and present, is explored. The SC builds and extends on the primary *Ta'lim* and 'explores Islam as both faith and civilisation in world history and in contemporary times. The content is drawn from the general Islamic context and the normative perspective of the Shia Ismaili Tariqah' (IIS 2010b: 7). The SC consists of eight curricula to be taught over a four-year period and is organised into thematic areas: *Muslim Societies and Civilisations, Cultural Encounters, Muslims in the Contemporary World, Intellectual Traditions, The Literature of Muslim Traditions and Cultures, Faith and Practice, The Qur'an and Its Interpretations, and Ethical Pathways to Human Development.*[7] The latter will be the focus of this chapter and will seek to explore how specific examples within this particular curriculum could help address challenges, such as discrimination, faced by students.

Each module mentioned above consists of a Student Reader and a Teacher's Guide; some modules also contain a Student Workbook. The Student Reader comprises the core content divided into three units with three explorations per unit, exploration summaries, objectives, key messages, visuals, age appropriate questions and further links to references. The Teacher's Guide complements the student reader by providing an overview of the philosophical principles and aims of the curriculum, pedagogical approaches, ideas for parental involvement, guides on using the supplementary materials, questioning techniques, and suggested ways to explore the text, including lesson ideas for teachers. The Student Workbook supplements the Student Reader with activities for students which relate to the subject matter.

Producing a curricular repertoire of materials to fit an international scope of students, rather than a national or localised curriculum already familiar to students from their daily secular school arena, poses certain challenges. In the diverse countries where this curriculum is taught there are various religious, political, social and economic sensitivities that need consideration when creating the curriculum and its related resources. Requiring a global universality would mean that the curriculum has to be broad enough to include relevant examples from multiple contexts. This breadth provides less structure for teachers, and allows for more flexibility for them to contextualise the content to the local context, thereby making the subject matter more relevant to students' everyday lives. This results in a fluid and dynamic curriculum, which is continuously being developed to suit the various RE contexts, as well as the differentiated learning needs of the students.

ROLE OF THE CURRICULUM

Broad Vision of Curriculum

As mentioned above, a curriculum is not simply confined to the text. To be effective it requires subject matter knowledge, pedagogical content knowledge (Shulman 1986) and an understanding of students' various learning abilities, as well as the physiological, emotional and social milieus surrounding their own frames of reference. A curriculum is written with the intention of representing a particular vision. Broadly speaking it is a living document designed, developed, implemented, assessed, evaluated and revised with the purpose of nurturing particular skills and competencies. These skills and competencies are usually underpinned by central values that students would obtain through various learning experiences set within a particular framework and wider context (UNESCO 2012). Information shared with students through textbooks and student readers provides a wealth of content information such as facts, figures, historical narratives, and powerful images, which can encompass a certain aspect of learning. This is one feature in ensuring quality education. However, the implementation process and the art of teaching the material is equally, if not more, important. The teacher has a vital role in trying to make the text come alive in a way that resonates with the world of the student and engages them in the process of learning. The role of the teacher is also to make connections between ideas as well as adding newer ideas or subject concepts to an existing repertoire of students' ideas, but also challenging perspectives (Ball and Bass 2000). This requires teachers to have the flexibility and creativity in integrating all areas of such knowledge into classroom interactions, discussions and worldviews; therefore, pedagogical approaches are as critical to this process as students' voices. Educational theorists, such as Dewey (1938) and Vygotsky (1978), looked at how students actively construct their understanding through the idea of student-centred learning. This type of learning moves students away from being merely passive recipients in education to active participants in the classroom by engaging in enquiry processes, constructing their own learning together with classmates and bringing in their prior knowledge and experience from varied contexts into the classroom space to be both deconstructed and reconstructed. In this manner, skills and competencies that speak to the larger curricular objectives come alive organically.

Turning to the BUI context, the *Ethical Pathways to Human Development* curriculum consists of a Student Reader with an intended vision of engaging students in issues of social development and its consequential global impact on economic, cultural, social, educational and health related areas. The content makes reference to social and ethical challenges that have been faced in the past and that continue to be faced today. The curriculum is designed around a series of educational aims, values and outlooks, as well as skills and competencies. These ideas are presented through the Readers' content material consisting of text, visuals, narratives, and questions that probe further thinking which are all powerful ways for students to understand content and feel a part of the narratives presented. The text helps connect students with their heritage, including the countries, cultures and lifestyles of their ancestors. The values inherent in this Reader assist students to realise the spiritual and ethical ideals that underpin the concept of development and the idea of being ethical beings, which is central to Islam, regardless of 'race', gender, ethnicity, culture and socio-economic status. It is a way to re-invigorate and appreciate their past while also breathing new hope into a future where the sanctity of the human being is valued in all its aspects. Education cannot be looked at in isolation from social factors. This curriculum provides students with a foundational understanding of what it means to live Islam, even within the classroom milieu. Hence, the BUI classroom experience is meant to provide a sense of community, a place of belonging and opportunities for students to grow in various skill sets. Working collaboratively, a skill set built into the curriculum, where learning how to engage with difference is the norm, provides an evolutionary process in helping to prepare students, not solely as Canadian citizens, but as global citizens, as they learn to appreciate diversity in thought, and different cultural and religious contexts, while engendering values of tolerance and respect (IIS 2010b).

With any curriculum, as previously mentioned, the teacher plays a vital role. The teaching style in BUI advocates for a student-centred approach valuing experiences, interests and contributions of each student while encouraging creative expression. Hence, student voice is an integral part of the teaching and learning process and the teacher must find ways to integrate the narrative of the content with the questions and realities raised by students, while at the same time retaining tradition and celebrating culture. How can a teacher create relevancy and make the curriculum come alive? Crucial to this question is understanding the context of the students, as well as their outlooks and the daily challenges they may face, such as living within a diverse society, and negotiating how to preserve their culture within a rapidly changing cultural landscape.

Contextualising content for students helps them to find and create meaning as well as provide an interrelatedness of ideas and actions (Johnson 2002). One significant aim of the curriculum is 'to create a positive sense of identity in students, and to inspire in them self-confidence and self-worth' (IIS 2010b: 13). As teachers, it is important to ensure that students do not feel that aspects of their identity are marginalised. In fact, supplementing the curriculum content by providing cultural specific examples that draw on the students' cultural ancestry helps to reinforce their identity while at the same time educating them to live an ethical life. The content in the *Ethical Pathways to Human Development* curriculum draws on ethical examples rooted in the Quran, and historical examples of how Prophet Muhammad's teachings and actions reflect the ethical spirit of Islam. Furthermore, Aga Khan IV has set up institutions such as the Aga Khan Development Network (AKDN), which is a contemporary endeavour to realise the social conscience of Islam through action where 'the ethical message of Islam can be translated into practical action for the well-being of all humanity' (IIS 2010a: 51). Its work exemplifies ethical service and generosity towards others regardless of faith, nationality or background (IIS 2000). The essence underpinning the historical and contemporary examples are considered timeless and can no doubt be applied to the challenges students face in contemporary times.

The following examples illustrate how I have highlighted this essence from the content in the curriculum in my classrooms using cultural specific examples to help students create links to their ancestral culture. At the same time, my role as the teacher has been to apply the essence of the content in a manner that will equip students to deal with challenges, such as discrimination, using an ethical framework that is grounded in their Islamic value system. The curriculum advocates that culture is core to human life and explains culture as being 'all around us, in the food we eat, the clothes we wear, the music we love, and the books we read. We find it in ... our language' (IIS 2010a: 70). Culture provides value and meaning in the lives of individuals. Throughout the curriculum, images of men and women in various parts of the world, including South Asia, Central Asia, the Middle East and Africa, help to display an array of traditional clothing and ways of life, including diverse occupations, such as agriculture, while taking into account harsh seasonal climates in various parts of the world (ibid.: 89).

Several examples relate to the Gujarati ancestry of many of the students. One image (ibid.: 67) depicts women from Kutch in a newly constructed house following a devastating earthquake where contemporary programmes emanating from the AKDN have helped communities in that area to rebuild their lives and achieve a better quality of life. Through these examples, while students cannot visualise the type of environment and culture that made up the everyday lives of their ancestors, it does, however, give them an overview of the work being done by the AKDN in the areas that form a link to the students' own ancestral culture. As a teacher, I have encouraged my students to use this opportunity to ask their parents and grandparents to convey personal narratives about their past. Drawing on various aspects of my students' ancestry, I have incorporated elements of their ancestral culture into my classrooms by building on the narratives conveyed by their families, thus creating more engaging and relevant lessons. The essence of such images from Gujarat teaches students about their ethical duty to help reconstruct the lives of others as modelled with the Aga Khan Planning and Building Services programme under the AKDN, exhibiting a contemporary example of extending help and generosity. Reconstruction does not have to be limited to restoring a physical building once someone loses their home; rather, the essence of the example from Kutch can be looked at in relation to the reconstruction of societies to help improve the quality of life of all its members. This idea is also supported by the example of the Prophet noted in the curriculum: 'he [Prophet Muhammad] drew attention to the needs of people who required help and care, and tried to lessen their suffering. He urged those who were wealthy and powerful not to ignore the poor and the defenceless' (ibid.: 34). In parallel to the Prophet's message, as stated earlier in the chapter, students continue to feel a sense of inferiority and defencelessness due to being discriminated against, which can be attributed to social and cultural inequalities that have arisen out of globalisation (Bovill and Leppard 2006). The content speaks about the effect of globalisation on culture including an increased interaction between peoples of different religious and cultural backgrounds. Even though we come from different backgrounds, Ismailis have been guided to 'understand and respect the faiths and cultures of different communities' (IIS 2010a: 127) so that we can all work towards the benefit of all of humanity.

Positively nurturing human co-existence is crucial to reforming societies. The curriculum points out that with globalisation, conflicts have arisen and the ability to live with one another peacefully has posed challenges; therefore, efforts are needed to cease the onset of conflicts. The curriculum draws on an example of how past communities from varying religious traditions, such as Christianity, Hinduism, Judaism, and Islam, have drawn on the ethics of their respective faiths to address tensions that have emerged over time (ibid.) as a result of increased interaction between different faiths and cultures. The curriculum further warns that 'In addressing these issues, we have to consider what beliefs and values will guide us towards better societies' (ibid.: 9). For Muslims, peace is highly valued and the idea of a common humanity is paramount, emphasising that individuals have an ethical responsibility as humans to see all individuals as equal no matter the challenges faced by others, including discrimination. This is highlighted in the Quran (49:13), which stresses that human beings have been created from a single soul uniting humankind: 'O mankind, We have created you male and female, and made you into nations and tribes, that you may know one another: Surely, the noblest of you in the sight of God is the best in conduct'.

To further support the idea of equality of all humanity, advice on ethical behaviour is also apparent in the *ginans*, the devotional songs of the Ismailis of Gujarati ancestry (Mawani 2007). *Ginans* have been a part of the religious life of the Ismailis emanating from the Indian subcontinent for centuries (Esmail 2002) and are sung on a daily basis in the *jamatkhanas* (place of worship) (Mawani 2006). Ismaili students who attend congregational prayers at the *jamatkhanas* are thus not only exposed to the recitation of *ginans*, but they may participate in the congregational singing, sometimes even leading the recitation (ibid.). Since *ginans* are composed mainly in Gujarati and also describe in poetic language vernacular components, such as the lifestyles and religious traditions that formed part of the traditional culture of Gujarati Ismailis (Esmail 2002), the *ginans* and their translations are frequently brought into the classroom to help reinforce the content as well as provide a linguistic ancestral link for students. For many, while they may not understand what they are singing, the *ginans* are a part of their cultural and linguistic heritage, which they have been brought up with since childhood: 'For the younger generation ... ginans ... act as symbols of the ... ethnic ancestry ... it is by participating in the ginans during congregational worship that the younger generation are able to identify with the Gujarati Nizari Ismaili tradition' (Mawani 2006: 459). The following verses (19, 22, 31–2) from the *ginan Bavan Bodh* (Kamaluddin and Kamaluddin 2010: 84–87), which speak about living an ethical life, were used to supplement the curriculum:

> *Vada nananl adabe rahie*
> Be respectful to the elders and those who are young
>
> *Bolavo bhare modhe parmano*
> Address everyone with sincere respect.
>
> *Sambhle rudo ne ochre bhundo*
> He who hears good and speaks evil
>
> *Te tame jano nische thaese bhundo*
> Know that he will surely be evil

In one of my classes, while relaying the ethical lessons present in the *ginans*, Naushin, a 14-year-old female student, became so enthused she commented, 'I cannot imagine my life without *ginans*. They are a huge source of guidance for me and my family and this tradition as well as the language has remained with my family for generations and I plan on passing this down to my children as well'. This demonstrates the centrality of the *ginanic* tradition for many Ismailis.

Students live in a context where human co-existence can pose challenges and they need to also find other ways in which to build ethical skill sets in order to understand and appreciate diversity. My students have often told me that what I mention above is really a secondary step to the process. The first step is for students to feel a strong sense of pride in their own religious and cultural identity. They advocate for the need to be a part of a safe space where they can feel a sense of belonging, self-worth and can take pride in their own culture. This is something that it appears is absent from the secular school setting, where, perhaps, fostering a Canadian identity is the priority. Taking into account the requests of my students, I introduced cultural days where students were invited to share parts of their culture with the rest of the class. Students of Gujarati ancestry proudly wore traditional Gujarati attire and brought Gujarati cuisine and sweets, which the whole class enjoyed during the lunch break. While students shared aspects of their culture, including teaching other Ismaili students from different cultural backgrounds humorous sentences in Gujarati and Kutchi, they were all encouraged to actively listen to one another, ask questions for clarification and understanding, and draw similarities (more so than differences) with other cultural traditions that they have been exposed to at school and in the wider community. At the end of the class, the students reflected on the entire process including the manner in which sharing took place, others' reaction to their ancestral culture and the ways in which they responded to others' questions. Through these cultural days I discovered that students had acquired a safe space in which to celebrate their cultural heritage with others in the class and did so in a manner that allowed them to exemplify the ethics of tolerance, open-mindedness, and respect.

For some students, they took the cultural day a step further and performed a dance for the Ismaili celebrations for Aga Khan IV's annual birthday celebrations. Students picked the song *Ame Africana Rehvasi Bwana Gurjar Gujarati* that humorously conveys the story of Gujaratis migrating from Gujarat to East Africa and how they had to negotiate their Gujarati culture with the East African culture. Essentially, the song highlights the fact that wherever Gujaratis go they will always preserve their heritage and faith and are proud to say that they are Gujarati. At the celebrations a Gujarati meal is served and the community, including the students in this study, rejoiced by participating in *garba* (Gujarati folk dance). The nature of the *garba* itself seeks to bring individuals together in a circling unison which fills the room with bright flowing colours, while also providing a space for students to learn and partake in a long-standing cultural tradition while sharing a communal identity. These students now have the confidence to perform cultural dances at cultural events in their secular schools. I believe the cultural days offered students the ethical skills, mindset, pride and comfort in their heritage to take these skills and frameworks outside of the Ismaili community to a more culturally diverse milieu, looking to build bridges with others through cultural education grounded in the principles of their Ismaili faith, rather than negatively responding to acts of discrimination. Learning about ethical content provides students with the necessary skills and background information to be able to respond to challenges in an ethical manner while drawing on historical and contemporary examples situated within their own cultural ancestral roots.

ADDRESSING ISSUES OF INEQUALITY AND DISCRIMINATION

Teaching about citizenship education, human rights and the making of cosmopolitan citizens is one of the ways in which challenges stemming out of discrimination can be addressed. Citizenship education, an overarching theme espoused in the IIS' secondary curriculum, is essential when considering the challenges of living as a visible minority community within a culturally diverse milieu like Canada (Lynch 1992; Osler 2005; O'Sullivan and Pashby 2008). Citizenship, according to Osler and Starkey (2005), can be defined as a status, an entitlement to rights, a set of duties and a practice which are all likely to be experienced as a feeling of belonging. Furthermore, it involves 'making connections between our status and ... the lives and concerns of others with whom we share a sense of community' (ibid.: 8). However, the notion of belonging and sharing within a community can be quite controversial when deciding on the criteria which entitles one to belong to a certain community (O'Sullivan and Pashby 2008). Nevertheless, what can be universally agreed upon is that every human shares an equal status of belonging to the human race.

The idea of common humanity is reflected in the curriculum: 'The Holy Qur'an calls upon human beings to recognise their common humanity and to act as guardians of one another' (IIS 2010a: 32). This suggests that the idea of a citizen is not only confined to nationalistic ideals. It extends to being a global citizen and implies a connection to a global community and the rest of humanity as also reflected in the Quranic verse (49:13) mentioned above. The notion of equality is central to citizenship education (Schugurensky 2006). The curriculum attempts to explain that equality should exist universally, regardless of 'race' or ethnicity, as everyone is bound by the commonality of belonging to the human race. The curriculum content highlights the importance of equality also as central to the institutional work of Aga Khan IV, which reaches out to all people who are in need, regardless of faith, nationality or background (IIS 2010a).

Citizenship education has inspired students to think about the first steps towards resolving issues inhibiting a positive civil society, such as intolerance. The Student Reader, quoting 13-year-old Imran, provides an example of how to overcome the issue of intolerance,

> One way of comparing people is like comparing groups to bubbles. Each bubble houses a different group complete with their own views and values. The occupants of these bubbles do not care for anyone outside of their bubble, because they do not know them. Sometimes, when these bubbles collide, they bounce off in a violent clash. It is up to us ... to pop these bubbles ... to make the world a better place. (ibid.: 7)

The notion of a common, shared humanity, also entitles each human to rights. Schugurensky (2006) emphasises that in order for citizenship education to address inequality the curriculum content must include education about human rights. Furthermore, Lynch (1992) and Spencer (2000) argue that human rights are the essence of moral and social responsibility and should lie at the core of citizenship education. In this way, responses to challenges stemming out of discrimination can find their grounding through the understanding of human rights. The Universal Declaration of Human Rights (United Nations 1948) recognises the need to protect against oppression and discrimination, advocating for basic standards of human dignity. It represents the coming together of diverse religious, cultural, political and economic opinions from across the globe and incorporates common shared values including principles, norms, and standards of living together, which promote equality and dignity for the human race. The curriculum does extensive work in outlining the importance of upholding the vision of human dignity calling Islam 'A humane religion' (IIS 2010a: 51). One heading in the curriculum titled 'Restoring and sustaining human dignity' states that 'Human dignity – restoring it, and sustaining it – is a central theme. Enabling individuals to recover and maintain their dignity ... is one of the main reasons for charitable action' (ibid.: 75). The curriculum mentions that the ethics of Islam requires Muslims to be compassionate and caring towards the vulnerable and weak in all societies and references the following example: 'The Prophet also encouraged his followers to respect the principles of fairness and justice. He placed on them the responsibility of building a strong community in which everyone had a place' (ibid.: 35). In keeping with the values espoused by the Prophet, the contemporary global humanitarian work of Aga Khan IV is examined in detail in the curriculum, including AKDN's programmes to help alleviate poverty, hunger, illiteracy, and ill health, with an overarching approach to improve the quality of life of these marginalised individuals and respect their dignity. Among many global examples of the outcomes of this approach include the initiation of early childhood education in Gujarat, and advice for maternal and infant health care for women in Gujarat with the aim of decreasing infant mortality rates (ibid.).

Learning about human rights can be a useful tool which students can draw upon when they experience situations of inequality and discrimination as it can give them a set of principles with which to identify. They can rely on their understanding of human rights to participate in a shared dialogue using the support of a commonly agreed upon global document (United Nations 1948), as well as supplement this with underlying values from the curriculum such as building understanding, tolerance and peaceful co-existence with the inherent principle that the human has to be valued in all respects, including their religion and culture. Osler and Starkey (2005) found that students who have an insight into human rights are able to promote peaceful and democratic communities, including solving conflicts arising out of discrimination within schools. Educating about human rights can also empower students to take responsibility to work as active global citizens. Tarrow (1992) supports this idea and feels that if society is educated on human rights, then inappropriate laws and practices can be challenged and this can bring about change, equality and justice.

The successful upholding and implementation of human rights requires the development of specific characteristics. For instance, Devine (2002) rightly argues that citizenship education should not just be confined to curricula studies, but should also recognise that students are actual citizens in the making which requires them to be assisted in order to develop themselves as cosmopolitan citizens. Anderson-Gold (2001: 1) defines a cosmopolitan citizen as someone who 'views herself as a citizen of a world community based on common human values'. According to Osler (2005: xvii) 'cosmopolitan citizenship ... requires a cosmopolitan and humanistic vision ... based on human rights, justice and equality'. Hughes (1994: 21) found that Canadians who possessed values such as 'open-mindedness, civic mindedness, respect, willingness to compromise, tolerance, compassion, generosity of spirit, and loyalty' were deemed as having characteristics of good citizenship and a vision towards the greater good for all. This kind of vision entails the necessity of teaching moral education grounded in the recognition of a common humanity (Carr and Steutal 1999). Osler and Starkey (2005) support the view that citizenship education that includes the teaching of common human values can be envisioned within a religious perspective which could provide a supportive framework for developing oneself into a cosmopolitan citizen. One of the debated issues in character education is the question around the need for universal virtues and values because they seem to be contextual. In fact, *The Heart of the Matter Guide* (2005) stresses the need for schools, jurisdictions or faith-based perspectives to individually identify what they constitute as their core values, thereafter using these agreed upon values as a guide for developing cosmopolitan citizens. It is therefore possible to culminate both a universal aspect and a contextual aspect towards the development of cosmopolitan citizens. The universal aspect would be the universal recognition of a common shared humanity. However, the means to obtaining such a vision, which would be through ethics and values, would then be contextually based, so long as the ethics and values within this context are guided towards this universal common vision. UNESCO's (1995) *Integrated Framework of Action for Education for Peace, Human Rights and Democracy* outlines core principles and characteristics related to the development of cosmopolitan citizens. These include demonstrating care and compassion for others, respecting diversity between people regardless of gender, ethnicity and culture, learning to negotiate with others on the basis of equality, and recognising one's own worldview is shaped by personal and societal history, and by cultural traditions.

Looking particularly at the Muslim context, the curriculum emphasises that in Islam there is 'a close link between faith and ethics' (IIS 2010a: 32) and that Islam 'teaches us that all human beings are part of one divine essence. It makes us aware that as human beings we have mutual responsibilities towards one another ... Religious communities can play an important part in the development of humanity' (ibid.: 127). Specifically relating to the Ismailis, the curriculum affirms 'The values of generosity, care and compassion, giving and sharing, service and sacrifice, have played an important role in the Ismaili tariqah' (ibid.: 47). This notion of having inherent values and principles towards the greater good has been inspired by the ethical message emphasised in the Quran (4:36), which discusses the responsibility even towards strangers.[8] Historical reference is made to values and principles espoused by the Prophet including feeding the hungry, building a new community in Medina, and advocating for a fair and just society for all, regardless of religious, cultural or socio-economic status (ibid.). Throughout Muslim history, numerous examples are cited in the curriculum around forms of help and care. These include multiple ways of giving generously by means of wealth, time, knowledge, skills and resources for the good of all. Some institutions that have arisen out of this generosity over time include places of prayer, libraries, hospitals and educational institutions (ibid.). Today, students have seen this type of cosmopolitan citizenship in the work of Aga Khan IV through the AKDN which includes a network of care in social, economic and cultural areas, its mandate comprised of values and ethics such as the ethic of inclusiveness, education and research, compassion and sharing, self-reliance, respect for life and health care, sound mind, sustainable environment and governance (IIS 2000).

Examples in Muslim history have inspired Ismailis to plan for the future and contribute as active citizens to the well-being of families, communities and societies (IIS 2010a). A forward outlook is critical, especially in the globalised world students live in today. The curriculum states: 'In the globalised age, there is an increasing need for human beings to work together. The global and local problems that affect all of us require close co-operation between societies, communities and individuals around the world' (ibid.:

127). There are many examples in the curriculum of how students are trying to reach out to various communities today and contribute as cosmopolitan citizens. These include raising awareness of children with special needs, rebuilding an orphanage and teaching about the effects of alcohol and drugs. Teaching values and ethics as a core factor of cosmopolitan citizenship can result in an increased student awareness of their role within humanity. The curriculum highlights the comments of Mushtari, aged 15, who states: 'I believe that everybody has the chance to change the world for better because God has given us ... intellect to think and act rationally for the good of humanity. The first step in this direction is to be the good citizen of our own country and contribute to its prosperity, and then bring about changes for the good of the entire world' (ibid.: 130). Teaching about citizenship, human rights principles, and drawing on the importance of understanding equality as a humanistic vision through this formal educational endeavour has shown that students are inspired and are already contributing towards cosmopolitan citizenship.

The content around citizenship education, human rights and cosmopolitan citizenship discussed above has emerged from the broader outcomes which the curriculum seeks. As mentioned earlier, there are various intentional aims which guide this curriculum and its narrative. It is important to note the other aims, which include developing in students a knowledge and understanding of their Ismaili tradition, history and culture, while also acquainting and engaging them with social and ethical issues facing Muslim communities and other religious traditions and societies of today. Moreover, it talks about the active engagement expected of students, such as examining and reflecting on their present and future roles within all areas of society, while also exercising civic values as responsible citizens. The curriculum further encourages students to share experiences and ideals that are held in common with other religious traditions (IIS 2010b: 9).

There have been a variety of ways in which students over the last few years have demonstrated the application of these above mentioned aims. The outcomes that I mention below demonstrate ways in which students have begun to think about, and live out their civic values as citizens while also reinforcing and strengthening their Gujarati Ismaili identity. The curriculum strongly emphasises community participation by bringing people together and asking how best to solve their problems as a collective. Students in my classroom discussed how the discrimination they were facing challenged and threatened their identity. The students felt that the first step in attempting to overcome this challenge should be to increase their knowledge of their own Gujarati cultural traditions by engaging with the older generation of Ismailis in a knowledge exchange programme. This exchange resulted in numerous positive outcomes from students refining their receptive and productive Gujarati language skills, thereby making the older generation more comfortable when sharing their personal narratives; to an awareness of the difficulties the older generation faces with various aspects of daily life, which caused some members of the older generation to question their own human rights and dignity. The plight of the older generation was somewhat troubling for the students and they decided to take these concerns to a seniors' action team in the community who have resources and networks to address seniors' concerns at a more individual level. This engagement was beneficial for both parties as it provided a forum for the students to hear how others in the community had overcome certain challenges in an ethical manner. At the same time, this engagement provided the older generation with a sense of worth and belonging.

Students have also drawn inspiration from Sabrina's voice highlighted in the curriculum in which she outlines how she hopes to make a difference: 'If I were to make a difference, I would enlighten people about different cultures and heritages people have … . If I could, I would go to schools to share our culture, tradition, and heritage with the students and teachers. I would also organise an event in which people of different religions would get an opportunity to learn about other cultures and religions' (IIS 2010a: 131). Students decided to put this idea into action and took the cultural days previously mentioned to a wider audience in a public space. The annual World Partnership Walk, organised by the Aga Khan Foundation Canada, raises money to help alleviate global poverty. The event itself hosts a variety show, for which my students volunteered to learn a *garba* routine and dressed in Gujarati attire to perform on stage in front of a multicultural public audience. In this way, students were able to learn aspects of their culture as well as celebrate this in front of other faith and cultural groups with pride. Moreover, this particular event continually exposes students and the wider public, including the many non-Gujarati Ismailis and non-Ismaili classmates that students invite from their secular schools, to view this display of Gujarati culture, as well as learn about AKDN's global work in areas such as Gujarat. Thus, the ethical call of Islam and its value system is translated in many visual representations for the general public in the work undertaken by the AKDN under the leadership of its Chairman, Aga Khan IV, to improve the quality of life for all people. The public, including the students' classmates, learn how the funds raised contribute to various development projects around the globe. It also gives them a venue to dialogue about the ethics and values inspired by their faith. The curriculum points out that 'We are aware of diverse cultures in our community … . We come to appreciate other cultures by learning more about them' (ibid. 70). The World Partnership Walk provides a way for different communities to interact and learn more about the Ismaili community, its values, and its heritage, including that of the Gujaratis.

However, not all interactions are positive. With the age of globalisation, change in its various aspects can also pose challenges. The curriculum stresses that 'Education is a vital factor in human development' (ibid.: 99) and helps one face challenges and adapt to change while also providing the tools to face issues within an ethical framework. The ethical use of the intellect is paramount: 'In the Ismaili tradition today, individuals contribute their resources, talents and knowledge to the Imam [spiritual leader] of the time for the welfare of the community as well as people in need' (ibid.: 40). A crucial part of developing a community is the development and empowerment of the young. Providing them a head start in learning processes through early childhood education, like the new centre set up by AKDN in Gujarat depicted in an image in the curriculum (ibid.: 99) is a necessary process in assisting students to construct their identity and negotiate social relationships, with the possibility of embracing the value of pluralism earlier in life (Robinson and Diaz 2006). Some of my students found this example intriguing and have sought to volunteer their time to tutor younger students, especially new Ismaili immigrants from different parts of the world, who sometimes feel marginalised and socially isolated in a new country. The curriculum encourages this and quotes a speech by Aga Khan IV stating that the best of charity can also be about sharing knowledge 'to help marginalised individuals build different and better futures for themselves' (IIS 2010a: 75).

CONCLUSION

While Canada's Multiculturalism Act seeks to promote equality, societal challenges particularly related to discrimination still affect Ismaili students, including those of Gujarati ancestry, and this necessitates intervention through formal education. This chapter has explored several ways in which the religious education curriculum, *Ethical Pathways to Human Development,* intended for the use of Nizari Ismaili students, can be used as a tool to address challenges students are facing in an increasingly global world. The content is grounded in curricular aims which aspire to develop an understanding of tradition, history and culture, as well as social and ethical issues, while also examining the students' own role in taking agency and ownership to improve societal challenges. The aims have been supported by relevant content that provides an array of ethical underpinnings of the faith, including examples of citizenship education, human rights and cosmopolitan citizenship. Additionally, the combination of student voice and the pedagogy of the teacher play a crucial role in contextualising content for students and connecting it to their cultural heritage. It is hoped that the content will provide students with the requisite reassurance that although they may be experiencing feelings of marginalisation and segregation, they can find moral and emotional security in the idea of belonging to a common humanity, while also feeling a proud sense of belonging to the global Ismaili community in general and their Gujarati heritage in particular. It is this foundation that will enable students to understand their place as Canadian Ismaili Muslims of Gujarati ancestry.

NOTES

1. Henceforth, the *Ethical Pathways to Human Development* curriculum will be referred to as 'the curriculum', 'new RE curriculum', or 'Ismaili curriculum' and is one of the eight modules comprising the secondary curricula.
2. Henceforth, the term 'discrimination' will be used in reference to phenotypical discrimination.
3. The Nizari Ismaili Muslims constitute the second largest Shia community after the Twelvers. Today, the Nizari Ismailis are a community of ethnically and culturally diverse peoples, living in many countries around the world and are united by their allegiance to their *Imam* (spiritual leader), His Highness Prince Karim Aga Khan IV (Daftary1990).
4. The Nizari Ismailis living in Canada are of diverse cultural backgrounds, the majority of whom are of Gujarati ancestry. Interaction between Ismaili students of Gujarati ancestry and their peers of Pakistani, Afghan, Tajik, Syrian and Iranian ancestry is evident inside and outside the classroom.
5. Henceforth, the term 'Ismaili' will be used in reference to Nizari Ismaili Muslims of Gujarati ancestry.
6. It should be noted that the Gujarati version is in use only in the state of Gujarat, India. The English version is used throughout Canada.
7. The curricula cater to the cultural diversity of the Ismaili communities worldwide and provide many textual and visual examples of various regions in the world where Ismailis reside, including Gujarat.
8. Quran (4:36): '(Show) kindness unto parents, and unto near kindred, and orphans, and the needy, and unto the neighbour who is of kin (unto you) and the neighbour who is not of kin, and the fellow-traveller and the wayfarer and (the slaves) whom your right hands possess. Lo! Allah loveth not such as are proud and boastful'.

REFERENCES

Alberta Education, Learning and Teaching Resources Branch. *The Heart of the Matter: Character and Citizenship Education in Alberta Schools*, Edmonton, Alberta, 2005, <http://www.edc.gov.ab.ca/charactered/PDF/intro.pdf> (15 June 2013).

Anderson-Gold, Sharon. *Cosmopolitanism and Human Rights*, Cardiff: University of Wales Press, 2001.

Ball, Deborah L. and Hayman Bass. 'Interweaving Content and Pedagogy in Teaching and Learning to Teach: Knowing and Using Mathematics', in *Multiple Perspectives on the Teaching and Learning of Mathematics*, edited by Jo Boaler, Westport, CT: Ablex, 2000, pp. 83–104.

Bovill, Catherine and Margaret Leppard. 'Population Policies and Education: Exploring the Contradictions of Neo-liberal Globalisation', *Globalisation, Societies and Education*, Vol. 4, No. 3 (2006): 393–414.

Carr, David and Jan Steutal (eds). *Virtue Ethics and Moral Education*, London: Routledge, 1999.

Daftary, Farhad. *The Ismailis: Their History and Doctrines*, Cambridge: Cambridge University Press, 1990.

Devine, Dympna. 'Children's Citizenship and the Structuring of Adult-Child Relations in the Primary School', *Childhood*, Vol. 9, No. 3 (2002): 303–20.

Dewey, John. *Experience and Education*, New York: Macmillan, 1938.

Esmail, Aziz. *A Scent of Sandalwood: Indo-Ismaili Religious Lyrics*, Surrey: Curzon, 2002.

Government of Canada. 'Canadian Multiculturalism Act', 1988, <http://laws.justice.gc.ca/eng/C-18.7/page-1.html> (2 January 2010).

Hughes, Andrew S. 'Understanding Citizenship: A Delphi Study', *Canadian and International Education*, Vol. 23 (1994): 13–26.

Institute of Ismaili Studies (IIS). 'Aga Khan Development Network (AKDN): An Ethical Framework', 2000, <http://www.iis.ac.uk/SiteAssets/pdf/akdn_ethical_framework.pdf> (1 June 2013).

——. *Ethical Pathways to Human Development: One World, Many Hopes – Student Reader*, London: Islamic Publications Limited, 2010a.

——. *Ethical Pathways to Human Development: One World, Many Hopes – Teacher's Guide*, London: Islamic Publications Limited, 2010b.

Johnson, Elaine B. *Contextual Teaching and Learning: What it is and Why it's Here to Stay*, Thousand Oaks, CA: Corwin Press, 2002.

Kamaluddin, Zarina and Ali Muhammad Kamaluddin. *Collection of Granths with English Translation and Glossary*, Karachi, Pakistan: Z.A. Printer, 2010.

Lynch, James. *Education for Citizenship in a Multicultural Society*, London: Cassell Education, 1992.

Mawani, Sharmina. 'Aapun Aap Pichano: The Ginanic Tradition of the Nizari Ismaili Muslims of Gujarati Ancestry', in *Gujaratis in the*

West: Evolving Identities in Contemporary Society, edited by Anjoom A. Mukadam and Sharmina Mawani, Newcastle: Cambridge Scholars Publishing, 2007, pp. 25–41.

——. 'The Construction of Identities amongst Young Adult Nizari Ismaili Muslims in Toronto and Mumbai', Unpublished PhD Thesis, SOAS, University of London, 2006.

Mukadam, Anjoom A. 'Sharing His Vision: Aga Khan IV and the Nizari Ismaili Muslims of Gujarati Ancestry', in *Gujarati Communities across the Globe: Memory, Identity and Continuity*, edited by Sharmina Mawani and Anjoom A. Mukadam, Stoke-on-Trent: Trentham, 2012, pp. 43–57.

O'Sullivan, Michael and Karen Pashby (eds). *Citizenship Education in the Era of Globalization: Canadian Perspectives*, Toronto: Sense Publishers, 2008.

Osler, Audrey. *Teachers, Human Rights and Diversity: Educating Citizens in Multicultural Societies*, Stoke-on-Trent: Trentham, 2005.

Osler, Audrey and Hugh Starkey. *Changing Citizenship: Democracy and Inclusion in Education*, London: McGraw-Hill, 2005.

Osler, Audrey and Kerry Vincent. *Citizenship and the Challenge of Global Education*, Staffordshire: Trentham, 2002.

Pereira, Cecil, Bert N. Adams and Mike Bristow. 'Canadian Beliefs and Policy Regarding the Admission of Ugandan Asians to Canada', *Ethnic and Racial Studies*, Vol. 1, No. 3 (1978): 352–64.

Raby, Rebecca. '"There's No Racism at My School, it's Just Joking Around": Ramifications for Anti-Racist Education', *Race, Ethnicity and Education*, Vol. 7, No. 4 (2004): 367–83.

Richardson, Robin. *Racism and Professionalism: Race Equality Teaching*, Stoke-on Trent, Staffordshire: Trentham, 2009.

Robinson, Kerry H. and Criss J. Diaz. *Diversity and Difference in Early Childhood Education Issues for Theory and Practice*, Maidenhead, England: Open University Press, 2006.

Schugurensky, Daniel. 'Adult Citizenship Education: An Overview of the Field', in *Contexts of Adult Education: Canadian Perspectives*, edited by Tara Fenwick, Tom Nesbit and Bruce Spencer, Toronto: Thompson Education Publishing, 2006, pp. 68–80.

Shulman, Lee. S. 'Those Who Understand: Knowledge Growth in Teaching', *Educational Researcher*, Vol. 15, No. 2 (1986): 4–14.

Spencer, Sarah. 'The Implications of the Human Rights Act for Citizenship Education', in *Citizenship and Democracy in Schools: Diversity, Identity and Equality*, edited by Audrey Osler, Stoke-on Trent: Trentham Books, 2000, pp. 19–32.

Statistics Canada. 'Visible Minority Immigrant', *Statistics Canada*, 2008, <http://www.statcan.gc.ca/pub/81-004-x/def/4068739-eng.htm > (21 February 2010).

Tarrow, Norma. 'Human Rights Education: Alternative Conceptions', in *Cultural Diversity and the Schools: Human Rights, Education and Global Responsibility*, Vol. 4, edited by James Lynch, Celia Mogdil and Sohan Mogdil, London: Falmer, 1992.

Twaddle, Michael (ed.). *Expulsion of a Minority: Essays on the Ugandan Asians*, London: Athlone Press, 1975.

United Nations. 'Universal Declaration of Human Rights (UDHR)', 1948, <http://www.un.org/en/documents/udhr/> (14 February 2010).

United Nations Educational, Scientific and Cultural Organization (UNESCO). 'Curriculum', *Education*, 1995–2012, <http://www.unesco.org/new/en/education/themes/strengthening-education-systems/quality-framework/core-resources/curriculum/> (25 May 2013).

——. 'Integrated Framework of Action for Education for Peace, Human Rights and Democracy', 1995, <http://www.unesco.org/education/nfsunesco/pdf/REV_74_E.PD> (1 October 2010).

Vygotsky, Lev Semyonovich. *Mind in Society: The Development of Higher Psychological Processes*, Cambridge, MA: Harvard University Press, 1978.

CHAPTER 11

Space, Representation and Belonging

A Swaminarayan Temple in Sydney, Australia

Laura Beth Bugg

This work examines the submission of a development application for a Hindu temple by a group of Swaminarayan Gujarati migrants on the rural fringe of Sydney, Australia in 2009. The application encountered significant opposition from residents and was denied planning approval by local government planners for reasons of incompatibility with the rural area. Using the Hindu temple as a case study and Soja's (1996) spatial trialectic as a theoretical lens, this chapter considers the way in which a minority place of worship serves as a contested site of belonging for transnational Gujarati migrants. I explore the way in which homogeneous Anglo-Australian space is codified, produced and maintained through planning practice and reinforced by the spatial practices and representations of local residents. These strategies to maintain material Whiteness are challenged, however, by the Hindu community, who contest a hegemonic representation of space on the rural-urban fringe and form new alliances with other marginalised groups. This work aims to extend research both on the way in which urban planning policies and procedures are underpinned by Anglo-Celtic understandings of space and community objections to social change (Sandercock 1997; Yiftachel 1998; Fenster and Yacobi 2005), as well as research on the way that Whiteness is maintained in the urban landscape (McCann 1999; Pulido 2000; Shaw 2006; Low 2009). It also aims to contribute to research on transnational religious belonging and the importance of place (Levitt 2004; Kong 2010).

METHOD AND CONCEPTUAL FRAMEWORK

This project is underpinned by Soja's (1996) spatial trialectic. Soja's (2000: 10) Firstspace is space that is open to measurement and description and consists of 'spatial practices that work together to produce and reproduce ... specific patternings of urbanism as a way of life'. Soja (1996: 76) argues that Firstspace epistemologies understand human spatiality 'defined primarily by and in terms of its material configurations', and see human spatiality 'as outcome or product'. Secondspaces, Soja (ibid.: 79) asserts, are 'distinguishable by their explanatory concentration on conceived rather than perceived space and their implicit assumption that spatial knowledge is primarily produced through discursively devised representations of space'. He adds that Secondspaces are 'projections into the empirical world from conceived or imagined geographies' (ibid.).

It was Soja's frustration with the explanatory power of the binary perceived/conceived notions of space, a frustration articulated by Lefebvre (1991) in the notion of representational space, that led to the articulation of Thirdspace, or a space of social and cultural resistance. This Thirdspace, Soja (1996: 163) states, is 'a simultaneously real-and-imagined, actual-and-virtual locus of structured individual and collective experience and agency'. Soja, drawing on, among others, Bhabha (1990) hooks (1990) and Rose (1993), argues that Thirdspace 'directly challenges ... all conventional modes of spatial thinking' and is meant to 'detonate, deconstruct, not be comfortably poured back into the old containers' (Soja 1996: 163). Soja (ibid.: 61) emphasises the importance of struggle, writing of the need to assert 'the third-as-Other [which] begins an expanding chain of heuristic disruptions, strengthening defenses against totalising closure and all 'permanent constructions'. In Thirdspace, the potential for old and dominant ways of being and doing are disrupted and there are possibilities for remaking the way space is both lived and conceived.

Drawing on the work of Soja, I argue that through the epistemologies of First and Secondspace, urban planners and local residents represent the rural-urban fringe as a space of Whiteness in which hegemonic practices of social and cultural privilege embedded in both conceived space and spatial practice 'refer back to the other, reinforce each other, and hide behind the other' (Lefebvre 1991: 27). Here I understand Whiteness to refer not only to 'race' but also to the systematic advantages of one group over another and the privileges of being part of a socially, not just racially, unmarked category (Lipsitz 1995; Fine et al. 2004). 'White privilege' thus takes as natural 'the privileges and benefits that accrue to white people by virtue of their whiteness' (Pulido 2000: 15) and may be understood as 'middle class privileges' not restricted by color, but also by 'class, gender, sexual orientation and place of origin' (Low 2009: 81). Here it is important to note the racialisation of religion, in which 'religion becomes a proxy for race' and 'race becomes a "marker" for religion' (Joshi 2006: 218). In countries throughout Europe and in the US and Australia, this has meant the conflation of Hinduism and Sikhism with Islam so that South Asians or those of imagined racial/ethnic characteristics are 'othered' (Singh 2003; Dunn et al. 2007; Hopkins 2007). In Australia this examination of Whiteness is particularly important because of the nation's colonial history and relatively recent end to the so-called 'White Australia' immigration and assimilationist cultural policies. It is also significant as a considerable number of Australians exhibit a 'substantial degree of intolerance of Muslim and Arab-Australians' and view non-Anglo Australians as 'problematic, by dint of supposed and generalised cultural practices' (Dunn et al. 2004: 426).

Going beyond First and Secondspace dualisms, I will examine the 'simultaneously real and imagined, actual-and-virtual space', (Soja 2000: 11) Soja's Thirdspace. In this Thirdspace the Hindu community negotiates with and attempts to subvert hegemonic conceived and perceived White space, opening up the 'possibility of reappropriating space and decentring institutionalized forms of spatial organization' (Lefebvre 1991: 373–74). In addition, the Hindu community forms new types of alliances and consolidates collective identity, revealing the ways in which 'the links between space, knowledge, power and cultural politics must be seen as both oppressive and enabling ... with possibilities for community, resistance and emancipatory change' (Soja 1996: 87).

In order to examine these representations of space I utilised Critical Discourse Analysis (CDA) as an analytical framework. In the last two decades discourse analysis has become an accepted way within urban research to demonstrate rhetorical strategies around power relations, social difference, economic development and ideological difference (for example, Marston 2002; Jacobs 2006; Vaara et al. 2010). In particular, CDA is concerned with the rhetorical strategies and effects of language (Hastings 1999), and aids in the understanding of texts as modes of social interaction rather than as neutral or systematic (Jacobs 2006).

CDA was conducted on the following planning policy documentation: development assessment reports, letters of submission from government agencies and from community members to local government planners regarding the development application, Statements of Facts and Contentions prepared by both local government planners and planning consultants on behalf of the temple, statutory land-use environmental plans and development controls. Fifteen fully transcribed, semi-structured interviews with local government land-use planners, professional land-use planning consultants, key community members and members of the temple were conducted during 2010–11. A grounded theory approach was used to analyse responses to open questions, and data was organised into a number of key themes (Strauss and Corbin 1990). During 2010–11, I also conducted site visits to the proposed temple location and conducted participant observation at worship services.

CASE STUDY CONTEXT

In March 2009, the Swaminarayans, a Hindu congregation made up of Gujarati migrants, purchased a piece of land in Box Hill, a rural-residential area on the rural-urban fringe of Sydney. Box Hill is overwhelmingly Anglo-Australian, with only 12 per cent of residents from a non-English speaking background (ABS 2006). The vast majority of Box Hill residents are either couples with children (54%) or couples without children (36%), and three quarters of all residents describe themselves as affiliated with a Christian denomination. In the last decade, Box Hill has seen the growth of a significant number of ex-urban in-migrants from nearby local government areas. These families have purchased rural mega-homes with multiple living and entertaining spaces and leisure facilities such as stables or hobby farms. The land that the Swaminarayans purchased was zoned rural but with places of worship permitted with the consent of the local government Council (Hills Shire Council 2009). The Swaminarayans then lodged a development application with the Council for a place of worship. Members of the Swaminarayan community told me in interviews that the land for the temple was purchased expressly because it was zoned for a place of worship, and thus the group's trustees expected to receive approval without great difficulty. The design proposed for the temple was rectangular in shape with concrete walls painted in earth tones to blend with the surrounding area, a hipped metal roof, and a small decorative dome. Additionally there was provision for parking, landscaping and a noise barrier. The temple proposed a maximum of 200 worshippers during regular weekend worship (ibid.).

After reviewing the application, Hills Shire planners refused the proposed temple because of unacceptable hours of operation, frequency of activities and number of people attending services, bulk and scale of the building, traffic and site coverage (ibid.). Planners concluded that the proposed development would 'unacceptably impact upon the amenity of adjoining and nearby land' and that the temple was contrary to the objectives of the rural zone. Following the refusal, the Swaminarayans lodged an appeal with the Land and Environment Court, the State's appeals court for building, development and planning matters. In July 2011 a Commissioner of the Court dismissed the Swaminarayans' appeal, arguing that there would be inadequate electricity supply to the temple (Shree Swaminarayan Temple v. Baulkham Hills Shire Council 2011).

'AN UNEXPECTED AND UNUSUAL FORM OF DEVELOPMENT'

The Secondspace of Land Use Planners

I begin my analysis with Secondspace, as this is where space is interpreted, mapped and controlled, 'a thoughtful re-presentation of human spatiality in mental form' (Soja 1996: 10). Secondspace refers to plans, codes and ideas articulated *about* space. Though abstract, representations of space impose order 'via control over knowledge, signs, and codes: over the means of deciphering spatial practice and hence over the production of spatial knowledge' (ibid.: 67). Critical Discourse Analysis of planning policy documentation related to the refusal of the temple along with interviews of planners who assessed the development application reveals that planners represented the rural zone as a space of low-density building, reserved for residential and agricultural uses. Land use planners represented rural space as aligned with particular functions and land uses, namely small hobby farms and rural residential properties. This was done through the use of zoning, by which planners declared particular uses in the rural zone orthodox and others unorthodox. Planners explicitly stated that the 'rural character of the surrounding area' was 'exclusively used for rural residential purposes' (Hills Shire Council 2009: 16). Second, planners were concerned about the destruction of viable agricultural land, and argued that a temple would not 'encourage the use of the land for agricultural and rural uses' (Wilshire Webb Staunton Beattie 2010: 7).

Planners conceived of the rural space as low-density, with buildings of minimal bulk and scale. They argued that any new development must be of the same bulk, scale, built form and design as the existing properties, maintaining a uniformity of visual impact (Hills Shire Council 2009). In rurally zoned areas, design controls ensure that development is carried out 'with regard to the rural and heritage character of the surrounding area' so that the 'scenic qualities of the area or the amenity of surrounding residents' are not adversely affected (Wilshire Webb Staunton Beattie 2010: 7). As one planner I interviewed stated,

> It's [the temple's] just generally rectangular in shape, pre-cast concrete, I mean, well, that doesn't fit in with anything around for a start ... . Now most of our blocks in the Hills [local government area] are less than 700 square metres, so we are talking about a building that would take up two housing blocks, and that is out of keeping with what's around in that area.

Planners also contrasted the noises, light and traffic of a temple to the 'predominantly quiet, peaceful, low scale and [of] somewhat undeveloped rural character' of the area (Hills Shire Council 2009: 17). When I asked a planner for clarification as to why a temple might be particularly disruptive if places of worship were allowed in that zone, he replied,

> There was a great deal of the unknown [with the temple] there that ... I think 10 ceremonies per year, or 10 festivals per year, *which is probably a point of difference from traditional churches* [my emphasis] ... We have a zoning that permits places of public worship; traditionally that has meant the bush church, you know ... I always think that people know what they are getting with traditional churches, and I guess my view is that it is a little more open ended with other religions.

As these statements from planners along with planning documentation illustrate, local government here clearly restricted the range of acceptable behaviours and aesthetics through zoning regulations and restrictive ordinances that limited maximum lot size, design elements, hours of operation and type of use. This resulted in what Lefebvre (1991: 382) terms, the 'abstract' spatiality of capitalism in which the idea of the rural is created by planners and all difference must be 'forced back into the system by constraint and violence'. In this case 'difference', understood as behaviours, building types and design antithetical to the Anglo-Australian, White rural landscape, threatened the reproduction of capitalism and the management of elite rural-residential space.

'WE HAVE A RIGHT TO THE LIFESTYLE WE'VE PURCHASED'

The First and Secondspace of Local Residents

Firstspace, Soja claims, is space that can be measured and mapped, the space of the 'real' and 'material' (Soja 1996). Critical Discourse Analysis of letters of submission to the Hills Shire by local residents of Box Hill, along with interviews of local residents reveals an understanding of space informed by both material spatiality and imagined representations of space (Secondspace). While residents articulated the measurable and material elements of their space – flora, fauna and streetscapes – these elements were linked to conceptions of rural space as peaceful idyll, as linked to particular Anglo-Australian values and to English colonial heritage.

First, local residents experienced rural space as peaceful and quiet. Residents contrasted the 'normal noises of animals, birds, dogs and all other wildlife that enjoys the peaceful surroundings' (Letters of Submission 2009) with the imagined sounds and even smells that a Hindu temple might bring. As one local resident stated, 'The noises and smells produced by other cultures are quite offensive to us' (ibid.). Several residents mentioned concern over culturally specific music, particularly that of 'sitars, drums and organs ... We are living in a rural environment!' (ibid.). Second, the material space of Box Hill consists of large rural homes in the style of English country manors as well as small-scale suburban agriculture or 'gentlemen's farms'. Local residents in turn conceptualised space as intimately tied to Anglo-Australian heritage. Letters from local residents to the Hills Shire noted that a temple 'is not in keeping with the heritage aspects of the area' (ibid.). Particular images of colonial history were mobilised to depict the area as one with ties to elite English landowners and pastoralists, with a form letter submitted by many residents noting connections between the area and prominent English colonial figures (ibid.). Finally, local residents represented and imagined rural space as absent of a minority ethnic presence. Namely, they experienced Box Hill as lacking a visible Indian community, thus rendering a Hindu temple unnecessary. Residents expressed concern that the temple would be 'of no benefit to local residents' and would be used as 'a community centre for people outside our area' (ibid.). One resident asked that the Local Government Area (LGA) 'enquire from the census figures how many families in the area are of the Hindu denomination' and concluded, 'I believe this application is not in the best interests of the local home owners and is in fact for the benefit of out of suburb worshippers' (ibid.).

Here in the First and Secondspace of local residents, there were several strategies of Whiteness clearly deployed. The first was the celebration of specific histories and the exclusion of others (the landed English gentlemen to the exclusion of indigenous or migrant histories), which implicitly excluded ethnic others from the landscape. The second strategy of exclusion could be characterised using Young's (1990: 141–42) understanding of 'aversive racism'. Aversive racism, in contrast to the dominative racism that prevailed during the 19th century, is marked by avoidance, disgust and negative reactions to things such as cultural practices, bodies and sights, smells and sounds of others. In the letters of submission it is clear that residents feared the smells, sounds and practices of the temple and the bodies who would inhabit it. Residents' reaction, as Young argues, using Kristeva's (1982) notion of the abject, was to place borders between themselves and those whom they considered potentially polluting or dangerous. The third strategy was to represent rural space as absent of persons of colour and to construct urban space as the appropriate location for the activities, sounds and smells of racialised bodies. This 'spacialisation of race' (Cohen 1993: 7) has led to an understanding of the rural as a space of white safety and the city or urban as the 'repository of non-white migrants and "aliens"' (Bonnett 2002: 356).

'THE CONGREGATION HAD TO ADAPT'

The Thirdspace of the Swaminarayans

In reaction to the limitations of binary First/Secondspace epistemologies, Thirdspace 'draws selectively and strategically from the two opposing categories to open up new alternatives' (Soja 1996: 5). I understand Thirdspace here to incorporate Lefebvre's 'lived spaces' (1991: 38–39), Foucault's 'heterotopias' (1986: 24), hooks' (1990: 41) 'homeplaces' and Bhabha's 'third space' (1990: 107). Important for all these understandings are notions of resistance, marginality and the articulation of identities. Because of the flexibility and creativity of Thirdspace, these new identities may be forged from 'new combinations of once dualized elements' (Anderson 2002: 304). Critical Discourse Analysis, participant observation and in-depth interviews with members of the Swaminarayan community capture a dynamic Thirdspace in which the Swaminarayans re-appropriated and subverted the hegemonic understanding of rural space through a transformation of discoursive frameworks around 'rurality'. The Swaminarayans also negotiated strategic alliances that resist cultural expectation through boundary crossing moves, while at the same time creating new cultural practices that reinforced group solidarity.

Local Anglo-Australian residents conceptualised the rural as constitutive of Anglo-Australian values, activities and heritage. The 'rural idyll' as a place of peace and quiet was depicted by local residents as one which was in stark contrast to the noise, lights, and smells of a Hindu temple. As a practice of resistance in Thirdspace, however, members of the Swaminarayan community articulated the rural as a space in which peace and tranquility are well suited to the activities of prayer and meditation. The Swaminarayans also understood rural space as a prime site for the transmission of cultural and religious practice. One letter to the local government from the Swaminarayans noted, 'Rural land is preferable for a temple. We need the site in a peaceful and rural area' (Letter of Submission 2009). Another argued, 'The land itself is in a peaceful and calm area, so it will be good for our worship and our practices. It is important for worshippers to have a silent and peaceful environment for prayers. It is obvious that prayers are always chanted in a silent environment' (ibid.). These practices, community members noted, are important not only for providing worship space but for 'safeguarding the next generation' and to 'learn our culture, so it is not lost' (ibid.). As one member wrote, '[The temple] gives us a peaceful place to relax our minds, unworry and connect to the Supreme Being. It will help us maintain our culture and pass it on to the next generation. Our culture preaches about kindness, honesty, independence, team work and respect' (ibid.). This letter was typical of many from within the community that pointed to the positive aspects of Swaminarayan culture and behaviours, including the Swaminarayans' strict abstinence from alcohol and drugs, support for community charity events, and high levels of university graduates. Using Anglo-Australian signifiers of the 'good citizen' (education, civic participation and values) the Swaminarayans articulated a cultural identity in defense of meanings imposed by local residents. The Swaminarayans also deployed the framework of cultural preservation and the preservation of 'traditional identity' used by local residents, but turned it on its head. While local residents understood the rural as a way to preserve Anglo-Australian settler history and ideology, the Swaminarayans understood the rural as a way to safeguard Hindu values and religious practice.

The Swaminarayans' efforts to secure space required the crossing of both perceived and real borders; this resulted in a Thirdspace of 'invention and transformational encounters' (Routledge 1996: 409) in which cultural barriers were collapsed. This may be seen in the alliance formed between the Swaminarayans and a local Muslim group that submitted a 2002 development application with the Hills Shire Council. The Muslim group's application for a prayer hall was extremely contentious, with more than 8000 objections lodged by local residents and the site subjected to repeated vandalism, including the appearance of severed pigs' heads at the site (Kerin 2008). The local government refused the application, however it was overturned on appeal to the Land and Environment Court. As new migrants to Australia, the Swaminarayans have little knowledge of the local government planning process. As one trustee stated, 'Apart from the land saying that it was zoned for a place of worship, we didn't have any prior knowledge of how things worked'. Because of the Muslim prayer hall application's success in the Land and Environment Court, the Swaminarayan trustees contacted the Muslim group for help. Based on the recommendation of the Muslim community leader, the Swaminarayan trustees hired a planning consultant who regularly represents Islamic places of worship and schools in local government planning disputes. This planning consultant both agreed to facilitate the Swaminarayans' development proposal with the local government and represent the temple in the Land and Environment Court. Planning theorists have noted the 'sinister' and regressive consequences of planning for minority ethnic groups, despite what may be the benign intentions of planners (Harvey 1973, 1992; Sandercock 1995; Yiftachel 1998). In the Thirdspace of Hindu/Muslim alliance a potential arena of emancipatory action emerges in which knowledge is shared collaboratively beyond traditional power elites. This widens participation in place-making activities through the transference of urban governance skills.

In addition to the sharing of knowledge, the Swaminarayans made a useful alliance with a minority religious group that is also spatially, socially and culturally excluded in the Australian context. What makes this significant in the dynamic restructuring of the 'Thirdspace' is both the historically contentious relationship of Muslims and Hindus in the Swaminarayans' state of origin, Gujarat, and the vexed relationship of Hindus and Muslims in Sydney. In 2002 Gujarat experienced one of the most significant forms of communal violence in Indian history in retaliation for the attack of an Ahmedabad-bound train carrying a large number of Vishwa Hindu Parishad (VHP, a right wing Hindu organisation) activists. In the end, over 600 Muslims were killed and more than 200,000 displaced because of the looting and burning of homes and property (Varadarajan 2002). Hindu nationalism in Gujarat has been a compelling force over the last few decades, and in the Gujarati Hindu cultural imagination Muslims are constructed as the 'other' (Pandey 1999). Tensions between Muslims and Hindus have played out in Sydney as well, with ongoing feuds between neighbouring groups in one area leading to vandalism and gunshots at Australia's oldest Hindu temple, located in a predominately Muslim area (SMH 3 April 2011). Despite this history of antagonism, in a situation of shared struggle to claim space and representation in the rural-urban fringe, a Thirdspace was created in which Muslims and Hindus were impelled to create a strategic alliance.

Finally, in the dynamic process of encounter that occurs in Thirdspace, the Swaminarayans fashion new and hybrid identities. As Bhabha argues in a quote favoured by Soja,

> All forms of culture are in a process of hybridity. But ... the importance of hybridity is not to be able to trace two original moments from which the third emerges, rather hybridity is for me the new 'third space' which enables other positions to emerge. The process of cultural hybridity gives rise to something different, something new and unrecognisable, a new arena of negotiation of meaning and representation. (Bhabha 1990: 211 quoted in Soja 1996: 140)

This notion of hybridity is particularly critical for the Swaminarayans, who have immigrated to Australia from several countries, namely India, the UK and Kenya (see Mukadam's chapter in this volume). As Williams (2001: 198) has noted in his extensive research of Swaminarayans worldwide, 'Swaminarayan Hindus have been particularly adept in moving successfully between several countries and in establishing the infrastructure and emotional ties that preserve their identity and gradually transform aspects of Swaminarayan Hinduism, which has become in the process a transnational world religion.' This strong sense of geographical displacement was noted in my interviews with temple members, and descriptions of personal identity were riddled with contradiction and caught between multiple understandings. All of the temple members whom I interviewed described themselves as Swaminarayans but also as Indian, Australian, and occasionally as Kenyan or British. As one woman who migrated from the UK to Australia stated,

> We've got Indians, Kenyans and Poms [British] like myself, three different cultural backgrounds. Although we're all Swaminarayan. But living in the country the Kenyans come from is different to the other countries, because Kenya, being a third world country, that's a different lifestyle over there and then the UK is a first world country and you've got a different lifestyle there. And then you've got India, which is not much different from Kenya but still different from Kenya. So although the Swaminarayan [religion] is still the same for them, the basics are the same but their lifestyle outside the Swaminarayan religion is different because the ones from the UK are more westernised, India a little bit westernised, Kenya is not westernised.

It is because of these multiple identities and locations as immigrants to Australia that the Sydney Swaminarayans must come together in a sense of unified belonging. In order to do this, temple members are adamant that they need a permanent place of worship. In diaspora settings, the construction of a temple is often understood as the most important step to the recognition of Indian communities (Barot 2002). In Swaminarayan communities outside of India, the temple 'may be the only place where Gujaratis gather in a dominant social position' (ibid.). For the Swaminarayans, the lack of permanently installed deities in a place of worship has had a significant effect on religious practice. As one man explained, the permanently installed deities 'have more spirituality than the mobile ones ... because they're obviously moving from one place to another. They're not looked after properly and they're put in a bag and all that kind of stuff.'

In order to accommodate their temporary worship location in a high school gymnasium, the Swaminarayans moved all ritual food preparations such as *prasad* (offerings for the gods), which must follow strict guidelines for preparation, to members' homes. In addition, members store the deities in their closets and garages, and host events in their homes that would otherwise be held at the temple. Because of the logistical feats required to organise and set up a mobile worship service each week, along with youth schools and other events regularly offered by the community, nearly every temple member has a significant role to play. This has resulted in a strong sense of group solidarity and significant level of pride expressed in cultural maintenance despite the circumstances. One woman who migrated from the UK stated,

> It does make a difference that we don't have a *mandir* [Hindu temple]. Everyone has that feeling. Everyone just compensates by doing more at home, even if it's not convenient .... In that sense, you have a *mandir* in your home and you have to believe your home is your temple and treat it like a temple and do *aarti* [devotional prayer] every single day. In many temples people might do *aarti* and then just go home and forget it. In ours, we will all rush back to do *aarti* after the mandir. We feel like we are neglecting the *Bhagwan* [Lord Swaminarayan] if we don't rush back and take care of him. That's how we do it in Australia.

In addition to hyper-maintenance of cultural practice, the dislocation from permanent space has resulted in a participatory spirit among members. 'It's hard to do *puja* [worship] in the gym because we have to be in and out in a certain time. A lot of work goes into it, into decorating, into preparing everything, doing the stages, getting the food. So when it comes to it the community spirit is there, we all muck in, do what we need to do to make it work and that's it. It's not, "You do that!" and, "You do that!" It's, "We are doing that". "We!"' This sense of unified participation has been particularly important to the Sydney Swaminarayan community, as differences in cultural and religious practice were observed between Kenyan, British and Indian members of the community around language (Gujarati or English), appropriate dress (including headcovering for women) and diet. As one woman who migrated with her husband from Kenya noted, 'You leave ... whatever you did back in Kenya, you leave whatever you did in India, you leave whatever you did in the UK, we're Australians, how do we move forward, and that's how we've moved forward, because we're Australians. We do everything together. Everybody had to change. We had to adapt. The congregation had to adapt'.

The statements above from temple members vividly illustrate Soja's (1996: 41) understanding of Thirdspace as the space where cultural in-betweens begin to articulate new ways of being, 'the place where alienation and mystification are played out, enacted, concretely inscribed'. In this reconceptualised space the Swaminarayans stand re-constituted in relation to home and homeland – Australia, the UK, Kenya and India. Displaced from what they previously understood to be full belonging in their local community and the wider nation, the Swaminarayans create oppositions to the 'real', material space they are denied through the subversion of hegemonic discourses of White space, the crossing of borders both perceived and real, and the fashioning of new identities.

CONCLUSIONS

Minority places of worship serve as sites of cultural reproduction and as symbols of the permanence of a minority ethnic and religious group in local communities. Thus controversies over these sites are not only about the distribution of resources such as land; they are also about the permanent presence of minority ethnic groups. This chapter has argued that using First and Secondspace epistemologies, hegemonic practices of social and cultural privilege are embedded in both the conceived space of urban planners and spatial practices of local residents. This finding accords with other scholarship that examines the nature of power and planning, particularly the relationship between planning, 'race' and ethnicity (Sandercock 1997; Trudeau 2006; Yiftachel 2006). The case study also illustrates the way in which local residents ensure the stability of their position as White Anglo-Australian elites in a rapidly changing spatial situation in which their foothold is not secure. A focus on the representation of space as unmarked White space (absent of ethnic presence, Anglo-Australian settler history) reveals how aversive racism works to shape place. Finally, it is important to acknowledge that the Swaminarayans remain spatially excluded from the site of their proposed temple. However, a Thirdspace approach offers the potential to see the in-between spaces in which the Swaminarayans' discoursive strategies transform and re-articulate dominant Anglo-Australian understandings of rural space. Their boundary-crossing and new spatial practices open up space – and possibilities – for meaning and representation.

REFERENCES

Anderson, Jon. 'Researching Environmental Resistance: Working through Secondspace and Thirdspace Approaches', *Qualitative Research*, Vol. 2, No. 3 (Dec. 2002): 301–21.

Australian Bureau of Statistics (ABS). *Baulkham Hills (A) Local Government Area Expanded Community Profile*, Canberra: Australian Bureau of Statistics, 2006, <http://www.abs.gov.au/ausstats/abs@.nsf/781eb7868cee03e9ca2571800082bece/10cbb5a1464c7862ca2571cb000c2fd0!OpenDocument> (23 March 2011).

Barot, Rohit. 'Religion, Migration and Wealth Creation in the Swaminarayan Movement', in *The Transnational Family: New European Frontiers and Global Networks*, edited by Deborah Bryceson and Ulla Vuorela, Oxford: Berg, 2002, pp. 197–216.

Bhabha, Homi. 'The Third Space: Interview with Homi Bhabha', in *Identity: Community, Culture, Difference*, edited by Jonathan Rutherford, London: Lawrence and Wishart, 1990, pp. 107–21.

Bonnett, Alastair. 'The Metropolis and White Modernity', *Ethnicities*, Vol. 2, No. 3 (Sept. 2002): 349–66.

Cohen, Philip. *Home Rules: Some Reflections on Racism and Nationalism in Everyday Life*, London: University of East London, 1993.

Dunn, Kevin, Natascha Klocker and Tanya Salabay. 'Contemporary Racism and Islamaphobia in Australia: Racializing Religion', *Ethnicities*, Vol. 7, No. 4 (Dec. 2007): 564–89.

Dunn, Kevin, James Forrest, Ian Burnley and Amy McDonald. 'Constructing Racism in Australia', *Australian Journal of Social Issues*, Vol. 39, No. 4 (Nov. 2004): 409–30.

Fenster, Tovi and Haim Yacobi. 'Whose City is it? On Urban Planning and Local Knowledge in Globalizing Tel Aviv-Jaffa', *Planning, Theory and Practice*, Vol. 6, No. 2 (June 2005): 191–211.

Fine, Michelle, Lois Weis, Linda Pruitt and L. Mun Wong. *Off White: Readings on Power, Privilege, and Resistance*, New York: Routledge, 2004.

Foucault, Michel. 'Of Other Spaces', *Diacritics*, Vol. 16, No. 1 (Spring 1986): 22–27.

Harvey, David. 'Social Justice, Postmodernism and the City', *International Journal of Urban and Regional Research*, Vol. 16, No. 4 (Dec. 1992): 588–601.

——. *Social Justice and the City*, London: Edward Arnold, 1973.

Hastings, Annette. 'Discourse and Urban Change: Introduction to the Special Issue', *Urban Studies*, Vol. 36, No. 1 (January 1999): 7–12.

Hills Shire Council. Development Assessment Unit 8 December 2009, DA NO. 1178/2009/HA – Place of Worship – Lot 2 DP 263960 – 33 Nelson Road, Nelson, 2009.

hooks, bell. *Yearning: Race, Gender and Cultural Politics*, Boston, MA: South End Press, 1990.

Hopkins, Peter. 'Young People, Masculinities, Religion and Race: New Social Geographies', *Progress in Human Geography*, Vol. 31, No. 2 (April 2002): 163–77.

Jacobs, Keith. 'Discourse Analysis and its Utility for Urban Policy Research', *Urban Policy and Research*, Vol. 24, No. 1 (2006): 39–52.

Joshi, Khyati. 'The Racialization of Hinduism, Islam, and Sikhism in the United States', *Equity and Excellence in Education*, Vol. 39, No. 3 (Aug. 2006): 211–26.

Kerin, Lindy. 'Islamic Centre Welcomed by Sydney's Annangrove Community', *ABC PM*, 29 May 2008, <http://www.abc.net.au/pm/content/2008/s2259708.htm> (20 March 2011).

Kong, Lily. 'Global Shifts, Theoretical Shifts: Changing Geographies of Religion', *Progress in Human Geography*, Vol. 34, No. 6 (Dec. 2010): 755–78.

Kristeva, Julia. *Powers of Horror: An Essay on Abjection*, translated by Leon Roudiez, New York: Columbia University Press, 1982.

Lefebvre, Henri. *The Production of Space*, Cambridge: Blackwell, 1991.

Levitt, Peggy. 'Redefining the Boundaries of Belonging: The Institutional Character of Transnational Religious Life', *Sociology of Religion*, Vol. 65, No. 1 (2004): 1–18.

Lipsitz, George. 'The Possessive Investment in Whiteness: Racialized Social Democracy and the 'White' Problem in American Studies', *American Quarterly*, Vol. 47 (Sept. 1995): 369–87.

Low, Setha. 'Maintaining Whiteness: The Fear of Others and Niceness', *Transforming Anthropology*, Vol. 17, No. 2 (Oct. 2009): 79–92.

Marston, Greg. 'Critical Discourse Analysis and Policy-Orientated Housing Research', *Housing, Theory and Society*, Vol. 19, No. 2 (June 2002): 82–91.

McCann, Eugene. 'Race, Protest, and Public Space: Contextualizing Lefebvre in the US City', *Antipode*, Vol. 31, No. 2 (April 1999): 163–84.

Pandey, Gyanendra. 'Can a Muslim be an Indian?', *Comparative Studies in Society and History*, Vol. 41, No. 4 (Oct. 1999): 608–29.

Pulido, Laura. 'Rethinking Environmental Racism: White Privilege and Urban Development in Southern California', *Annals, Association of American Geographers*, Vol. 90, No. 1 (March 2000): 12–40.

Rose, Gillian. *Feminism and Geography: The Limits of Geographical Knowledge*, Cambridge: Polity Press, 1993.

Routledge, Paul. 'The Third Space as Critical Engagement', *Antipode*, Vol. 28, No. 4 (Oct. 1996): 399–419.

Sandercock, Leonie. *Towards Cosmopolis: Planning for Multicultural Cities*, London: Wiley, 1997.

——. 'Introduction', *Planning Theory*, Vol. 13 (1995): 10–34.

Shaw, Wendy. 'Decolonizing Geographies of Whiteness', *Antipode*, Vol. 38, No. 4 (Aug. 2006): 851–69.

Shree Swaminarayan Temple v. Baulkham Hills Shire Council. New South Wales Land and Environment Court 1218, 2 Aug. 2011.

Singh, Jaideep. 'The Racialization of Minoritized Religious Identity: Constructing Sacred Sites at the Intersection of White and Christian Supremacy', in *Revealing the Sacred in Asian and Pacific America*, edited by Jane Iwamura and Paul Spickard, New York: Routledge, 2003, pp. 87–106.

Soja, Edward. *Postmetropolis: Critical Studies of Cities and Regions*, Malden, MA: Blackwell, 2000.

——. *Thirdspace: Journeys to Los Angeles and Other Real-and-Imagined Places*, Malden, MA: Blackwell, 1996.

Strauss, Anselm and Juliet Corbin. *Basics of Qualitative Research: Grounded Theory Procedures and Techniques*, London: Sage Publications, 1990.

The Sydney Morning Herald (SMH), 3 April 2011.

Trudeau, Daniel. 'Politics of Belonging in the Construction of Landscapes: Place-making, Boundary Drawing and Exclusion', *Cultural Geographies*, Vol. 13, No. 3 (July 2006): 421–33.

Vaara, Eero, Virpi Sorsa and Pekka Pälli. 'On the Force Potential of Strategy Texts: A Critical Discourse Analysis of a Strategic Plan and its Power Effects in a City Organization', *Organization*, Vol. 17, No. 6 (May 2010): 685–702.

Varadarajan, Siddarth (ed.). *Gujarat: The Making of a Tragedy*, New Delhi: Penguin Books, 2002.

Williams, Raymond. *An Introduction to Swaminarayan Hinduism*, Cambridge: Cambridge University Press, 2001.

Wilshire Webb Staunton Beattie. Statement of Facts and Contentions. Filed for Hills Shire Council, Land and Environment Court NSW 10147/2010, 2010.

Yiftachel, Oren. *Ethnocracy: Land and Identity Politics in Israel/Palestine*, Philadelphia: University of Pennsylvania Press, 2006.

——. 'Planning and Social Control: Exploring the Dark Side', *Journal of Planning Literature*, Vol. 12, No. 2 (May 1998): 395–406.

Young, Iris Marion. *Justice and the Politics of Difference*, Princeton: Princeton University Press, 1990.

CHAPTER 12

From Ahmedabad to Karnavati

Cultural Roots and Socio-Spatial Aspects of Intolerance

Tommaso Bobbio

The third consecutive election of Narendra Modi to the Chief Ministership of Gujarat in December 2012 can be read from many perspectives. Firstly, it definitely sanctioned the personal success of Modi as a political leader, both within his party – the Bharatiya Janata Party (BJP) – and in terms of public opinion. In spite of being a highly controversial figure, who was opposed by factions within his own party, Modi was selected again by the people for his image of a model of good governance, as well as efficient and transparent politics (Sud 2008; Bobbio 2012). Secondly, the vote testified once again to the fact that the 2002 anti-Muslim pogroms, and the proven involvement of state apparatuses in the carnage, did not represent a determinant factor in influencing vote patterns. While the 2002 electoral campaign focused on issues relating to the violence (Mehta 2006), the two subsequent campaigns (in 2007 and 2012) were mostly centred around economic themes, so that, for Modi, to show a positive record in terms of development and growth rates was more of a priority than answering all the accusations of being directly responsible for the massacres. Thirdly, the election results show that the victory of the BJP was based in the urban areas, where it obtained a huge majority, while in rural constituencies the BJP and the Congress Party were almost even (Shah 2012; Election Commission of India 2012). This neat cleavage between urban and rural areas is one of the most significant clues that the election results provide us in order to interpret the social and cultural background of the rise of Modi. As we will see, since the early 1990s, and more powerfully after 2002, the BJP and Modi constantly sought to build electoral consent on an agenda stressing concepts such as development, growth, modernisation and globalisation (see Guichard's chapter in this volume). These arguments, combined with the ideological base of Hindutva, proved successful in enticing the middle classes along with all those sectors of the urban population which aspired to benefit from the fruits of development policies. Lastly, although socio-cultural trends of this election will emerge more clearly in the long run, the BJP has built its success in promoting its idea of development as a cross-cultural, interreligious and inter-caste political culture. In this frame, all issues regarding economic inequalities, social and cultural marginalisation, and religious discrimination disappear in front of a progressive view of economic growth that is seen to possess an almost natural power to benefit people indiscriminately.

Looking back at the rise of the BJP as the leading political actor in Gujarat, this chapter argues that the main success of the party has been on a cultural level. Much before the rise of Modi as the undisputed leader of state politics, the BJP had laid the base for the promotion of a seductive, as well as a very adaptive public culture, in which traditional arguments of the Hindu right, equating the Indian nation with the majority Hindu community against the minority Muslim community, were combined with a 'modernist' propaganda following the adoption of a neo-liberal paradigm in economic policies after 1991. Both the political success of Modi and the overwhelming participation of 'ordinary people' in the state-sponsored 2002 pogroms can be understood in this frame. Moreover, the widespread assimilation of a rhetoric around development and growth allowed Modi, and the BJP, to completely shift the focus of their political propaganda after 2002, and to become keen advocates of an apparently all-inclusive model of development. Despite the fact that development patterns since the 1991 reforms generated more inequalities and exacerbated the marginality of the lower sectors of society (Mahadevia 2002, 2003; Sud 2007), in urban areas the shift towards a service-based, consumerist-oriented, model of development was seen as a promise of upward mobility and the symbol of a success story

(Joshi 2000). The industrial sector in urban areas, and in Ahmedabad in particular, had entered a declining phase in the 1980s. In the subsequent decade the adoption of neo-liberal reforms fostered a new wave of private investment in infrastructure and services that drove the recovery of the economy.

It is beyond the scope of this chapter to investigate in detail the shift from an industrial-based to a service-based economic model and its consequences to the urban milieu of Ahmedabad. However, one should keep in mind that these reforms came at the end of a decade of a deep economic crisis for Ahmedabad, in which most of the textile industries shut down, leaving some 120,000 workers jobless. Thus, the enormous impact of the reforms came in terms of the casualisation of the labour market, and the consequent loss of job security and income for large sectors of society.[1] The entrance of tens of thousands of people in the informal sector of the economy, as petty traders, or self-employed labourers has been welcomed as the triumph of self-entrepreneurship, as a result of the spirit of initiative and 'courage' of the people who drew Ahmedabad out of the crisis as a result of their efforts.[2] In this frame, the rhetoric about economic development became part of a discourse aimed at glorifying the ideal Gujarati middle-class. It is in such a construction that one can see what Prakash (2003: 1602) defined as the 're-imagination of the state' under the banner of Hindutva identity-politics. The peculiar aspect that this process had in Gujarat, in respect to the rest of the country, is that this whole ideological construction underpinned the definition of a local Gujarati cultural specificity combining Hindu values and neo-liberal argument.

The construction of such a culture borrowed typical elements of a so-called Gujarati cultural tradition, specifically from an upper-caste Brahmin and Baniya fold, mixing them with the stereotypical features of a globalised society, in order to create an image of the Gujarati population as more predisposed than others to enter the global economic markets and do business in a 'modern', post-industrial economy. The success of this narrative in becoming part of the public culture of the city lay in its intrinsic ambiguity. Development arguments are presented as the final step towards egalitarianism, as 'every community is reaping the fruit of development' (Thottam 2012: 4). Even secularism is now mainly understood in the frame of economic development, as Vishwanathan (quoted in Yadav 2011) pointed out: 'Secular-speak is always in the language of economic rationality. Investment can be calculated, so it is rational. Anything outside this is subjective, ethnic and irrational'. Inclusive as it may appear, such a rhetoric is in fact highly exclusive, as defining an idea of Gujaratiness following traditional high caste, Hindu and Jain values, makes its boundaries neatly marked along religious lines.[3]

From this point of view, the 'middle-class revolution', which revived the economy of Gujarat in the last two decades, marked at the same time the revival of a conservative and revivalist culture. An increasing intolerance towards the urban poor and the Muslim minority was hindered in the rhetoric of a strife to modernise Gujarati society (Patel 2002). The BJP's ability to represent both elements – progressive towards the economy and conservative towards culture and morals – lay at the base of the party's strong electoral success in state elections for two decades. At the same time, the slow but steady propaganda activity that the Sangh Parivar (the universe of Hindu extremist organisations moving around the Rashtriya Swayamsevak Sangh (RSS), the Vishva Hindu Parishad (VHP) and the BJP) conducted in most cities and districts of the state, allowed the consolidation of a shared culture that, claiming to revive central aspects of the local tradition and ethos, became in fact a culture of prejudice and intolerance against all those sectors that were not identified in this revivalist idea of Gujarati culture.

CULTURE, RELIGION AND THE INFILTRATION OF HINDUTVA IN THE DAILY LIFE OF AHMEDABAD

In the debate about the rise of the Hindu right in Gujarat, many scholars agree in identifying the state, since the mid-1980s, as a 'laboratory of Hindutva' (Patel 2002; Shah 2002a, 2002b; Yagnik and Sheth 2005, 2011; Shani 2007; Spodek 2010, 2011). In particular, Shani (2007) has pointed out that from the 1980s onwards, by taking advantage of the industrial crisis and the consequent loss of social and cultural points of reference for thousands of retrenched workers, the Sangh Parivar engaged in extensive campaigns to promote ethno-nationalist principles at a cultural and political level. Moreover, Hindu extremists also found a fertile ground among the local middle classes, mainly due to their ability to combine communal elements, based on an openly anti-Muslim agenda, with a more subtle component of identity politics that resorted to a standardised depiction of local higher-caste cultural traditions to define the terms of a Gujarati identity. Elements typical of the traditional upper-caste mercantile elites in the city, such as peace and harmony, vegetarianism, an entrepreneurial spirit, and a rather undefined attitude to combine traditional values with a modern business orientation thus became the widely recognised values defining the modern Gujarati ethos. The association of such a form of regional ethno-religious culture with a rhetoric of development and progress provided legitimacy for the BJP in front of all those sectors of the urban middle class that would have not aligned themselves with an extremist communal ideology, but enthusiastically supported a party that championed economic growth and globalisation.

Over the last two decades of the twentieth century, the main elements of such a political rhetoric became part of a shared culture among the lower-middle and middle classes of Ahmedabad. Regional chauvinism as well as an increasing intolerance towards the urban poor and the Muslim community are now part of the daily language of large portions of the urban population, and inform the management of the urban space at an administrative level.

The present section shows how such a culture of intolerance has become pervasive in Ahmedabad. By taking into account two relevant episodes that marked the public debate at the turn of the century, this chapter argues that not only did the BJP and all Hindu extremist groups favour the radicalisation of an aggressive and falsely progressive political rhetoric, but that they also contributed to crystallising forms of spatial segregation in the geography of a city like Ahmedabad. Firstly, the controversy about the possibility of changing the name of the city from Ahmedabad to that of a presumed antecedent urban centre called Karnavati (established by the Solanki King Karna I, AD c.1072–1094), found large coverage in the public and political debate during the 1990s.[4] Following other name changes in cities like Bombay, Calcutta and Madras, local BJP politicians sought to 'restore' the alleged original name of

Ahmedabad, but while those other examples showed forms of revivalism directed against British colonial rule, here the attempt was to rewrite history in order to erase the memory of the first five centuries of life of the city. Hence, the attempt to change the name of Ahmedabad can be understood as part of the construction of a larger propaganda discourse aimed at depicting the Muslims as alien, and equating them with the invaders of five centuries earlier.

Secondly, the proliferation of illegal roadside temples in the city provides an interesting angle to observe form and practices of a Gujarati-Hindu culture in the daily life of the city. More than representing places of worship, illegal temples have become places for socialisation and, more than accommodating the practice of religion, they provide stages for the display of religiosity. This will be looked at in further detail later in the chapter.

Ten years after the 2002 pogroms, collective violence and social conflicts have apparently made way for 'peace, harmony and development' (Modi 2011) in contemporary Gujarat. Whether this is true, and whether it can be considered to be the result of excellent growth rates is open to debate. But what needs to be highlighted is that in urban areas, where the BJP has made the greatest harvest of votes in the past elections, such a model of development contributed to the increase of inequalities and of the number of urban poor and slum dwellers (Shah 2012; NSS 2010). Understanding the cultural roots of the so-called middle-class revolution in Gujarat is the first step in untangling the political ambiguity of a party that built its strongholds in urban centres while, at the same time, creating the largest inequalities within the urban social and spatial landscape (Shinoda 2000). On the one hand, the BJP presented itself as the champion of modernisation and growth; on the other it gathered votes from across all sectors of society through a rhetoric that is highly exclusive and intolerant.

BEYOND THE MANCHESTER OF INDIA

Karnavati as the New Name for Global Ahmedabad

The name Karnavati has been associated with the city of Ahmedabad for a long time. Ancient histories and chronicles about the city often contained references to a former agglomeration named after the Solanki King Karna I, who ruled over the region between AD c.1072 and c.1094 (Forbes 1856). The presence of some sort of pre-existing human settlement, in the area where Sultan Ahmed Shah founded Ahmedabad in AD c. 1411, remains unquestioned in most narratives, although the definition of the spatial and demographic dimension, as well as the exact location of the supposed town or village remains vague. In post-independence times, references to the town of Karnavati had marginal space, as the matter had a highly destabilising potential for Hindu-Muslim relations. However, in documents and official reports of the Ahmedabad Municipal Council (AMC), the information was mentioned and the existence of a township older than Ahmedabad was assumed as historical truth.[5]

The issue burst into the realm of politics as soon as the BJP became a dominant political actor both in the city and in the state governments. After the party gained a majority in the AMC in 1990, the city's municipal board passed a bill proposing to change the name of the city to Karnavati: the resolution was rejected by the central government, but the issue remained central in the political debate of the city (*The Times of India* 2004). Within the main frame of the Hindu nationalist propaganda, the name change symbolised a restoration of justice, which the Muslim invasion of Gujarat (AD 1298–1299) had violated. At the same time, this political battle implicitly, but rather directly, characterised the Muslim population of Ahmedabad as the invaders (alien to the 'real' Gujarati ethos), who had allegedly destroyed a flourishing Hindu township. In this sense, the discourse around the change in the city's name was meant to endorse Hindutva's propaganda, providing historical depth to the claims about the supposed Hindu character of the local identity.

After the first refusal from the central government, the BJP, which remained in charge of the city's administration almost uninterruptedly for the whole decade, carried on campaigning for the restoration of the city's original name. Hitherto, these campaigns have not reached their goal and Ahmedabad has retained its name. The controversy has lost momentum as a political argument, but the narrative representing the city's past in a monochromatic Hindu light, and depicting the Muslim community as alien, has gradually entered the popular culture of the city. In fact, changing the name of Ahmedabad has gone beyond being a political issue and has become part of the cultural project of the Sangh Parivar. When the historical image of Karnavati entered the public domain as an established truth, it appeared relatively less important to insist on the political dimension of the issue. As another testimony of the success in the state of the cultural project of Hindutva, the supposed Hindu city of Karnavati has entered popular narratives about the city's past, gaining, at the same time, increasing importance in marking the landscape of modern expanding Ahmedabad. In this respect, two aspects are significant in understanding how Karnavati occupied a symbolic role in the attribution of a Hindu past to present-day Ahmedabad. Firstly, the wide use of the name for private and public places in the city, especially in the newly developed commercial areas on the western side of the Sabarmati river. Secondly, the consolidation of a narrative equating the controversy around the name in Ahmedabad to cities like Mumbai or Chennai, where the restoration of the original name was in opposition to British colonial rule. The justification of the claim over Ahmedabad's name in the same frame as the quest to change British colonial names automatically led to associating the Muslim community with the colonisers, and consequently to labelling the former as invaders, and alien.

Before considering these two aspects, it is useful to understand the controversy from a historical perspective. Did Ahmed Shah found his city on the site of a pre-existing township? Whether Karnavati was an important town or a small village, is it meaningful to characterise it as a 'Hindu' town as opposed to a 'Muslim' Ahmedabad? References to Karnavati in historical sources and chronicles about the city are vague and do not allow us to ascertain either the dimension or the exact location of a township with that name. In his 1856 *Ras Mala*, Alexander Kinloch Forbes (see Bhatt's chapter in this volume) includes the reign of Karna Solanki over the region now included in North Gujarat. Quoting Merutunga, a chronicler who lived at the court of Karna's successor Siddharaja (AD 1094–1143), Forbes (1856) says that Raja Karna was the first ruler who devoted his attention to fight the tribes of Bhils and Kolis that lived on the regions of eastern Gujarat between the Rann of Kutch and the Sabarmati river. Reportedly, these tribes consisted of 'hereditary and professional plunderers', and Raja Karna conducted a series of military campaigns against them (ibid.: 79). Among these, the major campaign was against a Bhil chieftain named Asha, who lived at Ashawal (or Ashapalli), 'near the city of Ahmedabad'. After defeating the Bhil ruler, Karna Solanki 'built in the same place a temple to a Devee, called Kochuruv'. Following Merutunga, Forbes goes on to state that after his victory, Raja Karna also founded a city, called Karnavati, the position of which 'cannot be decisively ascertained' (ibid.).

There are two interesting elements that emerge from this account: the first is that not only Karnavati, but also a city called Ashawal, the headquarters of a tribal group, was located on the banks of the Sabarmati. The second is the impossibility of ascertaining the location and dimension of Karnavati; if it appears likely that Raja Karna founded a township with his name, it does not seem that the settlement ever acquired any great importance. The capital of the Solanki Kingdom remained based in the city of Anhilvad (present-day Patan in north Gujarat), until the fifteenth century – after the first invasion of Gujarat (AD 1298) – when the new capital of Ahmedabad was founded. Arab and Persian sources of the same period, such as works by the Moroccan geographer al-Idrisi, mention the city of Ashawal as a populous and rich commercial centre at the end of the eleventh century, the time of Karna's campaign against the Bhils. Even chronicles of the fourteenth and fifteenth centuries mention the city, mainly as the place near which Ahmed Shah founded his capital, while there are no references to a township named Karnavati (Commissariat 1938). As no references appear in any of these sources of a possible conquest of Karnavati by Ahmed Shah, it appears difficult to think of Ahmedabad as having been constructed on the site of another city.

Spatial references that can help us locate those settlements point to the western bank of the Sabarmati river; the temple that Karna Solanki founded to celebrate his victory against the Bhil King Asha was called Kochuruv, which has survived until the present day, and is known as the village of Kocharab, an urban village of

Ahmedabad, near Paldi Bridge. Another source, the account of Emperor Humayun's invasion of Gujarat (1535–1536) by historian Nizam-ud-Din Ahmad refers to the fact that 'Mirza Askari and his nobles left Ahmedabad' and 'formed a camp in the rear of Asawal opposite Sarganj (Sarkhej)' (ibid.: 61). If these references are trustworthy then it is possible to argue that Ashawal was located on the western bank of the Sabarmati, on the opposite side of the site where Ahmedabad was then located.[6] There might have been another settlement, called Karnavati, placed on the eastern side of the river, opposite Ashawal, but there are no references to two large and important cities being placed one in front of the other. What appears more certain is that towards the end of the fourteenth century, the newly appointed governor of the province, Muzaffar Khan, stayed in Ashawal before marching towards the capital Anhilvad (1392), while no references at all to Karnavati are present in two important Persian chronicles on Ahmedabad, the *Mirat-i-Sikandari* (1611) and the *Mirat-i-Ahmadi* (c.1750–1760). This adds a further element to the question of whether Ahmedabad was founded on the ruins of a pre-existing Hindu city.

Townships on the Sabarmati river retained an important position in the commercial routes from the Gulf of Cambay to the regions in northern and central India, and that must have been one of the main reasons that attracted the attention of both Karna Solanki in the eleventh and Ahmed Shah in the fifteenth centuries. However, at the time when Ahmed Shah moved the capital of Gujarat from Anhilvad to the new site, the whole valley of the Sabarmati river was already under the control of the Muzaffarid Sultanate (Sikandar 1961). Thus, the only battle that may have taken place on those grounds was that between the Hindu Raja Karna Solanki and the Bhil chieftain Asha, in the eleventh century. In this light, the rhetoric about a Hindu-Muslim clash in relation to the city loses much of its strength.[7]

The claim by Hindu extremists, including Modi, that Karnavati should be restored as the original name of the city is devoid of any historical basis. In fact it represents a case of substitution of history with propaganda in public debate, in order to erase traces of the Muslim heritage from the city's past and rewrite its history according to the mainstream Hindutva narrative.[8]

Interestingly, in the reconstruction of a Gujarati-Hindu past of the city, not only did the Hindutva main narrative erase the name Ahmedabad, but it also concealed the city of Ashawal, for which there would be much more solid evidence to claim its precedence over Ahmedabad. What disqualified Ashawal to be chosen as the 'real' original name of Ahmedabad was probably that the town was originally the capital of the Bhil tribe, which is still a consistent Adivasi group in Gujarat, and this would have stained the image of a glorious Hindu past.

Although Ahmedabad still retains its name, the controversy has had a strong impact on the political debate in the city over the past two decades. The name Karnavati has progressively become part of public memory and of the spatial organisation of contemporary Ahmedabad. People often refer to Karnavati suggesting that the name change should be pursued, as it was for many other Indian cities that regained the name they had before British rule. In this sense, changing the name of the city would symbolise eliminating the main element that was reminiscent of a non-Hindu identity of the city. Moreover, in the definition of Gujarati culture, to associate with the modern and globalised aspirations of the local middle classes, the claim of a Hindu past for the city supported the assertion of a local culture that was exclusively Hindu. In recent times, the proliferation of places in the city that are named after the ancient Hindu city can be seen as another testimony of the penetration of a Gujarati-Hindu rhetoric within the urban culture. The emergence of a number of housing societies, tenements, shops and a large sports club named after Karnavati can be seen as a significant sign of a deep penetration of the mainstream Hindutva narrative, and its symbols, in the core of the city's public culture.

Roadside Temples and the Emergence of a New Religiosity

Roadside temples are phenomena that have gathered increasing importance in the past years in Ahmedabad. Constructions of this kind are usually illegal, and arise on roads or junctions with an intense transit of vehicles and people throughout the day. The presence of illegal temples in Ahmedabad is not new in itself, but in recent times a large number of new constructions have surfaced on the sidewalks of some of the most crowded avenues in the middle class commercial areas of the western city, attracting an increasing number of visitors every day. Moving around the city it is possible to spot many of these temples at various stages of development: usually they start as small idols placed on a stone or on a tree alongside the road; in the second stage of development a small altar is constructed around the idol, where people can start placing offerings and where *puja* (worship) can be offered daily; finally, as time passes, the temple 'owner' starts building a semi-permanent structure around the altar, always in tacit collaboration with local municipal or political authorities, and the spot is gradually transformed into a temple.[9]

One such example is the small temple of Hanuman located on one side of IIM Crossroad, on Dr Vikram Sarabhai Marg, beside the entrance of the old campus of the Indian Institute of Management (IIM). The temple rises literally on the road, in one of the most congested junctions of western Ahmedabad, and it receives thousands of visitors every day: morning visitors are usually workers who stop there to offer prayers on the way to the office; throughout the day many college students and professors often stop for a brief visit; in the evening and at night the temple attracts even more visitors and becomes a social pole of attraction for large groups of people. Beside the temple there is a tea stall, open from early morning until late at night, and the proximity between the two has transformed that corner into one of the most popular places for nightlife in the area. Almost every day, from early evening to late at night, the corner is populated with groups of people who come to visit the temple and then indulge in drinking tea and chatting on the side of the road. On average, the visitors conform to a standard prototype of the middle- and upper-class society in the city. Youngsters come to the temple on their brand-new motorbikes, dressed in western fashion accessorised with status symbols, such as mobile phones, western branded clothes, sunglasses, etc., typically associated with the middle- and upper-classes. Besides them, many adults and families arrive at the temple by car, park chaotically on the road, and drink tea leaning up against their vehicles before driving back home. The temple is always packed with visitors and the sound of the temple bells mixes with the noise from the traffic and people chatting. Despite the large number of visitors, the atmosphere during the evenings at the IIM Crossroad is far from religious.

The connection between the temple and the tea stall makes this spot a perfect representation of a new form of religiosity and devotion that has spread among the urban middle class in correspondence with the consolidation of Hindutva as a cultural and political ideology. From the 1970s onwards, the emergence of new middle-class neighbourhoods in western Ahmedabad has been paralleled by a growing display of religious symbols and exterior forms of religious devotionalism among the middle class. As historian Devrat N. Pathak states, lower caste middle class people seek legitimacy for their wealth by associating themselves with religion: 'these new middle class Gujaratis do not love religion but they love religiosity – for demonstration' (Citizens for Justice and Peace 2002: 214). This attitude towards religion became more evident towards the end of the century, as the Sangh Parivar sought to enlarge and mobilise its social base through the organisation of religious demonstrations, processions, rallies and all sorts of public display of religious symbols. In Gujarat this led to a decade of 'politics of yatras' between the mid-1980s and the mid-1990s, where the constant organisation of moments of public religiosity provided local middle-class people with many opportunities to demonstrate a sense of unity, and, at the same time, offered the security of a political representative (Yagnik and Sheth 2005: 257-ff). Hence, religion and religiosity at a social level became forms of legitimisation for the upwardly mobile middle caste and class in the city. The increasing number of illegal temples, as well as the massive attendance at public religious moments, such as festivals and processions, is testimony to the importance that religiosity acquired in defining spaces of sociability in the new areas of the city.

Forms of devotion associated with roadside temples appear as an affirmation of the 'politics of yatra'; people visit the temple as a way of iterating their affiliation to a community, to show that they belong to a well-defined group, one defined through the distorted lenses of Hindutva. Evening gatherings at the IIM Crossroad constitute daily representations of such an affiliation to the Gujarati-Hindu community, as people publicly, on the side of a congested road, leave their token to the deity before joining the city's nightlife. At the same time, the proliferation of illegal temples contributes to shaping the landscape of the changing city. These constructions, other than being places for displaying devotion, are private enterprises: 'running' a roadside temple means managing an informal, and illegal, business. Temples collect large amounts of money in the form of offerings from devotees and, in some cases, determine the wealth and power of families who own the land where temples are built. Moreover, illegal temples are unplanned and unregulated constructions and represent obstacles to the implementation of planning projects. In many cases, the presence of a temple becomes a matter of controversy in the realisation of infrastructural projects, as in the case of slum clearance or in the construction of new roads: if a new project runs over the structure of an illegal temple, local people often organise opposition groups to stop the project, mobilising citizens at the neighbourhood level. For instance, in February 2000, a mob of VHP activists ransacked the office of Ahmedabad's mayor (himself a BJP member) to protest against the planned demolition of a temple in Maninagar (*The Hindu* 2000). This suggests elements of a dualistic relationship between the rise of illegal temples and the emergence of Hindutva as a cultural phenomenon. On one hand, these temples represent important nodes in the network of associations and groups linked with the Sangh Parivar: they are strongly rooted in the territory and play an important role in mobilising people around religious and political issues. On the other hand, the organisations or the individuals that own the temples also acquire greater economic power due to the offerings that people leave daily, and this increases their influence at a local political level. In this way, roadside temples can be seen as a further element that consolidates the relation between the spread of a culture based on an ethno-religious, exclusivist idea of Hinduism (or Gujaratiness) and a political party, the BJP, which aims at representing the interests of those who identify with this culture.

CONCLUSION

Middle Class as a Code of Conduct

The idea of a middle class, as it has been referred to in this chapter, aligns with the conceptualisation made by the BJP and by the whole range of Hindu extremist associations in order to attract a large section of the electorate. As we have seen, the definition of the middle class encompasses different elements: the promise of unending progress and development; a blind faith in the universal benefits of economic growth; an ideal representation, based on consumerism, of the way of living of the middle classes in the western world; a strong attachment to a constructed form of religious orthodoxy; and the revival of regional cultural stereotypes to legitimise the claim to a local subnational identity. Rhetoric about the Gujarati-Hindu identity and ethos has dominated public culture in Ahmedabad from the late 1980s, and consolidated the myth of a successful middle-class society creating out its own space in the globalised world.

From the beginning of the 1990s, such a conceptual frame has become increasingly dominant not only as the outcome for a political culture, but also as a public culture shared by large sectors of the urban society. On the one hand, the electoral successes of the BJP in the state and municipal elections since the late 1980s are indicative of how political propaganda based on a mix of economic, religious and cultural aspects could attract the votes of different socio-economic groups. On the other hand, the typical symbols of globalised consumerism have acquired a central role in the definition of the physical (with the rise of shopping centres, Western chain restaurants and shops) and socio-cultural (with the adoption of consumer goods as status symbols) landscape of Ahmedabad. The parallel radicalisation of religious intolerance in the city is evidence of the relationship between economic upward mobility and religious and cultural sectarianism.

However, while in the idiom of the emerging political culture the expression 'middle class' has gained centrality, as a formula recalling a well defined economic and cultural imaginary, the same expression lost part of its weight in identifying and quantifying a specific social group. As it was shaped by the Sangh Parivar, the rhetoric about the 'rising middle class' in Gujarat proposed an image which corresponded to a rather restricted portion of society – the highly skilled workforce employed in financial and service activities. However, larger segments of the population could see their aspirations represented in that image. In order to understand this dichotomy between a 'real' and an 'imagined' middle class it is important to consider when and how people label themselves as part of this group. The category middle class appears, then, as a rather heterogeneous group in terms of wealth, life standards, social position, caste and real access to the market of 'western-type' consumer goods of its members. The range of people considering themselves as middle-class citizens stretches to enclose a large variety of people: from the Brahman physician living in a bungalow in Navrangpura, to the family of a bank clerk in a row house in Ghatlodiya, to the retired college professor living in an apartment near Nehru Nagar, to the migrant shop-keeper in Maninagar. For different reasons these people would all include themselves in the middle class, although they would have very little in common as regards daily life.[10]

One aspect that seems to link all these different versions of the middle class is an ambiguous relationship that its members have with ideas such as modernity and development: on the one hand they aim at the western symbols of wealth, through the adoption of various goods that can associate them with a western lifestyle (see Mawani's chapter in this volume). On the other, they constantly assert a specificity that distinguishes them from the West, in a 'quest for equality through difference' (Hansen 1999: 232) that betrays a sense of peripherality and the desire to be integrated in the globalised world. In these terms, Hansen (ibid.: 235) has spoken about an 'unease with modernity,' considering it as the prerogative of the rise of Hindu nationalism from the 1980s onwards. I would suggest that the heterogeneity of their social and economic background, as well as the different behaviours and political orientations that the middle class label includes, are outcomes for long-term transformations of the urban social milieu, within which the textile crisis and the reconstruction of the city's economy during the 1990s represented two critical moments. In this perspective, the Sangh Parivar and the BJP emerged as the most successful actors in framing the contours of a political culture shaped around an 'identity-mania' (Daechsel 2006: 6).

The BJP appropriated the reference to a middle class, filling it with ideas of modernity and globalisation, the rediscovery of a local identity and of a religious morality, to constitute a symbolic landmark for a broader portion of the electorate. In this sense, the category started to define more an ethos than a homogeneous social background: people started to conform to exterior canons, in order to be part of the middle-class revolution that constituted the core rhetoric of the Hindu right at the turn of the century. The adoption of certain symbols, from modern consumer goods to the public display of religiosity, became a discriminant in the definition of new 'class' boundaries. Hence, by describing themselves as middle class, people referred to their various ways of adapting to that ethos, more than implying an affiliation to a politically and sociologically compact group.[11]

Talking of a 'middle-class culture' refers to this range of instances among different social groups, which the Sangh Parivar sought to enclose under the umbrella of a political culture that interwove identity politics, religious extremism and the vision of a path towards progress and modernisation. Projecting itself as the legitimate political representative of all these instances, the BJP fostered a political rhetoric around ideas such as modernity, progress, and globalisation, in combination with a rediscovery of the cultural elements recalling a Gujarati tradition. As part of this propaganda, Ahmedabad became the social and physical space where these contrasting elements merged in the creation of a 'modern', 'globalised', 'Gujarati' society, at the base of which lay an increasing intolerance towards all social groups that did not fit that narrative, like the urban poor and religious minorities.

NOTES

1. The economic aspects relating to the industrial crisis in Ahmedabad during the 1980s and the impact of neo-liberal reforms have attracted wide scholarly attention and there is not enough space to summarise them here. For a thorough analysis of the economic and political aspect, see Hirway (2000), Mahadevia (2002, 2003), Jhabvala et al. (2003), Breman (2004), and the interesting and very detailed report SEWA (2000).
2. The term 'courage' recurred many times in the narration made by former BJP MLA and Speaker of the Gujarat Legislative Assembly Ashok Bhatt. In his view, the Gujarati people's courage, more than economic reforms, determined the recovery of the economy (Shinoda 2000; Interview with Ashok Bhatt, Ahmedabad, 30 May 2008).

3. As it emerged from the testimony of many social workers and activists, in Ahmedabad, the equation between Hindu and Gujarati identities became so rooted among certain sectors of society that native Gujarati Muslims were automatically classified through their religious affiliation instead of their regional origins, or mother tongue.
4. The city of Ahmedabad was founded in 1411 by Sultan Ahmed Shah, of the Muzaffarid dynasty, who reportedly laid on the ground the first brick for building the new capital of the Gujarat Sultanate.
5. See, for instance, Town Development Department (1975). The first controversy around the name rose in 1973, when the director of the Jamalpur telephone exchange (in a Muslim area of the old city) proposed to name it after Karnavati (*The Times of India* 1973). At that time, the debate did occupy some space in local newspapers, but it did not become a central issue in the city's public debate, as it did during the 1990s.
6. All these reflections need the support of archaeological surveys, which are still to be conducted. New rulers often made use of building materials taken from other towns or temples to build their cities, so it is unlikely that the ruins of a pre-existing city will be found anywhere around Ahmedabad (Commissariat 1938).
7. Even more so if one considers that during the reign of Karna Solanki many Sufi saints were reported to have settled down in the Solanki's capital, Anhilwad (Yagnik and Sheth 2005). Moreover, Hindu and Jain communities flourished mainly in the Muslim Mughal period.
8. It is important to mention that this is not a unique case, and there are other towns in Gujarat, such as Pirana, which are encountering similar challenges (Khan and Moir 1999; Khan 2004).
9. The story of many illegal temples in the city presents an interesting tangle of business, politics and the underworld, which has followed the expansion of the urban area of Ahmedabad. An analysis of such dynamics is beyond the scope of this section, which analyses illegal temples as places where a new form of Hindu religious devotionalism has found expression over the past decade. The subsequent description is based on direct observation, iterated over a fourteen-month period (October 2007-December 2008), as well as on interviews with local visitors to the temple and municipal officers.
10. This is in line with current research carried out in the UK on the class system in which the middle class forms the largest group and the second wealthiest (BBC 2013).
11. This understanding of the BJP's political propaganda and of the category of middle class provides a useful perspective to interpret

one of the most puzzling aspects of the 2002 pogroms in Ahmedabad. During the most intense phase of violence in the first week of March, while attacks on the Muslim community were taking place all over the city, many people took advantage of the situation to loot shops and malls, irrespective of the religious affiliation of the shopkeepers. As many sources reported, in the early days of the riots many people from the 'middle to upper-middle income bracket' took part in raiding shopping centres: as it happened, the closed-circuit televisions placed in the shops captured the unusual scene of people arriving at the shops by car and helping themselves to a vast range of consumer goods, from clothes to microwaves and jewellery (Bhatt 2002; Mathew 2002; Roy 2002). Such a materialistic frenzy, which apparently shared nothing with the bloodthirsty mobs that were engaged in slaughtering Muslims, may be explained in an opportunistic way, considering that people, under the cover of large scale rioting, took advantage of the situation to pursue personal interests (Brass 2003). The fact that looting was directed at those kinds of consumer goods, which are usually identified as belonging to the middle class, shows how such a category was more defined by the adoption of certain symbols than by sharing a range of interests and common values. The main characterisation that those symbols confer is the definite differentiation from another broad group, that of the urban poor, who are occupying increasing space in the construction of modern Ahmedabad.

REFERENCES

BBC News. 'The Great British Class Survey: Results', 3 April 2013, <http:www.bbc.co.uk/science/0/21970879> (5 April 2013).

Bhatt, Sheela. 'Sane Voices in Ahmedabad Call for Reason', *Rediff.com*, 2 March 2002, <http://www.rediff.com/news/2002/mar/01train17.htm> (25 January 2010).

Bobbio, Tommaso. 'Making Gujarat Vibrant: Hindutva, Development and the Rise of Subnationalism in India', *Third World Quarterly*, Vol. 33, No. 4 (2012): 657–72.

Brass, Paul. *The Production of Hindu-Muslim Violence in Contemporary India*, New Delhi: Oxford University Press, 2003.

Breman, Jan. *The Making and Unmaking of an Industrial Working Class: Sliding Down the Labour Hierarchy in Ahmedabad, India*, New Delhi: Oxford University Press, 2004.

Citizens for Justice and Peace. *Concerned Citizens Tribunal, Gujarat 2002*, Vol. 1, Mumbai: Citizens for Justice and Peace, 2002, <www.sabrang.com/tribunal> (Nov. 2004).

Commissariat, Manekshah Sorabshah. *A History of Gujarat: Including a Survey of its Chief Architectural Monuments and Inscriptions*, Bombay: Longmans, Green & Co., 1938.

Daechsel, Markus. *The Politics of Self-Expression: The Urdu Middle-Class Milieu in Mid-Twentieth Century India and Pakistan*, London: Routledge, 2006.

Election Commission of India. 'Results of Assembly Election Gujarat 2012', *Election Commission of India*, 2012, <http://eci.gov.in/eci_main1/Result_Gujarat.aspx> (3 January 2013).

Forbes, Alexander K. *Ras Mal: Hindoo Annals of the Province of Goozerat in Western India*, Delhi: Low Price Publications, 1856.

Hansen, Thomas Blom. *The Saffron Wave: Democracy and Hindu Nationalism in Modern India*, Princeton, NJ: Princeton University Press, 1999.

Hirway, Indira. 'Dynamics of Development in Gujarat: Some Issues', *Economic and Political Weekly*, Vol. 35, No. 35/36 (26 Aug. 2000): 3106–20.

Jhabvala, Renana, Ratna M. Sudarshan and Jeemol Unni. *Informal Economy Centrestage: New Structures of Employment*, New Delhi: Sage Publications, 2003.

Joshi, Vidyut. 'Cultural Context of Development', *Economic and Political Weekly*, Vol. 35, No. 35/36 (2000): 3165–69.

Khan, Dominique-Sila. *Crossing the Threshold: Understanding Religious Identities in South Asia*, London: I.B. Tauris, 2004.

Khan, Dominique-Sila and Zawahir Moir. 'Coexistence and Communalism: The Shrine of Pirana in Gujarati', *South Asia*, Vol. 22 (1999): 133–54.

Mahadevia, Darshini. 'Interventions in Development: A Shift Towards a Model of Exclusion', in *Poverty and Vulnerability in a Globalising Metropolis: Ahmedabad*, edited by Amitabh Kundu and Darshini Mahadevia, New Delhi: Manak Publications, 2002, pp. 80–132.

——. *Globalisation, Urban Reforms and Metropolitan Response: India*, Ahmedabad: School of Planning, Centre for Environmental Planning and Technology, in association with Manak, 2003.

Mathew, Vinod. 'The Middle Class Show-Up', *The Hindu Business Line*, 9 March 2002, <www.thehindubusinessline.in/2002/03/09/stories/2002030900051200.htm> (25 January 2010).

Mehta, Nalin. 'Modi and the Camera: The Politics of Television in the 2002 Gujarat Riots', *South Asia: Journal of South Asian Studies*, Vol. 29, No. 3 (2006): 395–414.

Modi, Narendra. 'Letter from Gujarat CM Narendra Modi to Citizens', 13 September 2011, <http://narendramodi.in/news/news_detail/1622> (Sept. 2011).

National Sample Survey (NSS). *Some Characteristics of Urban Slums 2008–2009 (NSS Report No 534)*, Ministry of Statistics and Programme Implementation, Government of India, 2010.

Patel, Girish. 'Narendra Modi's One-Day Cricket: What and Why?', *Economic and Political Weekly*, Vol. 37, No. 48 (2002): 4826–37.

Prakash, Aseem. 'Re-Imagination of the State and Gujarat's Electoral Verdict', *Economic and Political Weekly*, Vol. 38, No. 16 (2003): 1601–10.

Roy, Arundhati. 'Democracy: Who's She When She's at Home?', *Outlook*, 6 May 2002, <http://www.outlookindia.com/printarticle.aspx?215477> (25 January 2010).

Self Employed Women's Association. *Voices from the Streets: The National Vendors Campaign in India*, Ahmedabad: SEWA, 2000.

Shah, Ghanshyam. 'Caste, Hindutva and Hinduness', *Economic and Political Weekly*, Vol. 37, No. 15 (13 April 2002a): 1391–93.

——. 'Contestation and Negotiations: Hindutva Sentiments and Temporal Interests in Gujarat Elections', *Economic and Political Weekly*, Vol. 37, No. 48 (30 November 2002b): 4838–43.

Shah, Rajiv. 'Urban Gujarat: The Incumbency Riddle', *The Times of India*, 27 December 2012.

Shani, Ornit. *Communalism, Caste and Hindu Nationalism: The Violence in Gujarat*, Cambridge: Cambridge University Press, 2007.

Shinoda, Takashi. 'Institutional Change and Entrepreneurial Development: SSI Sector?', *Economic and Political Weekly*, Vol. 35, No. 35/36 (26 Aug. 2000): 3205–16.

Sikandar ibn Muhammad Manjhu ibn Akbar. *The Mirat-i-Sikandari: A History of Gujarat*, Baroda: Maharaja Sayajirao University of Baroda, 1961.

Spodek, Howard. 'In the Hindutva Laboratory: Pogroms and Politics in Gujarat, 2002', *Modern Asian Studies*, Vol. 44, No. 2 (2010): 349–49.

——. *Ahmedabad: Shock City of Twentieth Century India*, Bloomington: Indiana University Press, 2011.

Sud, Nikita. 'Constructing and Contesting a Gujarati-Hindu Ethno-religious Identity through Development Programmes in an

Indian Province', *Oxford Development Studies*, Vol. 35, No. 2 (2007): 131–48.

——. 'The Nano and Good Governance in Gujarat', *Economic and Political Weekly*, Vol. 43, No. 50 (13 December 2008): 13–14.

The Hindu. 'Temple Demolition Sours VHP-BJP Ties', 22 February 2000.

The Times of India. 'Ahmedabad is Karnavati Only in Speeches', 1 February 2004, <http://articles.timesofindia.indiatimes.com/2004-02-01/ahmedabad/28337392_1_bjp-leaders-resolution-bjp-councillor> (Dec. 2010).

——. 'New Name for Telephone Exchange Resented', Ahmedabad edition, 17 May 1973.

Town Development Department. *Revised Development Plan 1975–1985 Draft*, Ahmedabad: Ahmedabad Municipal Corporation, 1975.

Thottam, Jyoti. 'Boy from the Backyard', *TIME*, 26 March 2012, <http://www.time.com/time/printout/0,8816,2109164,00.html > (January 2013).

Yadav, A. 'The Truth Behind the Stage Show', *Tehelka*, 1 October 2011, <http://www.tehelka.com/the-truth-behind-the-stage-show/> (Nov. 2011).

Yagnik, Achyut and Suchitra Sheth. *The Shaping of Modern Gujarat: Plurality, Hindutva and Beyond*, New Delhi: Penguin Books, 2005.

——. *Ahmedabad: From Royal City to Megacity*, New Delhi: Penguin Books, 2011

Index

Adam, Robina, 125
Africanisation, 121, 147, 193
Agger, Ben, 90
Ahluwalia, Montek S., 25
Ahmed, Aftab, 46
Albrow, Martin, 79
Alemu, Abreham, 49
Alibhai-Brown, Yasmin, 196
Allen, Calvin Jr., 42, 46, 47, 50
Amin, Ash, 21
Amory, Deborah, 174
Anderson, Benedict, 21, 94
Anderson, Jon, 34, 244
Anderson-Gold, Sharon, 225
Anthias, Floya, 67, 72
Antholis, Wiliam J., 33
Anwar, Michael, 199
Anwar, Muhammad, 71, 121, 124, 129, 159
Appadurai, Arjun, 34
Asani, Ali S., 61, 62, 66, 68
Ashcroft, Bill, Gareth Griffiths and Helen Tiffin, 130
Asian Voice, 80
Atkinson, Anthony Barnes, 13
Backhaus, Norman, 24
Ball, Deborah L. and Hayman Bass, 216
Ballard, Roger, 121, 123, 124, 129, 130, 132
Barot, Rohit, 248
Barry, Monica, 13
Barth, Fredrik, 90, 127
Bauman, Zygmunt, 32
Baumann, Martin, 91
BBC, 61
Beck, Ulrich, 5
belonging
  creation of a sense of, 2,
    impact of migration on, 6;
    role of language in, 8–9;
    effect of culture on, 9–10
  elements of, 3–4,
    interconnection between, 4
  notion/process of, 1, 2–3, 4
Bhabha, Homi, 130, 134, 237, 247
Bhachu, Parminder, 122, 147
Bharati, Agehananda, 172, 173, 195, 196
Bhatti, Ghazala, 161
Bibby, Reginald W., 69

Blackledge, Adrian and Aneta Pavlenko, 146
Blair, Tony, 203
Bobbio, Tommaso, 31, 255
Bonnett, Alastair, 244
Boulter, Razia-Begum and Sadrudin Nanji, 60, 61
Bourdieu, Pierre, 181
Bourne, Jenny, 122
Bovill, Catherine and Margaret Leppard, 219
Brah, Avtar and Annie Coombes, 130
Brah, Avtar, 45, 121, 124, 129, 132, 199
Brenner, Neil, 21, 22, 24
British migration policy, 192
Brown, Colin, 201
Bucholtz, Mary, 146
Buck, Anthony, 198
Büschi, Michaela, 29

Canada, 211
  and multiculturalism, 211
Canagarajah, Suresh, 146
Caplan, Pat and Farouk Topan, 185
Carr, David and Jan Steutal, 226
Cassirer, Ernst, 8
Castells, Manuel, 183
Castles, Stephen and Alistair Davidson, 4
Chakravarti, Ritadhi, 25
Chambers, Iain, 133
Chandhoke, Neera, 32
Chauhan, Jaya, 172
Ching, Leo, 36
Chiriyankandath, James, 36
CIA, 61
Citizens for Justice and Peace, 267
Clayton, Anthony, 174
Clifford, James, 169
code-mixing, 87, 134
Cohen, Philip, 43, 244
Cohn, Bernard S., 113, 114
collective consciousness, 1
Collier, Mary Jane and Milt Thomas, 146
Commodification, 135
congressional Research Service (CRS), 33
Connor, Walker, 23
Conversi, Daniele, 90
Copland, Ian, 205
Corbridge, Stuart and John Harriss, 25
Cornell, Stephen and Douglas Hartmann, 1
cosmopolitan citizen, 226
Coward, Harold G., John. R. Hinnells and Raymond Brady Williams, 121
Creese, Angela et al., 151
cultural identity, 10, 146
cultural reconstruction techniques, 91
culture, 9, 90
  and ethnic identity, 90–91
  definitions of, 9

Daechsel, Markus, 270
Daftary, Farhad, 61
Dahya, Badr, 129
Dalpatram, Daya, 104, 106, 107, 109
Dasgupta, Manas, 31, 33
Dave, Mahendra, 109

De Fina, Anna, Deborah Schiffrin and Michael Bamberg, 146
De Vos, George A., 127, 146
de- and re-territorialisation movement, 22
  in India, 25, beginning of, 25; impact on Gujarat, 26–28
Deffner, Veronika and Carmella Pfaffenbach, 46
Deleuze, Gilles and Félix Guattari, 35
Democratic Republic of the Congo (DRC), 61
  Gujarati Ismailis in, 61–62, struggle for identity in, 62–28
Desai, Meghnad, 80
Desai, Neera A., 11
Desai, Rashmi, 121, 123, 190, 191, 193, 195, 196, 200, 201, 202
Desai, Usha, 148, 151
Deshgujarat, 27
deterritorialisation, 22
  in Gujarat, 26–30
Devine, Dympna, 225
Devnaa, 139
Dewey, John, 216
Dharker, Anil, et al., 33
diaspora studies/discourses, 43
  on women, 44
diaspora
  concept of, 44
  in the Arabian Gulf, 45
diasporic Asian feminism, 44
Dillon, Michele, 62
Dirks, Nicholas, 114, 171
Dobbin, Christine, 59, 60, 64, 66
Douglas, Mary, 171
Dove, L.A., 124
Dunbar, Robin, 85
Dunn, Kevin, James Forrest, Ian Burnley and Amy McDonald, 238
Durkheim, Émile, 1
Dutta, Chandrabali and Bula Bhadra, 90
Dwivedi, Manan, 172, 182
Dwyer, Rachel, 88

East India Company, 104
Easterby-Smith, Mark, Richard Thorpe and Andy Lowe, 64
economic reforms
  in India, 25
Edwards, John, 146
Esmail, Ally, 60
Esmail, Aziz, 220
ethnic group, 199
ethnic identity, 146
  cultural expressions of, 91–94
  culture and, 90–91
  symbols of, 2
ethnic minority research
  trends in, 125–26
ethnic, 63, 90
ethnicity
  and religion, relationship between, 63–64
  concept of, 63, 90, 146
Exclusion, 12
  approaches, 10, 12
  Components of, 12
  forms of, 12
  process of, 12

federal market economy, 25
Fenster, Tovi and Haim Yacobi, 236
Fenton, John Y., 91
Fenton, Steve, 90

Fine, Michelle, Lois Weis, Linda Pruitt and L. Mun Wong, 238
Fischler, Claude, 84
Fishman, Joshua, 146
Fonow, Mary M. and Judith A. Cook, 64
Forbes, Alexander K., 104, 105, 108, 109, 112, 115, 261, 262
Foucault, Michel, 244
Friedman, Thomas, 81
Frübing, Judith, 148

Gardner, Andrew M., 45
gendering/feminising diaspora
  process of, 43–44
Ghosh, Nirmal, 88
Ghuman, Paul A.S., 86, 91, 118
Giddens, Anthony, 5, 103, 115
Gidoomal, Ram, 118, 122, 123, 125, 126, 159
Giles, Howard and Kimberly A., 87
Gillan, Michael, 36
Gilroy, Paul, 130, 134
global society, 79
Globalisation, 4, 24, 78, 89, 94
  and migration, 6
  definitions of, 5, 78–79, 103
  effects of, 5–6
  in India, 80
  phenomenon of, 5
  qualities of, 5
globality, 5
glocal, 21, 22
glocalisation, 21, 80–81
  forms of, 81, in Mumbai, 81–82
Goldschmidt, Myra M., 149
Gómez-Peña, Guillermo, 130
Goodin, Robert, 13
Goswami, Rahul, 32
Government of Gujarat, 29
Gray, John, 130, 131
Gregory, Robert., 59, 66, 172, 177, 179, 197
Gujarat, 21, 103
  de- and reterritorialisation movements in, 23, 36–28
Gujarati community
  in Singapore, 147, 148
  in South Africa, 147–48
  in the UK, 147, 191
  in Zanzibar, 169
Gujarati diaspora, 2
Gujarati Ismaili community
  migration of, to East Africa, 59; to Belgium Congo, 60–61
Gujarati women diaspora
  in Oman, 49–55
Gupta, Desh, 193, 197

Hall, Stuart, 10, 130, 134, 134, 146
Hallam, Elizabeth and Brian V. Street, 12
Hammond, Philip E. and Kee Warner, 63
Hannerz, Ulf, 91
Hansen, Randall, 193
Hansen, Thomas Blom, 270
Harvey, David, 246
Hassan, Robert, 136
Hastings, Annette, 239
Herberg, William, 73
Heyl, Barbara S., 65
Hills Shire Council, 240, 241, 242
Hinglish, 87
  popularity of, reasons for, 88–89
Hirway, Indira, 271
Hirway, Indira and Neha Shah, 32
Hollingsworth, Lawrence W., 66

hooks, bell, 237, 244
Hopkins, Peter, 238
Hua, Anh, 44, 49
Hughes, Andrew S., 226
Hussein, Ilias, 46
Hussein, Yasmin, 45
Hutnik, Nimmi, 91
hybrid identity, 87
hybridisation, 128
hybridity, 129, 134
  types of, 134

identity creation
  role of food in, 82–84
  role of language in, 84–87
identity
  definition of, 145
Ilieva, Gabriela Nik, 158
imagined community, 94
inclusion
  aim of, 13
  consequences of, 13–14
  definition of, 13
  notion of, 13
Inda, Jonathan X. and Renato Rosaldo, 79
Indian corner shops, 125
Indian diaspora
  in the Middle East, 43, studies on, 41–47
  in the UK, 148
Indian Express, 34
Indobrit, 126
Ingerson, Alice, 128
International Organization for Migration, 6
Internet revolution, 4
Isajiw, Wsevolod W., 2, 153, 161
Isaka, Riho, 205

Jackson, John A., 120
Jackson, Ronald L. and Thurmon Garner, 146
Jacobs, Keith, 239
Jain, Shobha, 44
Jaspal, Rusi, 149
Jhabvala, Renana, Ratna M. Sudarshan and Jeemol Unni, 271
Johnson, Elaine B., 217
Jones, Stephanie, 174
Joshi, Khyati, 238
Joshi, Vidyut, 257
Judd, Elliot L., 9

Kalka, Iris, 84
Kamaluddin, Zarina and Ali Muhammad Kamaluddin, 221
Kapadia, Aparna, 114
Karayil, Sajitha, 46
Karst, Kenneth L., 3, 4
Kasinitz, Philip, John Mollenkopf and Mary C. Waters, 118
Kavi, Nanalal, 106
Kelly, Melissa, 151
Kerin, Lindy, 246
Keshodkar, Akbar, 169, 173, 174, 178, 179, 182, 183
Khan, Dominique-Sila, 272
Khan, Dominique-Sila and Zawahir Moir, 272
Khan, Verity S., 133
Khare, Harish, 34
Khemlani-David, Maya, 146
Kong, Lily, 236
Kristeva, Julia, 244
Kroeber, A.L. and Clyde Kluckhohn, 90

Kronauer, Martin, 13

Labov, William, 48
Lal, Brij V., et al., 148
language, 8, 84
  and culture, connection between, 9
  and identity, 84–87
Larsen, Kjersti, 173
Leach, Neil, 4
Lefebvre, Henri, 237, 238, 242
Lenski, Gerhard, 73
Leow, Bee Geok, 148
Lévi-Strauss, Claude, 82
Levitas, Ruth, 12
Levitt, Peggy, 236
Lipsitz, George, 238
Lofchie, Michael, 172
Lovell, Nadia, 4
Low, Setha, 236, 238
Lustig, Myron and Jolene Koester, 146
Lynch, James, 223, 224

Macaulay, Thomas B., 111, 114
Mahadevia, Darshini, 256
Maira, Sunaina, 136
Majumdar, Dipesh, 30
Majumdar, Ramanuj, 88
Malkki, Liisa, 23
Mallison, Françoise, 205
Mancherji, Kavasji, 113
Mangat, Jagjit S., 173
MAP, 62
Marmot, Michael, 14
Marquez, Gustavo et al., 13
marriage diaspora, 45
Marston, Greg, 239
Martin, Esmond B., 174
Marzbanji, Furdunji, 110
Massey, Doreen B., 4
Mathew, Vinod, 273
Mattausch, John, 140, 192, 200, 201, 203
Mawani, Sharmina, 61, 62, 63, 67, 70, 91, 93, 149, 153, 212, 220
McCann, Eugene, 236
McLachlin, Beverley, 129
Mehrotra, Meeta, 155
Mehta, Kalyani K., 148
Mehta, Nalin, 255
Mehta, Nandshanker, 109
Michaelson, Maureen, 191
middle-class culture, 271
middle-class revolution in Gujarat, 258
migration, 6, 123
modernity, 103
Modi, Narendra, 27, 28, 260
Modood, Tariq, 91, 204
Modood, Tariq et al., 203
Mosley, Charles, 104
Mukadam, Anjoom A., 61, 62, 91, 92, 118, 119, 129, 149, 158, 159, 171, 199, 213
Mukadam, Anjoom A. and Sharmina Mawani, 66, 69, 70, 80, 88, 119, 126, 137, 139, 147, 148, 172

Nagel, Joane, 90, 91
Nager, Richa, 172, 173, 181, 182
Nandy, Ashis, 30
Nanji, Azim, 59, 61, 62, 68
Nayak, Ratilal, Somabhai Patel and Prasad Brahmbhatt, 107
Nelson, Linda Williamson, 48, 129

Nesbitt, Eleanor, 158
network society, 7
Neumann, Iver B. and Jennifer M. Welsh, 11
Nielsen, Jørgen S., 129
Niles, John., 48
Norrick, Neil R., 48

Ó Tuathail, Gearóid, 22, 34
O'Sullivan, Michael and Karen Pashby, 223
Okaya-Lakidi, Dent, 197
Oonk, Gijsbert, 171, 172, 173, 182, 195
Osborne, Hilary, 206
Osler, Audrey, 223, 226
Osler, Audrey and Hugh Starkey, 223, 225, 226
Osler, Audrey and Kerry Vincent, 212

Paasi, Anssi, 23
Pandey, Gyanendra, 247
Pandya, Natvarlal, 107
Parekh, Bhikhu, 120, 123, 124, 131
Parekh, Hiralal T., 111
Parker, Emma, 44
Parmar, Vijaysing, 30
Patel, Girish, 258
Pathak, Jayant, 109
Peek, Laura, 63
Pendleton, Scott, 83
Pennycook, Alastair, 9
Penrose, Jan, 23
PepsiCo, 82
Pereira, Cecil, Bert N. Adams and Mike Bristow, 211
Phinney, Jean S., 146
Pieterse, Jan N., 79
Popay, Jennie et al., 13
Poros, Maritsa, 147, 148
post-diasporic generation, 119
post-structuralism, 130
Powell, Enoch, 121, 122
Pradhan, N.S., 46
Prakash, Aseem, 257
Price, Glanville, 147
Pulido, Laura, 236, 238

Raby, Rebecca, 212
Rahman, Anisur, 46
Rai, Rajesh, 148, 154
Raja, Sheena, 154
Randeria, Shalini, 24
Rawlinson, Henry G., 109
Rayaprol, Aparna, 159
Rediff.com, 30
Resenhoeft, Annette C., 48, 49
reterritorialisation, 22
  and subnationalism, in Gujarat, 30–35
  in Gujarat, 26–28
Richardson, Robin, 212
Ritzer, George, 80
Robinson, Kerry H. and Criss J. Diaz, 231
Rodgers, Gerry, 13
Rodriguez-Pose, Andrés and Nicholas Gill, 24, 25
Rose, Gillian, 237
Routledge, Paul, 246
Roy, Arundhati, 273
Rudolph, Susanne H. and Lloyd I. Rudolph, 25
Runnymede Trust, 132, 149, 200, 201

Safran, William, 43
Saharso, Sawitri, 146
Sahoo, Ajaya, 182
Said, Edward, 11
Sandercock, Leonie, 236, 246, 250
Sandhu, Kernial Singh, 147
Sangameshwaran, Prasad, 96
Sangh Parivar, 258
Savage, Mike, Gaynor Bagnall and Brian J. Longhurst, 4
Schugurensky, Daniel, 223, 224
second-generation Indians/Gujaratis
  in Britain, 119, 126, 133, hybridity employed by, 135–36
SEZ(s), 29
  in India, 30
Shah, Ghanshyam, 258
Shah, Rajiv, 255, 260
Shani, Ornit, 258
Shaw, Alison, 133
Shaw, Wendy, 236
Sherman, Edward D., 83
Shinoda, Takashi, 260
Shukla, Sonal, 205
Shulman, Lee. S., 215
Sikandar ibn Muhammad Manjhu ibn Akbar, 264
Simmel, Georg, 169
Simpson, E. and Aparna Kapadia, 108
Singh, Jaideep, 238
Sinha, Aseema, 24, 26, 27
Smith, Anthony D., 23, 63
Smolicz, J.J., 91
Søderberg, Anne-Marie, 128
Soja, Edward, 15, 236, 237, 238, 241, 242, 244, 247, 250
Sood, Atul, 32
South Asian diaspora
  in Britain, 122–23, 126, growth of 123–24
spatial neighbourhood, 35
Spencer, Sarah, 224
Spivak, Gayatri, 44
Spodek, Howard, 258
Steger, Manfred B., 5
Stopes-Roe, Mary and Raymond Cochrane, 129
Storey, David, 23
Strauss, Anselm and Juliet Corbin, 239
Street, Brian, 128
subnationalism, 30
  in Gujarat, 30–31
Sud, Nikita, 28, 32, 255, 256
Sue, S., J. Ito and C. Bradshaw, 125
Swyngedouw, Erik, 35

Tagore, Rabindranath, 140
Tangri, Roger, 197
Tarrow, Norma, 225
Taylor, J.H., 159
territoriality, 23
Thaker, Dhirubhai, 107
Thomson, Gardner, 59
Thottam, Jyoti, 258
Tololyan, Khachig, 43
Tomlinson, John, 79
Torri, Michelguglielmo, 205
Tripathi, Dhirendra, 81, 82
Trudeau, Daniel, 250
Twaddle, Michael, 147, 172, 194, 211
Twamley, Katherine, Anthony Pryce and Karina Kielmann, 155
Tweed, Thomas A., 72

twice migrants, 122
Tylor, Edward, 90

UNESCO, 215
United Kingdom
  immigrants in, 120, history of, 120–25
United Nations, 224, 225
US Department of State, 61, 62

Vaara, Eero et al., 239
van den Berghe, Pierre L., 172
Varadarajan, Siddarth, 247
virtual neighbourhood, 35
visible minority, 211, 223
Vohra, Neha, 45
Vygotsky, Lev Semyonovich, 216

Walji, Shirin, 59, 61, 62, 70
Walji-Moloo, Parveen, 172, 173
Walker, Alan and Carol Walker, 12
Warburg, Margit, 79
Warde, Alan, 83
Watson, James, 118, 159, 199
Weller, Robert, 128
Werbner, Pnina, 133
Westernisation, 4, 89
Williams, Raymond B., 63, 248
Wilshire Webb Staunton Beattie, 241
Wise, Amanda, 73
Woodruff, Phillip, 104, 107
Woolard, Kathryn A., 146

Yadav, A., 258
Yadav, Anumeha, 32
Yagnik, Achyut and Suchitra Sheth, 205, 258, 267
Yashashchandra, Sitanshu, 107
Yiftachel, Oren, 236, 246, 250
Yinger, John M., 63
Young, Iris Marion, 244